TIME RIDERS

2001 1912 1957 1941 2066

ALEX SCARROW used to be a graphic artist, then he decided to be a computer games designer. Finally, he grew up and became an author. He has written a number of successful thrillers and several screenplays, but it's YA fiction that has allowed him to really have fun with the ideas and concepts he was playing around with when designing games.

He lives in Norwich with his son, Jacob, his wife, Frances, and two very fat rats.

Become a TimeRider at www.time-riders.co.uk

TIME RIDERS

ALEX SCARROW

PUFFIN

To Jacob, my proofreader.
And in memory of Bullseye . . . a wonderful rat.

PUFFIN BOOKS

Published by the Penguin Group
Penguin Books Ltd, 80 Strand, London WC2R 0RL, England
Penguin Group (USA) Inc., 375 Hudson Street, New York, New York 10014, USA
Penguin Group (Canada), 90 Eglinton Avenue East, Suite 700, Toronto, Ontario, Canada M4P 2Y3
(a division of Pearson Penguin Canada Inc.)
Penguin Ireland, 25 St Stephen's Green, Dublin 2, Ireland (a division of Penguin Books Ltd)
Penguin Group (Australia), 250 Camberwell Road, Camberwell, Victoria 3124, Australia
(a division of Pearson Australia Group Pty Ltd)
Penguin Books India Pvt Ltd, 11 Community Centre, Panchsheel Park, New Delhi – 110 017, India
Penguin Group (NZ), 67 Apollo Drive, Rosedale, North Shore 0632, New Zealand
(a division of Pearson New Zealand Ltd)
Penguin Books (South Africa) (Pty) Ltd, 24 Sturdee Avenue, Rosebank,
Johannesburg 2196, South Africa

Penguin Books Ltd, Registered Offices: 80 Strand, London WC2R 0RL, England

puffinbooks.com

First published 2010
001

Set in Bembo Book MT Std 11/14.5 pt
Typeset by Palimpsest Book Production Limited, Grangemouth, Stirlingshire
Made and printed in England by Clays Ltd, St Ives plc

British Library Cataloguing in Publication Data
A CIP catalogue record for this book is available from the British Library

ISBN: 978–0–141–34481–2

www.greenpenguin.co.uk

CHAPTER 1

1912, Atlantic Ocean

'Anyone left here on deck E?' cried Liam O'Connor. His voice echoed down the narrow passageway, bouncing off the metal walls. 'Anyone down here?'

It was silent save for the muffled cries and clatter of hasty footsteps coming from the deck above and the deep mournful creak of the ship's hull, stressing and stretching as the bow end of the ship slowly dipped below the ocean's surface.

Liam braced himself against the gradually steepening angle of the floor, holding on to the doorframe of the cabin beside him. The chief steward's instructions had been clear – to ensure every cabin at this end of the deck was empty before coming up and joining him.

He wasn't sure he wanted to; the screaming and wailing of women and children that he could hear coming down the stairwell from above sounded shrill and terrifying. At least here on deck E, amid the second-class cabins, there was an eerie sense of peace. Not quite silent, though. Far away, he could hear a deep rumble and knew it was the sound of the freezing ocean cascading into the stricken ship, roaring through open bulkheads, gradually pulling her down.

'Last call!' he cried out again.

A few minutes ago he had roused a young mother and her daughter cowering in one of the cabins wearing their life jackets.

The woman was paralysed with fear, trembling on her bed with her daughter wrapped in her arms. Liam ushered them out and led them to the stairs to deck D. The little girl had quickly kissed his cheek and wished him luck as they parted on the stairwell, as if – unlike her confused mother – she understood they were all doomed.

He could feel the angle of the floor increasing beneath his unsteady feet. From the top of the passage he heard the crash of crockery tumbling from shelves in the steward's room.

She'll be going under soon.

Liam uttered a quick, whispered prayer and craned his neck into one last cabin. Empty.

A loud groan rippled through the floor; it vibrated like the song of a giant whale – he felt it more than heard it. His eyes were drawn to something flashing past the cabin's small porthole. He saw nothing but darkness, then the fleeting quicksilver flutter of bubbles racing past.

Deck E's below the water line.

'Sod this,' he muttered. 'I'm done here.'

He stepped back out into the passageway and saw at the end a ripple of water only an inch or two deep, gently lapping up along the carpeted floor towards him.

'Oh no.'

The lower end of the passage was his only way out.

You stayed too long, Liam, you fool. You stayed too long.

He realized now the girl and her mother had been his fateful warning to get out. He should have left with them.

The ice-cold water met his feet, trickled into his shoes and rolled effortlessly past him. He took several steps forward, wading deeper into the water, feeling its freezing embrace around his ankles, his shins, his knees. Up ahead, round the bend at the end of the passage, was the stairwell he should've been climbing five minutes ago. He pressed forward, whimpering with agony as the icy water rose round his waist and soaked through his white steward's tunic. His breath puffed past chattering teeth in clouds of vapour as he struggled forward.

'Ah *J-Jayzzzusss* an' Holy Mary . . . I d-don't want to drown!' he hissed, his voice no longer the recently broken timbre of a sixteen-year-old, but the strangled whimper of a frightened child.

It was getting too deep to wade now. Ahead of him, where the passage turned right for the stairwell, the water had reached the wall lights, causing them to spark and flicker.

The stairwell's probably flooded.

He realized that round the corner the water had to be lapping the ceiling and at least one flight of the stairs would be completely submerged by now. His only way out would be to hold his breath and hope it would last long enough for him to fumble his way up that first flight to the landing.

'Ah *J-J-Jay*-zus!' His blue lips trembled at the thought of floundering in the darkness, beneath the surface – losing his way, feeling the growing desperation and then finally sucking churning seawater into his lungs.

It was then he heard it – the sound of movement from behind him.

CHAPTER 2

1912, Atlantic Ocean

He turned to look up the passageway and saw a man standing ankle-deep in the water, holding on to a wall rail to prevent himself tumbling down the passage towards him.

'Liam O'Connor!'

'We're s-stuck!' Liam replied. 'There's no . . . there's no way out!' His voice sounded shrill.

'Liam O'Connor,' the man said again, his voice calm.

'*What?*'

'I know who you are, lad.'

'Whuh? . . . We need to –'

The man smiled. 'Listen, Liam.' He looked at his watch. 'You have just under two minutes left to live.' The man looked around at the vanilla-coloured metal bulkheads of deck E. 'This ship's spine will snap in about ninety seconds. She'll break two thirds of the way along. The bow end, the larger section, the bit you and I are in, will sink first – like a stone. The stern will bob for another minute and follow us down, one and a half miles to the bottom of the ocean.'

'Ah, p-please no. No, no, no,' Liam whimpered, realizing that he was crying.

'As we sink, the water pressure will quickly mount. The hull will buckle under it. The air pressure will burst your eardrums.

The rivets in these walls,' he said, running his hand over a row of them, 'will fire out of the bulkheads like bullets. This passage will instantly fill with water and you'll be crushed before you can drown. That's at least a small mercy.'

'Oh *Jay*-zus, no . . . H-help us.'

'You'll die, Liam.' The man smiled again. 'And that makes you *perfect*.'

'P-perfect?'

The man took several steps forward, wading waist-deep into the water towards Liam.

'Tell me, do you want to live?'

'*What?* . . . Is th-there another w-way out?'

The lights in the passageway flickered out in unison. Then a moment later came back on.

'Sixty seconds until she buckles, Liam. Not long now.'

'Is th-there another w-way out of –?'

'If you come with me, Liam,' he said, holding out a hand, 'there is another way. You'll live an invisible life. You'll exist as a phantom, never quite in this world of ours. Never able to make new friends, never able to find love.' The man softened that with a sympathetic smile. 'You'll learn about *things* that . . . well . . . that can ultimately lead to madness if you let it mess with your mind. Some people choose death.'

'I w-want to live!'

'I must warn you . . . I'm not offering you your *life*, Liam. I'm offering you a way out, that's all.'

Liam grabbed hold of the candelabra of a flickering wall light and pulled himself backwards up the slanting passage, his feet finding the floor once more. A shuddering groan rippled around them – deafening.

'She's dying, Liam. The *Titanic*'s back is going to break in just a few seconds. If you believe in God, you might wish to join him now. If you stay here, I assure you, it'll all be over very quickly for you.'

Drowning. It was Liam's worst nightmare – for as far back as he could remember. He'd never learned to swim because of his terrible fear of water.

Liam looked up at the man, looking at his face for the first time: deep sad eyes surrounded by wrinkles of age. And then a thought occurred to him.

'Are you . . . are y-you an a-angel?'

He smiled. 'No. I'm just an old man.' His hand remained steady, outstretched towards Liam. 'I'd understand if you chose to stay and die. Not everyone decides they want to come.'

Liam felt a shudder. The floor beneath his feet convulsed and the air around them was filled with the shriek of tearing sheet metal, the pop of unbuckling seams, as deck after deck above them began to give way one after the other.

'Here it is, Liam. We've arrived at decision time.'

Liam pulled himself forward, up out of the water, desperately reaching out for the old man's proffered hand. If there was time, if his mind wasn't in a free fall of panic, he might have wondered who this man was, and how exactly he intended to save them both. Instead, right now, he could think only one thing.

I don't want to die. I don't want to die.

The lights suddenly winked out, leaving them in complete darkness.

Liam flailed with his arm blindly. 'Where's your hand? Please! I don't want to drown!'

His fingers brushed the old man's. The old man caught it and held on.

'Say goodbye to your life, Liam,' he shouted above the thunderous din of the ship splitting in two.

The last sensation that Liam was aware of was the vibrating metal floor of the passageway beneath his feet giving way, and falling . . . falling through darkness.

CHAPTER 3

2001, New York

Falling, falling . . . falling.

Liam jerked awake, his legs kicking out. His eyes still clamped shut, he felt with his hands – material, dry and warm covering him. It was quiet, almost silent, except for the soft rustle of breathing next to him, and a distant muted rumble somewhere far above him. He knew that he was mysteriously *somewhere else* – that much was obvious.

He was on a bed or a cot. He opened his eyes to see an arched ceiling of crumbling bricks above him, whitewashed long ago with paint that was now flaking off like dandruff. From the top of the arched ceiling a single flickering light bulb dangled from a dusty flex of cable.

He lifted himself up on to his elbows.

He was in a brick alcove, somewhere underground, perhaps. Beyond the pool of light coming from the bulb above, a damp concrete floor spread out from the alcove into darkness.

Where am I?

He sat up, feeling groggy and light-headed, and found himself looking across a gap of three feet at a bunk bed. In the lower bunk, he could see a girl a few years older than him stirring in an uneasy sleep. He guessed she might be eighteen, perhaps nineteen. More a young woman than a girl.

Her eyes rolled beneath the lids; her voice whimpered

pathetically. Her legs twitched and kicked, making the bunk squeak and rattle with every lurched movement.

Where the hell am I? he silently asked himself again.

CHAPTER 4

2010, somewhere above America

Maddy Carter reached round awkwardly and hit the flush button. The toilet hissed with a vicious suction and for a moment she wondered whether a person unlucky enough to accidentally snag the button while still sitting on the seat might be sucked down the u-bend and blasted out at forty thousand feet to free fall amid a shower of turds.

Nice thought.

Maddy cleaned herself up as best she could within the cramped confines of the toilet cubicle. She stared down at the last of the vomit swirling round the toilet basin and down the hole, feeling better now that the aeroplane meal was out rather than still churning in her gut.

She wiped her mouth dry with the back of her hand and checked in the mirror for any telltale blobs of puke caught in her hair. A tall, gawky, pale-faced girl stared back at her; nerdy freckles she hated so much dappled across her cheeks beneath the frames of her glasses. Her strawberry-blonde hair dangled lifelessly to her skinny shoulders, on which hung a drab grey T-shirt with the Microsoft logo stitched on the front.

Yeah, one hundred per cent geek. That's what you are, Maddy.

A geek-ette . . . something of an oddity; a female into messing around with circuit boards, tricking-up her PC, hacking her iPhone to give her free internet access . . . a girl-geek. A girl-geek who got the *screaming terrors* every time she boarded a plane.

She unlocked the door, popped it open and stepped out. Her eyes glanced up the central aisle of the plane at a sea of headrests and the bobbing forms of several hundred heads.

She felt a hand on her shoulder and spun round to see an old man standing beside the bank of toilet cubicles.

'Uh? What?' she said, removing small hissing headphones from her ears.

'You're Madelaine Carter from Boston. Booked into seat twenty-nine D.'

She stared at him, bemused. 'What? You want to see my ticket or –?'

'I'm afraid you've got only a few minutes left to live.'

She felt her stomach lurch, getting ready to eject another torrent of half-digested food. A phrase like 'a few minutes left to live' was the last thing a nervous flyer like her needed to hear right now. It ranked alongside words like 'terrorist' and 'bomb' as something one should never utter on a packed passenger plane mid-flight.

The old man had the harried look of someone running late to catch a train.

'In a few minutes everyone on this plane will be dead.'

She figured there were only two types of person who might say something like that: a complete whacko in need of medication or . . .

'Oh my God,' she whispered, 'you . . . you're not a t-terrorist?'

'No. I'm here to rescue you, Madelaine,' he spoke quietly, then cast a glance at the sea of heads either side of the aisle, 'but only you, I'm afraid.'

She shook her head. 'What? . . . Who? I . . . uh –' Her mouth was flapping pointlessly.

'There's not much time.' He looked at a wristwatch. 'In about ninety seconds a small explosive charge will detonate midway along the right side of the plane. The explosion will knock a hole through the fuselage, the plane will instantly decompress and roll into a steep dive. Twenty seconds later the starboard wing will sheer off, filling the inside of the plane with aviation fuel, which will ignite.' He sighed. 'The impact with the woodland below thirty-seven seconds later will kill those who haven't already been incinerated.'

Maddy felt the blood drain from her face.

'I'm sorry,' he added, 'but I'm afraid no one will survive this.'

'Uh . . . this is . . . this is some kind of sick joke, right?'

'No joke.' He continued: '*You* alone have a choice. You can choose to live.'

He's serious. And something about him told her he wasn't on meds. She found herself gasping, instinctively reaching for her inhaler. 'N-ninety s-seconds? A bomb goes off?'

'Less than that now.'

Not a whacko, then . . .

'Oh God, it's *your* b-bomb. What do you want from us?'

'No, it's not mine, and I'm not a terrorist. I just happen to know this plane will be destroyed by a device. A terrorist group will claim responsibility for it tomorrow morning.'

'Is there t-time? Could w-we find the *b*omb and throw it off?' she asked, her voice raised in panic. She'd said the 'b' a little too loud and it had carried forward. Several heads up the aisle turned quickly to look back at her.

He shook his head. 'Even if there was time, I can't change events. I can't change history. This plane has to go down.'

'Oh God,' she whimpered.

'The only thing I can do is take you off before it does.'

She looked up the plane. More heads were turning. She could hear a rising ripple of voices and the word 'bomb' as a whispered tidal wave rolled from seat row to seat row.

'If you take my hand,' he said, offering it to her, 'you'll live. And in return I'll ask for your help. Or you can stay. You get to choose, Madelaine.'

Maddy realized there were tears of panic rolling down her cheeks. The man seemed sane. Seemed calm. Seemed deadly serious. And yet . . . how could *anyone* be taken off this plane mid-flight?

'I know you don't believe in God,' he said. 'I've read your file. I know you're an atheist. So I won't try to tell you I'm an angel. I know you have a fear of heights, that you're not great on planes either. I know your favourite drink is Dr Pepper, I know you have a recurring nightmare about falling from a yellow-painted tree house . . . I know so many more things about you.'

She frowned. 'How . . . how do you know th-that?'

He looked down at his watch. 'You have thirty seconds left.'

A stewardess was now striding down the aisle towards them, her eyes widened with concern.

'I know you're an avid reader of science fiction, Madelaine, so perhaps it'll be easier for you to understand if I tell you I'm from the future.'

Her mouth opened and closed. 'But . . . but that's impossible!'

'Time travel will become possible in about forty years' time.' His hand extended towards her. She looked down at it uncertainly.

'Twenty seconds, Madelaine. Take my hand.'

She looked up at his lined face. 'Why? Why –?'

'Why *you*?'

She nodded.

'You fit the skill profile exactly.'

She swallowed nervously, felt her breathing becoming laboured and erratic. Confused, panic-stricken, unable to think of a useful next question.

'We need you,' he said, looking at his watch. 'Fifteen seconds. It's time to decide.'

'Wh-who are y-you?'

'I . . . or I should say *we* . . . are the people who fix broken things. Now, take my hand, Madelaine. Take it now!'

Instinctively, she stretched out towards him.

A stewardess pulled up a few feet short of them. 'Excuse me,' she cut in, 'someone has reported the pair of you loudly using the "B" word . . . *bomb.*' She whispered the word quietly. 'I'm sorry but you just can't use language like that on a passenger plane.'

The old man looked up at her and smiled sadly. 'No . . . *I'm* the one who's sorry, ma'am. I truly am.'

Maddy looked at him. 'This is for real?'

He nodded. 'And we have to leave right now.'

'OK,' she uttered, grasping his extended hand tightly.

The stewardess tipped her head on one side curiously, her forehead furrowed, her lips pursed. She was about to ask how they planned to leave the plane exactly.

Then the world suddenly was a blinding white and Maddy snapped her eyes shut.

CHAPTER 5

2001, New York

She was screaming, at least that's what she thought the sound was. It might have been her. It might have been the sound of a wing tearing itself from the plane.

It might even have been the stewardess; she wasn't sure.

A terrifying dropping sensation, dropping away into darkness.

'No-o-o-o-o!' she found herself crying with a voice that sounded like the ragged death-squeal of a slaughtered pig.

She lurched suddenly and violently.

'Oh Jay-zus-Christ-Almighty!' a male voice beside her gasped.

Maddy's eyes opened wide and locked on to a flickering light bulb dangling from a brick ceiling, then on to the rusty springs of a grubby bunk bed directly above her. Finally, to her right, her eyes drifted to the smooth face of a young man sitting on a scruffy metal-framed bed across from her, dressed in what looked like a waiter's uniform.

'Jay-zus-Christ-Almighty, you made me jump there,' he uttered. 'One second you were sleeping all peaceful, the next you're up like a screamin' banshee.'

Maddy felt her breath rattling like a startled moth caught in a wire cage. Wheezing, she looked down and saw she was still clasping her inhaler, just as she had been a moment ago aboard the plane. She took a long pull on it and then managed to find enough air in her lungs to sit up slowly.

'I'm dead. I must be dead.'

The young man managed a weak and awkward smile. 'Me too . . . I think.'

They looked at each other for a moment. 'I wonder,' he said, 'do you think –?'

'That this is heaven?' she finished his question. 'No such thing. If there is . . . then it looks a bit rubbish to me.' The bunk bed in which she was lying creaked with movement from above. Maddy looked up at the springs and mattress.

'Is there somebody else up there?'

Liam nodded. 'Yeah, a young dark-skinned girl. She's asleep.'

'Her name's Saleena,' a voice called out of the darkness.

They both jerked round to look out into the gloom beyond the light thrown down from the bare bulb.

They heard footsteps on the hard concrete floor, and then, faintly at first, they saw a man emerge from the darkness, carrying a tray.

'Coffee?' asked the old man.

'Oh my God!' gasped Maddy, recognizing the face.

Liam's jaw dropped. 'You! You're the man on deck E.'

'That's right,' he replied calmly. 'My name's Foster.'

He joined them, setting the tray of chipped mugs and a carton of doughnuts on the floor between the beds. He sat on the bed next to Liam.

'And you're Madelaine Carter, and you're Liam O'Connor.' He nodded towards the top bunk. 'The girl up there's Sal Vikram. She's only young, thirteen. The poor girl will be terrified when she comes to. Here.' He handed Liam and Maddy a mug of coffee. 'You could both probably do with a little pick-me-up.'

'Mr Foster, is it?' asked Liam.

He smiled. 'Foster . . . Mr Foster, I'm not fussed.'

'Mr Foster, where are we?'

Maddy nodded. 'I should be dead. There's no way you could've got me off that plane. No way.'

Foster turned to her. 'Time travel, remember?'

She narrowed her eyes. 'But that's impossible.'

'No, it's not –' he shook his head – 'unfortunately.'

'What's *time travel*?' asked Liam.

Maddy cocked her head at him. 'You're kidding me, right?'

'Go easy on the lad,' said Foster. 'He's from 1912. They didn't have much in the way of sci-fi shows and comics back then.'

She turned back to Liam, looking more closely at his clothes: not a waiter, but a ship's steward. She spotted *White Star Lines* stitched on a breast pocket.

'1912? You're serious?'

'Very,' added Foster. 'Liam here was aboard the *Titanic*.'

Her mouth flopped open.

'What?' Liam looked confused. 'Why're you staring at me like that?' he asked her.

'Because, Liam,' said Foster, 'you're from Ireland a hundred years ago.' The old man laughed. 'And she's from New York, the year 2010.'

Liam's dark eyebrows lifted in unison.

'And Saleena Vikram, up there on the top bunk, she's from Mumbai, India, the year . . . 2026.' Foster offered a grin that made his old face crinkle like greaseproof paper. 'And as for me, well –' he smiled – 'let's say I come from Never-neverland.'

Maddy leaned forward. 'Oh my God, come on, when? The twenty-second century? Further on?'

His smile told her nothing.

'Do they have spaceships in your time? Has mankind colonized the solar system? Has warp drive been invented yet –?'

He held a hand up to shush her. 'Another time, perhaps. Right now there are more important things to attend to.'

Before either of them could reply, they heard a stirring from the bunk bed above them.

'She's coming round,' said Foster. 'She'll be even more disorientated, more frightened, than either of you.'

Maddy slurped a hot mouthful of coffee from the mug in her hands. 'I seriously doubt that.'

The girl's murmuring turned to a frightened whimpering that quickly intensified. Foster stood up and leaned over the top bunk.

'Shhh . . . it's OK, Saleena,' he cooed reassuringly. 'It's all over. You're safe now.'

The girl's mewling voice became a sudden shrill shriek as her eyes snapped open and she sat stiffly upright on the bunk.

Foster held her narrow shoulders firmly. 'Saleena.' He spoke quickly and softly. 'You're safe; no one can hurt you here. It's over.'

The girl's breath came in short stuttering gasps. Her eyes, thickly rimmed with dark eyeliner, widened behind a drooping black fringe that slanted across her narrow face. They darted from one thing to another, for the moment it seemed making sense of absolutely nothing.

'It's over, Saleena,' said Foster again. 'You're safe now.'

Her gaze settled on the old man. She flicked her fringe away from an almost ashen face; her coffee-coloured skin was drained to an almost corpse-like grey.

Liam stood up and peered over the edge of the bunk, cocking a bemused eyebrow at her strange appearance: a dark hooded top with some scruffy wording splashed in neon orange across it; thin drainpipe jeans ripped and patched, with patches on top of patches; and boots that looked two sizes too big for her, laced up past her ankles . . . And a small stud pierced her upper lip.

'Uh . . .' He did a double take before extending a hand in greeting. 'My name's Liam O'Connor. Pleased to –'

'Give her a moment, Liam,' said Foster. 'Just a moment . . . her extraction was particularly traumatic.'

'Is it you?' Her voice was small, shaken, uncertain. 'The man . . . the man in the flames.'

'That's right.' He smiled warmly. 'It's me, Saleena.'

'Sal,' she replied. 'Sal . . . Only my mum and dad call me Saleena.'

'Sal, then,' he said, helping her up. She swung her legs over the side of the bunk and silently studied the other two: a boy dressed like a hotel porter, and a lank-haired teenage girl with glasses.

'Hey,' said Maddy, 'welcome to Weirdsville.'

'Just give her a bit of room there. Let her catch her breath.'

'You got an odd accent, so you have,' said Liam curiously to Sal.

'That's rich,' snorted Maddy, 'coming from you.'

'She's from a city called Mumbai, in India, Liam. You'd know it as Bombay.'

'But she speaks *English*, so she does.'

'Well, duh,' said Maddy, rolling her eyes, 'they all do. It's a bilingual nation.'

CHAPTER 6

2001, New York

The coffee was gone and one last unwanted doughnut sat in the box.

'We've been . . . did you say *recruited*?' Maddy repeated.

'Yes, that's right. You're working for the agency now.'

Liam leaned forward. 'Uh . . . Mr Foster, sir, what exactly is *the agency*?'

'Let me go through everything I need to say first. Then you can all ask as many questions as you like. It'll be much quicker if we do this my way.'

They nodded.

Foster pointed out at the darkness beyond the alcove. 'I left the other lights off in here so you wouldn't see it all – this place, the equipment – and be overwhelmed by it. Right now let's just pretend there's only this little brick archway, that light bulb, the four of us and these beds . . . and that's where I'll start.'

He took a deep breath.

'Time travel exists, boys and girls.'

He left that statement hanging in the air for a few moments before continuing.

'A theoretical physics paper demonstrating the possibility was written in 2029. The first successful prototype machine was constructed in 2044.' He sighed. 'Now that we've opened that can of worms we can't close it.'

He studied them with deep stern eyes hidden between furrowed eyebrows and sallow cheeks etched with criss-crossing wrinkles.

'Mankind was *never* meant to dabble with time. Never! But now that we know how to somebody needs to make sure that nobody actually *does* so. And, if some fool does go back in time, then it's someone's job to fix the damage caused as quickly as possible.'

There was a faint tremor in his rasping old-man's voice.

'Time travel is a terrifying weapon, far more powerful than anything ever before conceived,' he said grimly. 'Mankind just isn't ready for that kind of knowledge. We're like children casually playing toss and catch with an atom bomb.'

Liam cocked his head questioningly. 'What's an atom b–?'

'I'll explain later,' replied Foster. 'Which brings me to you three, and this place,' he said, gesturing at the darkness beyond the pool of light. 'The fact is there are too few of us TimeRiders – groups like us dotted around the world, dotted through time, watching and waiting patiently.'

'Watching for what?' asked Maddy.

'For a shift.'

'A *shift*?'

He nodded. 'It starts as something ever so slight, almost unnoticeable to the eye. You catch it then, when it's just a ripple. You have to because, before you know it, it becomes a tidal wave; it becomes unstoppable, uncontrollable. And then we're all truly screwed.'

Sal's eyes had been lost in the darkness, still far away, but she turned to look at Foster. 'What is a shift?'

'A shift is the result of time being disturbed.'

Foster pursed his lips in thought for a moment. 'OK, think of it like this: *time* is like a still pool, or a bath. Have you ever tried stepping into a bath without creating a ripple? It's impossible, isn't it?'

The three of them nodded as the bulb above them flickered and fizzed ever so slightly.

'In the same way, it's impossible to step through into the past without creating a ripple. But the problem is the ripple spreads and grows from the point at which someone steps in. From that we get a tidal wave that increases in size and destroys everything in its way to replace it with a new world . . . a universe that *might have been*.'

Liam shook his head. 'Not sure I understand.'

'I get it,' said Sal. 'If you change the past a little, you'll change the present a lot.'

Foster nodded. 'That's exactly right, Sal.'

The light dimmed for a moment, then winked on and off. Foster looked up at it, irritated. 'The bulb's worked loose again.'

He stood and, carefully covering his hands with the sleeve of his jumper, twisted the bulb. The flickering stopped.

'We need to rewire this place . . . but there never seems to be enough time.'

Maddy looked around. 'Where are we? It looks like some skanky old railway arch.'

Foster smiled. 'That's pretty much what it is. It's actually a –'

The light dimmed and flickered once more and his eyes suddenly widened.

'Oh no.'

The others looked up at his face, all of a sudden a shade paler.

'What's up?' asked Maddy.

'It's here . . .' he whispered.

'A shift?' asked Liam.

'No –' he shook his head – 'worse.'

CHAPTER 7

2001, New York

Foster's eyes remained on the fizzing and flickering light bulb. 'It's draining the energy. I thought it was the damned light bulb on the fritz. Stupid of me,' he hissed.

'*What's* draining the energy?' asked Maddy.

The strained tone in Foster's lowered voice unsettled the others.

'I thought the thing had gone.'

'What *thing*?' asked Liam.

Foster turned to him, raising a finger to his lips to hush them. 'A *seeker*. It should've faded by now . . . It must have been leeching power somehow, just enough to keep it alive.'

The old man reached up with one hand and found a switch on the brick wall. He snapped it off and instantly the bulb winked out, leaving them in complete darkness.

Sal's small voice cut the silence softly. 'Er . . . it's dark.'

'Shhh, it's all right,' Foster whispered. 'We're going to sit tight for a little while. As long as we're still, we'll be just fine.'

A long silence stretched out, disturbed only by the sound of their ragged breathing. Then Liam saw something faint moving in the darkness, the slightest glow, barely an outline . . . of . . . *something*.

'A seeker,' Foster uttered quietly. 'It's very weak now – on its last legs.'

Maddy stirred. 'It looks like a ghost.'

'We don't know what they are exactly,' replied Foster, 'but every now and then when you open a time portal . . . it's possible to attract one, accidentally trap one of them and bring it back with you.'

The undulating outline pulsed and flickered like a loose cluster of fireflies, embers dancing above a campfire.

'That's what happened here. The last team . . .' Foster's whisper quietened to nothing.

'The last team *what*?' asked Maddy.

'I must have brought one back with me . . . the last mission I took into the past,' he replied. 'I went out for some food, came back a few hours later . . .' He paused for a moment, considering how to continue. 'What was left of them wasn't very nice to look at.'

Liam heard Maddy's breath hitch.

'They're pure energy. But they *can* take physical form if they're charged up enough. It's not good when that happens.'

The pale blue cloud drifted across the darkness in front of them, a spectral form like a lost spirit in a graveyard, a wisp of morning mist in a deep, dark wood.

'But this one's grown weak. I thought it had gone, faded away to nothing.' He shook his head with disbelief. 'I was cleaning up the mess, looking up your files on the computer, preparing to send myself into the past to find you and bring you back. And all that time the thing was lurking here in this place . . . quietly watching me.'

The shape stopped moving. It hovered just a few yards away, a dull pulsating glow that in fleeting moments seemed to find a shape that reminded Liam of mythical creatures – a centaur, a unicorn, a dragon – before becoming a pale cloud once more.

'I'd say it's too weak to take a physical form. It's dying. But we're best just keeping back for now.'

'Does that thing know we're here?' asked Maddy.

'Perhaps.'

Liam licked his dry lips anxiously. 'Where did it come from?'

'Another dimension,' Foster replied, 'another dimension overlaying ours, perhaps, attracted to the energy of a time portal like a moth is to light. These things are another reason we should never have messed with time to begin with.'

The entity moved again, this time drifting ponderously towards them.

'Er . . . it's getting closer,' whispered Sal.

'Yes, I do believe it is.'

'But we're *safe*, right, Mr Foster?' asked Liam. 'You said it's too weak to hurt us?'

Foster's silence in the pitch black was less than comforting.

'We should leave,' he finally replied. 'We've got over thirty hours before we need to return, before the arch's time bubble resets. I can't see this thing surviving that much longer.'

'Time bubble?'

'I'll explain outside. Everyone grab a hand. There's a mess of things in here to get tangled in. I need to lead us out.'

Liam, Maddy and Sal reached out and fumbled in the dark, each finding desperate probing hands and grasping them tightly.

'Whose hand have I got?' asked Foster, squeezing as he asked.

'Uh . . . mine,' replied Liam.

'You holding someone else's?'

'Mine, I think,' whispered Maddy. 'And I've got Sal's.'

'Good . . . let's move, slowly and quietly.'

Foster clambered to his feet and Liam felt a gentle pull. He followed, his eyes remaining on the pale cloud a few yards away. It was hesitant now, still finding curious fleeting outlines and just as quickly abandoning them.

Liam felt his feet catch on something snaking across the floor and stepped gingerly over it, fearful of tripping and making a noise. Behind him he heard Maddy and Sal treading lightly.

Through the pitch black, Foster led the way stealthily until finally Liam sensed they had arrived at a wall.

'The door's here somewhere,' hissed Foster.

He heard the old man patting the crumbling brick wall with his palms and then the rattle of knuckles on something metal.

'Found it.'

Liam turned to look over his shoulder. The seeker was little more than a faint blotch in the darkness.

Foster cursed under his breath. 'With the power off I'll need to crank the shutter-door open by hand.'

'Will it take long?' asked Sal quietly.

'Not too long.'

'Good, because I think it's moving our way.' She looked at the others. 'Oh my God, can you *hear* it? It's whispering!'

Liam cocked his head as he studied the faint bluish blur. He couldn't hear anything but Foster working the crank handle. 'No . . . but you're right about it coming this way.'

The manual winch was squealing like it needed oil badly while the metal shutter rattled noisily in its frame as it inched slowly upwards.

He felt a draught of cool outside air on his legs and saw a crack of pale light at the bottom of the shutter.

'She's right, it's definitely coming closer, Foster,' said Maddy urgently. 'Can you do that any faster?'

The shutter clunked and rattled up noisily, the sliver of light coming from outside widening much too slowly.

'There . . . that's enough to duck through,' he uttered, winded from the exertion.

'Ladies first,' offered Liam. He turned to look back over his shoulder, almost instantly regretting his chivalry. The seeker was making fast progress gliding towards them . . . almost upon them now, no more than a dozen feet away. The amorphous cloud of scintillating particles seemed to rear up as it drew across the floor, forming the momentary outline of some kind of face. An angelic, childlike face, a little girl . . . Then the face decayed into some kind of nightmarish creature with empty eye sockets and an elongated jaw.

Liam wondered whether this thing was as *spent* as Foster had claimed, or whether it was still capable of doing harm.

'Under you go, Liam,' said Foster, tapping his shoulder, 'quickly now.'

Liam dropped down and squeezed under the shutter door, joining the girls outside. Foster emerged a moment later, and with far less difficulty using the handle outside, worked the shutter down again. It rattled against the ground just as a faint tendril of blue light had begun to feel its way out through the gap.

'It's weakened enough that it won't get through,' he said with a smile.

He took a deep breath, and grinned apologetically. 'Sorry about that. Now then,' he continued, turning to gesture at the world around them with both hands. 'Welcome to your new home.'

Liam turned from the corrugated metal shutter, daubed with messy paint – that he would later find out was called *graffiti* – to witness a giant suspended iron bridge right above him, crossing the glistening waters of a wide river towards a glowing metropolis set against the blood red of an evening sky. He was stunned by a million lights glowing and buzzing, flickering and changing colour, beautifully reflected in the calm water in front of them.

'Oh Jay-zus-'n'-Mary . . . that's . . . that's . . . ' His voice faltered at the sight of the futuristic scene.

‘Oh *jahulla*! I know that,’ uttered Sal. ‘It’s New York . . . At least, how it used to be.’

‘That’s right,’ said Foster. ‘Let’s go get something to eat. I know a great burger place just over the bridge.’

CHAPTER 8

2001, New York

Half an hour later the four of them were sitting in a window booth, perched on tall stools around a table and tucking into double cheeseburgers and fries.

Liam's initial reaction to the plate of food had been one of bemusement. The fries looked like no potatoes he'd ever encountered before and the burger bun – waxy and brown – reminded him, oddly, of varnished wood. The savoury smell wafting up, however, soon overcame him and, warily watching the others hungrily tucking in, he followed suit.

As he clumsily manhandled the well-stacked cheeseburger into his mouth, his eyes were on the intersection outside: the pulsing lights of a billboard, the busy throng of pedestrians, cars that looked as sleek as dew drops, the neon glow from lamp posts and a sky, barely visible above the tower blocks, filled with the winking red and green lights of planes criss-crossing the night sky.

'It looks *so* different now,' said Sal. 'Just like Mumbai. My dad brought me here on a business trip once – it was depressing. The roads empty, and so many buildings, like, dark and empty.'

Foster nodded. 'The year you come from, Sal – 2026 – New York was already a dying city. People moved out, whole neighbourhoods were left deserted and began falling into decay.'

Maddy finished a mouthful of burger. 'It doesn't look that different to me, though.'

'That's because right now we're in 2001, only a few years before your time, 2010,' Foster replied. 'The global economic crash had only really just started.'

Liam turned from the window to look wide-eyed at Foster. 'I can't believe this is almost a hundred years in *my* future!'

'For you, Liam, yes. For Maddy it's just nine years ago, for Sal . . . it's eleven years before she was even born.' He sipped a mouthful of cold, frothy beer from a tall glass. 'This is where you, as a team, will be stationed. The archway under the bridge is your base of operations: your *field office*.'

Maddy looked at him. 'Are there other field offices?'

He wiped his mouth and nodded. 'But you'll never meet them or communicate with them.'

'Why not?'

He picked at the fries on his plate. 'It's just the way it is.'

Sal chugged a mouthful of Dr Pepper. 'I still don't get why we're here. What exactly you want us for.'

'You are *police* . . . sort of,' Foster replied. 'Here to police *time*. To stop trespassers from the future changing things in the past. The agency is top secret. It really isn't supposed to exist, so we don't have a proper job title. But inside the agency, we call ourselves *TimeRiders*.'

'TimeRiders?'

Foster hunched forward and stroked his chin thoughtfully.

'Look . . . think of time as a river. A river that always flows downhill. Well, we can ride up it or down it. Ride time. Timeride. Just like being in a river boat with a paddle, we can go against the flow. And your job will be looking for other people on the river going against the flow when they have no business to. You'll look for them, find them, terminate them and tidy up whatever damage they've done.'

'How're we going to do that?' asked Maddy.

'Well, I'll be training you, of course.' Foster smiled tiredly. 'As quickly as I can. We need this field office to be operational again as soon as is possible.'

Sal looked up from her food. 'The team before us . . . what were they like?'

Foster's smile faded. 'A little like you once, I suppose.' The old man looked away guiltily to gaze out of the window. He chewed on his lips for a moment. 'Young, inexperienced and frightened at first . . . and, ultimately, very unlucky.'

'That thing really killed them?'

He nodded. 'Seekers are rare. And normally we do a density scan before pulling someone back from a mission. That last time we didn't and . . .' Foster's words faded into an uncomfortable silence.

'So,' Liam cut in, 'when do we start this training you mentioned?'

Foster turned to them.

'Now.'

He sipped his beer again, took a deep breath. 'I think we should start with a little bit of a history lesson – the history of time travel.'

CHAPTER 9

2066, New York

Dr Paul Kramer looked out at the dark streets of the city, the boarded-up buildings, the discarded vehicles left rusting down the backstreets. Every so often their coach passed a pedestrian, a small scruffy corner shop, a light glowing through a grimy window.

New York was a rundown relic of the thriving city it had once been. There were whole blocks that were now little more than deserted shells, populated by feral packs of dogs and pigeons.

The coach was heading down Central Park West, off Broadway. Kramer had seen films made sixty years ago that showed these streets full of life and colour and hope. Now it was a dismal and grey place, a city dying piece by piece, block by block.

The coach slowed down as it passed a police precinct building, the windows protected by metal grilles.

'No need to drive too cautiously, Karl,' said Kramer. 'You'll make the police suspicious.'

Karl Haas, driving, picked up the speed a little.

Kramer twisted in his seat and looked back down the coach. His men, two dozen of them, sat quietly in their seats, lost in thought, pensive. All of them fighting fit, wearing combat fatigues, ready for their mission. The aisle between both rows of seats was clogged with their kit: crates and canvas carry-bags full of weapons.

He smiled proudly.

Good men, aren't they, Paul?

'We're nearly there,' he said to Karl.

Karl nodded and then barked out to the men behind them: 'Make ready!'

They stirred immediately and he could hear the rattle of firearms being racked and readied to use. They were all experienced, many of them ex-military . . . all of them firmly committed to Kramer's plan. None of them married or leaving children behind.

A one-way trip away from this dying world clogged with nine billion people – most of them starving. What Kramer was offering these young men was *hope*, a chance to change things for the better.

In the thigh pocket of Kramer's combat pants was the one little thing that was going to make that possible for them: a black notebook.

Karl turned a corner on to 79th Street. The intersection was busier than normal with a few pedestrians hunched over and miserable, shuffling their way home. Ahead of them was the grand building itself – the American Museum of Natural History. Like so many others, it was boarded up, covered in pigeon droppings and mostly dark, waiting in vain for better days.

Kramer felt his heart sink at the sight of its once-proud entrance now darkened with urban grime and defaced with graffiti. This once-great nation deserved better; this city deserved better. The museum was a pitiful reminder of a grand time when Manhattan really was the centre of the world.

He could cry, honestly . . . he really could.

CHAPTER 10

2001, New York

'It began with theory: a paper written in 2029 by a talented Chinese mathematics graduate called Edward Chan,' said Foster. 'According to him, on paper at least, it was possible to bend space and time in such a way as to create a *hole*. But it took another fifteen years, and someone else, to construct a prototype that sort of worked. The man's name was Roald Waldstein, a quite brilliant amateur physicist.

'There were all manner of huge corporations and military research teams working day and night to be the ones to make the first time machine. But it was Waldstein, working in little more than a garage, who managed to overcome the practical difficulties of turning the theory into a functioning device. It was Waldstein, one man on his own, who beat corporations and governments to the prize.'

Maddy laughed. 'The billionaires of tomorrow always seem to start out in garages, don't they?'

Foster shook his head, eager to continue. 'The story goes that he tested his own machine, went back to somewhere in the past. However, he returned *a completely changed man*.'

'Why?'

'He claimed he saw *something* on his trip that scared him.'

'What?'

'Waldstein never told anyone what he saw. But whatever it

was it convinced him that his work on developing a working time machine was dangerous. He became obsessed with preventing any further work on time travel. Over the years, Roald Waldstein became rich from other inventions, became an influential voice and campaigned very publicly to ensure this technology died.'

Maddy slurped her Dr Pepper. 'And obviously it wasn't halted.'

'Obviously.'

'So what happened?' asked Liam.

CHAPTER 11

2066, New York

Karl parked the coach outside the rear of the museum where the loading bay and trade entrances were. The men clambered off silently, efficiently, weapons slung over their shoulders, crates and kit bags carried between them.

Kramer helped one of his men with a canvas sack full of ammo clips. It was heavy enough to ensure his arms were aching by the time they carefully placed it on the ramp leading up to the museum's shuttered loading bay.

He looked around quickly.

The cover of night and sparse lighting from a sputtering arc light almost certainly meant no one had spotted them yet.

Yet.

Soon enough, though, there'd be armed police descending upon them.

Karl, a lean and muscular ex-marine in his thirties, approached him. Once upon a time he'd been *Technical Sergeant* Karl Haas – that was before the army spat him out, surplus to requirements. Karl was Kramer's second-in-command. While Dr Paul Kramer might be the brains – the *visionary* – it was Karl to whom the men would turn once the fighting started.

'Dr Kramer, sir?'

'Yes, Karl.'

'You're absolutely certain it's here?'

He couldn't blame the man for asking. Once they broke into the museum, and sealed themselves inside, there wasn't going to be any turning back.

Kramer patted his shoulder. 'It's here, my friend. Trust me.'

They worked the loading-bay door open with a sledgehammer, smashing the locking bar and pushing the heavy aluminium doors in. Almost immediately a bell began to ring somewhere inside the dark cavernous building.

'It's OK,' said Kramer, 'there are only a few security guards inside.' He looked over his shoulder at the night sky and the distant glow of a police hoverjet sluggishly patrolling the dead skyline of Manhattan. 'The police, on the other hand, will be with us soon, I'm sure. We should get everything inside as quickly as possible.'

Karl nodded. 'Yes, sir,' he said, and turned smartly away.

He helped drag in the crates and bags of equipment. Once everything was inside, they pushed the loading-bay doors closed. The area, stacked with wooden packing crates, flickered to life in the dazzling, strobing light of a welding torch sealing the service door shut.

'Make sure that's properly secured,' ordered Kramer. He turned to Haas. 'Karl, take a dozen men and round up the security staff. Bring them to me.'

The man nodded and headed towards the doors to the museum's galleries, quickly picking some men to go with him.

Kramer felt the item in his pocket: his small notebook. He silently prayed that he wasn't making a horrendous mistake.

You know it's hidden here, Paul.

So many reasons why he could be wrong. Maybe it wasn't down in the basement of the museum, but instead in some other building . . . Maybe the code was copied down incorrectly . . . Maybe he really did destroy it . . .

Have faith in your instincts, Paul.

If he'd got it wrong, though, they were going to be nothing more than a couple of dozen angry idealists trapped in a dusty old building full of priceless museum exhibits boxed away in the hope of better times.

He guessed the armed police might be wary of using heavy-calibre or incendiary weapons for fear of damaging the nation's irreplaceable heirlooms. But they'd be coming in, one way or another, and there'd be gunfire.

They'll shoot first and worry about the chipped pottery later.

CHAPTER 12

2001, New York

'Waldstein destroyed his machine. He smashed it up, as well as burning all his notes and files. Fifteen years of hard work . . . destroyed because he suspected time travel would ultimately harm this world.'

'Wow,' gasped Maddy. 'That's a bit over the top, isn't it? It's like deleting all the code for a game just to kill one bug.'

Sal looked up from her food, so far barely touched. 'So, why did he want to make a time machine in the first place?'

'His wife and son died in 2028. He made no secret of what was driving him to go back in time.'

'To save them?'

'No, to *see* them one last time, to say goodbye to them. Waldstein knew he couldn't save them – he couldn't *alter* history – but he could at least tell them he loved them both moments before their lives were to end.'

Liam shook his head slowly. 'That's a tough one, so it is. To have the chance to save those you love, yet not do it because that's the right thing to do.'

Foster nodded. 'Yes. Waldstein was a very principled man.'

'Did he manage to see them when he went back?' asked Sal.

'No one knows if he was successful. He never spoke about it. He returned, as I mentioned, a very changed man, immediately afterwards destroying all his work. He began a campaign for all research in time technology to be halted. His desperate warnings that the world could be destroyed by time travel began to find an audience and in early 2051 an international law was passed strictly forbidding the development of the technology. Waldstein became a recluse after that, rarely seen in public, but content that his campaign had put an end to time travel.'

Foster sighed. 'But, of course, it didn't.'

He finished his beer. 'It was obvious that every major corporation, every country, every tin-pot dictator, *anybody* with the money, the resources and manpower, was *secretly* working on their own time machine. Waldstein had shown it was possible and that was enough.

'So, in direct violation of the international law, this agency was set up. Quietly, secretly, working on their very own machines.'

'Let me guess,' interrupted Maddy, 'to go back in time to kill Waldstein?'

Foster shook his head. 'No. Just as Waldstein couldn't save his family, so the agency can't go back in time to prevent him from making his machine. History *cannot* be violated, it cannot be changed – that's the *tidal wave* I mentioned a while back, remember?'

They nodded.

'You see, time can cope with very small changes. History can sort of *heal* itself of very, very minor alterations, because there's a momentum to events, a momentum to history. It's as if history *wants* to go a certain route. But,' said Foster with a cautionary glance up at them, 'but, a more significant change, for example going back in time and talking Waldstein out of building his machine, or even killing him . . . well, something like that would be enough of a change to cause a tidal wave.'

He looked out of the window at the busy street aglow with

neon light spilling down from a billboard advertising Nike sportswear.

'The agency was set up to be ready for what they knew was coming: future time travellers, those who'd want to change the past and rewrite the present – terrorists, religious fanatics, megalomaniacs, the criminally insane. Anyway –' he pushed his stool back and stood up – 'that's enough of the history lesson for now. I think it's time I took you three outside and showed you a little of the world out there, the time and place in which you're going to be based. Particularly you, Liam.' He smiled. 'You'll need to play a little catch-up if you want to familiarize yourself with the world of 2001.'

Maddy shrugged. 'It doesn't look so different. Just as busy, noisy, smelly as 2010.'

'Oh, but this *is* a very different New York,' said Foster.

Maddy looked out of the window. 'Not really . . . I see the same ol', same ol' out there: adverts for Burger King and McDonald's, Nike and Adidas, yellow cabs and guys trying to sell cheap AA batteries that don't work.'

'I think I'd better show you something, Maddy. I think it'll mean a lot more to *you* than Sal and Liam.'

CHAPTER 13

2066, New York

Kramer studied the museum's six security guards, rounded up by Haas and his men without so much as a shot fired. They stared fearfully back at him, eyes darting anxiously down at the weapon slung over his shoulder. A couple of them were tousled-haired and bleary-eyed as if they'd been roused from sleep.

Kramer shook his head pityingly.

Great security guards.

'My name is Dr Paul Kramer. It's very simple, gentlemen. We want the major media networks assembled outside and I want to do an interview with them, which will be broadcast across the nation's networks, live. We also want a hoverjet landed on the roof of the museum, in which we intend to leave, untouched, when our work here is done. If we *don't* get what we want, we will destroy the museum and all of its incredibly valuable and irreplaceable contents.'

Kramer smiled. 'There. I said it was pretty simple.'

The security guards stared at him, dumbstruck.

'Now,' he continued, 'we will be letting one of you go to take our demands out to the police, who I'm sure are already on their way by now. The rest, I'm afraid, will be required to stay here with us as our hostages.'

One of the guards cleared his throat. 'The government won't negotiate with terrorists – you must know that.'

'We shall see. There are too many valuable national heirlooms in this building. Even in these godforsaken times – people starving, people living in shanty towns across this country – there's still a pride in our heritage, our grand past. The people will lynch the authorities if this place ends up burning to the ground.' Kramer shrugged almost apologetically. 'I'm pretty sure they'll negotiate.'

The guard's face stiffened. 'You'd *really* destroy this place?'

'Oh yes.' Kramer smiled sadly. 'I'm afraid I most definitely would.' He took a step towards the security guard. 'What's your name?'

'Malone, Bradley Malone.'

Kramer appraised the portly guard silently. In the distance they could hear the *whup-whup-whup* of police hoverjets already approaching and the wailing sirens of ground response units converging.

'Well, Bradley, I like that you spoke up. I really do. You seem to have more balls than the others. So why don't we let *you* be the one to go out and give the police our demands? You make sure you tell them that we're prepared to wait two hours for things to be arranged. *Not a minute more*. If they're late . . . this whole place will go up like a Roman candle.'

Bradley Malone nodded.

'And if they try something dumb, like – ooh, I don't know – a surprise assault, they'll be very sorry. As I'm sure you've noticed, my men and I are armed to the teeth and, while I'm more of a desk man myself, Karl here, and his boys, have quite an impressive amount of combat experience between them.'

Malone nodded once more. 'I'll be sure to tell them.'

'Good. Well, it's been a pleasure talking with you, Bradley.' Kramer nodded to one of his men. 'Send him out the front entrance.'

He watched them go, then turned to Haas.

'Karl, have the other guards taken into the basement; we'll hold them down there. And let's get our kit down there too. No time to waste – the clock's ticking now.'

'Yes, sir.'

The men moved quickly and efficiently, hustling the hostages through double doors labelled with a fading sign: TO STORAGE BASEMENT: STAFF ACCESS ONLY. The rest of them began to lift their crates and canvas sacks of equipment after them, banging clumsily through the swing doors and grunting with effort as they hefted them down concrete steps to the basement.

The sound of the hoverjets and sirens had grown louder, and through the metal grilles that covered the building's grand front windows he could see the blue flash of police lights. Apart from a couple of his men, stationed by the windows, keeping an eye on the police assembling outside, weapons unslung and ready to fire, Kramer stood alone in the dim interior of the Museum of Natural History's main hall.

'That should keep everyone busy enough, for now,' he muttered quietly.

CHAPTER 14

2001, New York

Foster pointed up at the New York skyline. 'Do you see something there that *shouldn't* be there?'

Maddy gasped. 'Oh my God . . . the Twin Towers!'

'That's right,' said Foster, 'the World Trade Center.'

She looked at him. 'Does this mean history's changed already? That they *won't* be destroyed by terrorists?'

The old man shook his head sadly. 'Sorry, no. History remains unaltered . . . remains in this case – regrettably – as it should be.'

'Oh man.' Her eyes moistened. 'I'd forgotten how beautiful they looked, all lit up at night like that.'

'The agency picked this time and this place for a very good reason,' Foster continued. 'Today's date is the tenth of September. Tomorrow is the eleventh.'

Sal looked up at him. Her eyes widened, suddenly registering something. '*Nine-eleven!*' she said. 'I remember, we studied that in school. That's going to happen tomorrow?'

Foster nodded.

Liam looked from one face to another, bemused. '*Nine-eleven?* What's that? What's going to happen?'

'*Nine-eleven* is how people refer to the terrible thing that will happen tomorrow morning, Liam.'

Foster gestured up at the glowing skyscrapers towering above Manhattan's cityscape like sentinels. 'Tomorrow, at eight forty-five a.m. precisely, a plane full of people will be deliberately crashed by terrorists into the side of the north tower, and about eighteen minutes later another will be crashed into the side of the south tower. By ten thirty a.m., both towers will have collapsed in on themselves and about three thousand people will have lost their lives.'

Liam looked at Maddy and noticed the glistening trail of tears running down her cheeks.

Foster took a deep breath. 'Many people in New York lost someone they loved, someone they knew. The nation was traumatized. Tomorrow, Liam, this will feel like a very different city.' He placed a comforting hand on Maddy's arm. 'I'm sorry. I know from our computer records that you lost family in there.'

She nodded. 'A cousin. Julian. He was cool.' She could have told the others how she'd had a childhood crush on him. How he'd made her laugh till she cried whenever he came to visit. He'd run the computer network for one of the banks. Julian died along with three thousand others. Died, and left them nothing to bury.

'I know this is painful for you,' continued Foster, 'but for practical purposes this is an ideal location for an agency field office.'

'Why?' she asked, wiping her cheeks dry. 'Why does it have to be here? . . . Why now?'

Foster paused for a moment, thinking how best to explain.

'The archway you awoke in, the field office, exists in a time bubble of forty-eight hours. Two days. Monday tenth and Tuesday the eleventh of September 2001. Come midnight on Tuesday it automatically resets back to the beginning of Monday. You, as a team, will live within that time bubble. You will live those two days over and over again, whilst for the rest of the world those two days will come . . . and go.'

'But why does it have to be *these* two days?' asked Maddy. 'I remember that day. I was nine. My mom and dad both cried the whole day, that Tuesday. Why *then*?'

'Because everyone's attention will be on what happened. No one will ever notice the comings and goings from that little archway beneath the bridge. No one will ever remember –' Foster glanced at Liam – 'this young man dressed in a steward's uniform, wandering around the night before. Your existence here will never affect time, never *contaminate* time . . . you'll never be remembered by anyone. All anyone will ever recall of today and tomorrow will be the horrendous images of the planes striking the towers, the towers coming down, the dust-clogged streets, the grief-stricken survivors emerging from the smoke.'

He shrugged. 'I'm sorry, but it's how we stay unnoticed, Madelaine, it's how we keep the agency a secret. It's how we keep from contaminating time ourselves.'

She nodded silently, new tears beginning to fill her eyes.

He rested a hand on her arm. 'I'm truly sorry. Do you remember the day before?'

She shook her head.

He smiled. 'The day before, the Monday, really was beautiful. A warm and sunny day, Central Park filled with tourists and New Yorkers enjoying the warmth without a care in the world. Take comfort in that, Madelaine, at the end of every grim Tuesday, because for you the world *resets* and that Monday waits to happen once more.'

Maddy wondered if that meant she might one day catch sight of Julian striding to work in his smart office clothes, be able to talk to him again. Warn him not to turn up for work?

No . . . No, I guess I can't. She shook the tempting notion from her head, knowing that it would come back again to taunt her.

Foster glanced at his watch. 'It's been a few hours now. The seeker should have faded away.'

Liam swallowed anxiously. 'You're sure of that, Mr Foster?'

'Yes. It was already dying when we left. I left everything powered off, even that light switch. It'll have faded away by now. We should head back. There's much for the three of you to learn, and learn quickly.'

Maddy drew her eyes from the towers and studied Foster intently. 'Why the rush?'

'And why *us*?' asked Sal.

'Why you? It's simple. All three of you have the specific skills we need. Now we have you, though, I need to train you for the work at hand.'

Foster took a moment to consider what to say next. 'And I'll not lie to you . . . it's going to be dangerous.' He looked at them sombrely. 'I lost the last team because of a silly mistake, a simple, stupid mistake. They should have scanned before pulling me back. They didn't. So this time the training's going to be more thorough. All three of you will need to work hard. You'll need to understand how time works, know what you're doing or . . .' He paused, looking away.

'Or what?' asked Sal.

'Or you'll end up like the last team.'

They stood in silence, watching the busy street, listening to the bustle of cabs, the thumping bass of a passing sound system, the distant squawl of a police siren bouncing off skyscraper walls of glass and steel.

'Mr Foster,' Liam said after a while, 'what if we *don't* want to do this?'

The old man offered them a sad, pitying smile. 'Then there's only one place you can go . . . back where I found you. For you, Liam, back on deck E, just as that poor broken ship starts its descent to the bottom of the Atlantic Ocean.'

Liam shuddered involuntarily at the thought.

'I'm sorry. It's not much of a choice, is it?'

'Not really,' muttered Liam.

He spread his hands. 'I'm afraid that's the way it is.'

Maddy shook her head. 'Well, there's no way I'm going back on to a plane that's about to crash and burn.'

'If you decide to stay,' cautioned Foster, 'there's no leaving. If you decide to stay, you're in for good.'

'Until we die in the service of this agency?'

He nodded sombrely. The three of them regarded the old man in stony silence.

'Right,' he said, 'we should probably head back. There's one more member of the team I want to introduce you to.'

Liam cocked his head. 'Someone like us?'

'Not exactly . . . no.'

CHAPTER 15

2066, New York

It's down here somewhere in the dark, Paul. Can't you feel destiny tugging at your sleeve?

He didn't. What he felt were the eyes of Karl and his men upon him, anxiously, impatiently, watching him thumbing through his little black notebook.

Through the open door, leading on to the stairwell up to the main hall, he could hear the muted echo of a loudhailer coming from outside. Apparently they already had a negotiator out front trying to establish contact. If he wasn't so preoccupied down here, it would have been fun to be upstairs in the museum's main hall watching the growing circus building up out there.

'Sir,' Karl prompted under his breath, 'there's only half an hour left of your deadline. They will surely come in soon if they think negotiation isn't getting them anywhere.'

'I know,' he replied, looking down at the pages of his scrawled handwriting. 'It'll take just a moment.'

Karl looked around the basement. It was filled to the high ceiling with crate after wooden crate of varying shapes and sizes, each stamped with a unique catalogue number. There were hundreds, no, thousands of them stacked down here on long rows of metal brackets and wooden-slat shelving.

Kramer looked up and noticed the concern on Karl's face.

'Karl, these boxes are all categorized. It may appear random, but they were very careful when they closed down the museum to store the exhibits by department, by sub-department, by genus, by species.'

Kramer waved the black book in front of Haas. 'He wanted to be able to locate it easily, quickly – not have to sift through a thousand wooden cases.' Kramer looked around. 'We'll find exactly where it's located,' he added. 'The answer's in this little notebook. Trust me.'

Kramer flicked through a few pages, finally running his finger down a page filled with fading handwriting.

'And here it is. CRM, three-zero-nine, one-five-six-seven, two-zero-five-one.'

Karl Haas turned to inspect the nearest crates, but Kramer grabbed his arm.

'We don't have the time to check *every* box. We can work out where to start looking from the number.'

'How?'

'CRM is the prefix code for the scientific exhibits. Three-zero-nine is the palaeontology department.' Kramer turned round and approached the huddled security guards.

'Tell me, gentlemen, where are the dinosaur exhibits stored?'

They shook their heads nervously. One of them, a frail old snowy-haired man who looked ten years past retirement age, nodded towards a nearby wall.

'Th-there's a chart just th-there.'

Kramer smiled. 'Ah yes . . . I see, thank you.'

He stepped over, tore it off the wall and examined it quickly. 'Right. It's down there, I think.' He pointed along an aisle that faded away into darkness. He pulled a torch out of his backpack and switched it on, heading at a swift trot into the narrow passageway flanked on either side by shelves laden with wooden and cardboard boxes of all shapes and sizes.

After a minute he stopped and checked the code stamp on the box nearest him. 'Two-zero-seven, we're getting closer,' he whispered to himself, and set off again at a trot.

Footsteps behind him.

He turned to see Karl, his torch a swinging beam of light lancing out in front of him. 'Sir? Can I help?'

Kramer stopped. 'Yes. Get the men to bring the Porta-Gen down this way. As soon as we locate this thing, we'll need that generator cranked and ready to go.'

'Yes, sir.'

Kramer continued into the darkness a while further, then once more drew up and checked the catalogue stamp on a nearby box.

'Three-zero-six,' he wheezed, winded by the exertion.

Geology . . . very close now.

He walked swiftly, panning his torch across boxes that were increasing in size, from small shoeboxes to crates that could fit an armchair, and even larger ones in which one might fit a small car . . . *or even a dinosaur.*

He grinned. This was it, palaeontology.

It's got to be somewhere here.

Kramer checked his watch. They had about twenty minutes left until the deadline he'd given expired. There was no guarantee the police were going to hold back until then, of course. But he suspected they probably would, and then stall a while longer after that, fine-tuning their plans to storm the museum and take down the terrorists inside with the minimum amount of damage to the nation's treasures.

He swung his torch from one box to the next, quickly scanning the catalogue numbers.

Getting close.

He clambered up on to the lowest crate and swiped the beam of his torch across the ones stacked on the shelf above.

'Come on, come on,' he found himself hissing, 'where the hell is it?'

His eyes darted from one number to the next. 'It's got to be here somewhere.'

It is, have faith.

As if in answer to a prayer, his torch spilled across a CRM-309 number. He quickly swung the torch back and read the next four digits.

'One . . . five . . . six . . . seven . . .'

He looked down at his notebook.

CRM-309-1567-2051.

He looked up at the crate again and his lean face creased with relief that the old man, Waldstein, had been smart enough not to smash up his machine as he'd publicly claimed . . . but instead to have secretly arranged to hide it down here while the museum was being mothballed.

There, didn't I say have faith?

Kramer nodded. His instinct always seemed spot on.

CHAPTER 16

2001, New York

Liam looked unhappily at the graffiti-sprayed metal shutter. 'Are you certain it's safe to go back in there, Mr Foster?'

The old man nodded assuredly. 'We left nothing on in the arch that the seeker could leach from. No power for six hours. It'll have faded to nothing by now.'

He grabbed the bottom of the metal shutter. 'Liam, crank the manual winch at the side there, would you?'

Slowly, creaking noisily, they winched it up and found themselves staring into the ominous pitch-black interior of the archway.

From above the arch a deep rumble made the girls and Liam jump.

'Train from Manhattan to Brooklyn,' chuckled Foster, 'runs over the Williamsburg Bridge above. Come on, there'll be no spooks in here now.'

The old man stepped inside, out of the litter-strewn backstreet, and disappeared into the thick darkness.

Maddy nodded at Liam. 'You first.'

He managed a wavering smile. 'There was me thinking *ladies first*.'

'Not in a million freaking years,' she replied.

They heard a switch being thrown inside somewhere and immediately several flickering fluorescent lights, dangling on dusty flex suspended from the archway's ceiling, winked to life, bathing a damp cold floor inside with a pale, unwelcoming glare.

Maddy made a face.

That's our 'field office'?

The floor was an uneven, cold concrete; stained with oil; gouged, scarred and pitted from a lifetime of previous tenants. Across the floor she could see loops of thick cable running from one side of the archway to the other. Inside she guessed it was just about big enough to park two single-decker buses tightly beside each other.

Along the left wall a bank of computer monitors haphazardly filled a grubby workbench. A few yards along from it in the corner she could see a large perspex cylinder filled with liquid, like some kind of giant test tube.

The back wall was laced with entwined drooping cables hitched up off the floor on hooks and running towards a hole in the wall through which they disappeared. Beside the hole was a sliding door of corrugated metal. She presumed that led to another room.

On the right she noticed the little brick alcove they'd awoken in several hours ago. Beside the alcove was a wooden kitchen table, and a scattering of mismatched chairs. A couple of armchairs were arranged over a threadbare throw rug. Another alcove contained an electric stove, a kettle, a microwave and a skanky-looking sink. Beyond that, an open door led on to an uninviting toilet.

It reminded Maddy of her older brother's grubby shared flat in Boston; all it needed was a floor knee-deep in dirty laundry and discarded pizza boxes.

'It's a mess,' said Maddy.

Foster stepped over a rats' nest of network cables gaffer-taped to the floor.

'It's your home,' he said. 'Come on in.'

They stepped gingerly inside. Sal scooped her fringe out of her eyes and surveyed her surroundings with a barely concealed expression of distaste on her face.

'Can we decorate?' she asked.

Foster laughed. 'By all means. A few more cushions, posters and throw rugs won't do any harm. Sal –' he pointed – 'would you hit that switch there?'

She turned round and looked at the wall beside her. 'This one?'

'That's right.'

She did so and, with a cranking whir, the metal shutter wound down behind them, clattering noisily as it hit the bottom.

While the three of them stood motionless, trying to find something to like about their new surroundings, Foster strode across the floor, stepping carefully over snaking cables, towards the metal sliding door on the back wall.

'What is all this stuff, Mr Foster?' asked Liam, pointing towards the computer monitors on the workbench and the large cylindrical water tank.

'All in good time, Liam. First, I'm going to acquaint you with the fourth member of your team.' He reached for a handle, slid back a locking bolt and pushed the door noisily aside.

Sal, Maddy and Liam stepped cautiously towards Foster, looking through the opening into the dark space beyond.

'Come on, nothing's going to bite you,' he said, waving them over. 'Your other team member's in here.'

'So, er . . . why's our teammate hiding alone in a dark closet?' asked Maddy suspiciously. 'He's not some kind of weird albino freak, is he?'

'He's . . .' Foster hesitated. 'Well, perhaps the best thing is for me to just introduce you. Follow me.'

He took a step into the darkness. Sal swallowed nervously as she heard his shoes clacking across the hard floor inside.

'We normally keep the lighting very low in here. The in-vitro candidates are very sensitive to bright lights, especially the smallest ones. Just a second . . .'

They heard Foster moving around, fiddling with something in the darkness. Then, very gently, a couple of wall lights began to glow red softly. With that, they could just make out half a dozen tall cylinders in front of them, each about eight feet tall. As the soft crimson glow from the lights above increased, Maddy decided to lead the way in.

She could see tall cylinders of clear perspex. Inside each she could just about make out some dark, solid mass.

'So, uh . . . what's in those tubes?'

'I'll give you a little more light,' Foster spoke in the gloom. They heard him flick a switch and then, in the bottom of each cylinder, an orange spotlight winked on, illuminating the contents.

'Oh my God!' She recoiled. 'That's . . . utterly gross!'

Each cylinder contained what looked like a watery tomato soup in which floated a gooey sediment and strands of soft tissue that dangled and wafted like snot in a toilet bowl. In the middle of the murky stew of the nearest tube floated something small and pale and curled up on itself. Strands of umbilical tissue connected to it so that it looked like a pale larva caught in a glistening web of entrails.

'That's a . . . that's a human foetus! Isn't it?' said Maddy, stepping towards it and peering closely through the glass. Liam and Sal joined her.

'Prenatal phase. That one is in pre-growth stasis. It'll remain like that until we need it.'

'Here,' he said, standing by the next tube along, 'we have one that is approximately one third of the way through the growth cycle.'

They looked into the murky water of the second tube to see what appeared to be a boy of eleven or twelve years of age, hairless, naked and tucked into a similar foetal curl. Like the foetus, umbilical cords connected to it and curled down to the bottom and up to the top of the cylinder.

Liam found himself recoiling at the sight. Horrified, disgusted and curious at the same time.

'That's not a *real* boy in there . . . is it?'

'No, it's an artificial,' Foster said. 'Grown from engineered human genetic data.'

Liam shrugged. The word 'genetic' meant absolutely nothing to him, but he was reassured by Foster's answer that he wasn't looking at a *real* child floating like a pickled egg in a vinegar jar. He leaned closer to get a better look at the still form of the boy.

And then its eyes suddenly snapped open.

CHAPTER 17

2001, New York

'Oh Jayzus!' Liam blurted as he and the girls lurched backwards in horror.

'It's OK,' said Foster. 'It's OK. It's not going to leap out and get you.'

All three of them gathered their breath. Sal giggled nervously. Maddy shook her head. 'Oh my God, it's like something out of *Aliens*.'

They watched in silent fascination as the boy's eyes slowly swivelled round to look at them through the murky fluid.

'I think it's seen us,' said Maddy.

'Yes,' replied Foster, 'it's seeing us, but there's no intelligence there. The body's motor responses are handled by a small organic brain at this stage. It has the brain capacity of a mouse. Real cognitive processing, in other words . . . *thinking*, that's incorporated later when they're nearly full term.'

The boy's mouth opened and closed silently.

'Is it trying to talk?' whispered Sal.

'No. That's just a reflex action.'

Liam watched the cloudy liquid drift in and out of the boy's open mouth. 'How can it breathe?'

'Oxygenated liquid solution. It's breathing the liquid into its lungs, just like we breathe air.'

Liam shuddered at the thought of that. 'But that must feel just like drowning.'

Foster nodded. 'I suppose it would feel like that if you were unused to it. But this unit has known no different.'

The boy in the tube cocked his head.

'Jahulla!' gasped Sal, leaping back. 'Did you see that?'

Maddy stepped closer to the glass tube. 'Are you sure it's not . . . you know . . . *thinking*?'

Foster nodded. 'Trust me. There isn't enough brain matter in there to *think*. Yes, it's awake and looking at us, but it's not wondering who we are.'

She shook her head. 'It looks just like a normal little boy. That doesn't seem right to me.'

'Come on,' said Foster. 'We're here to meet your colleague.'

With some difficulty he managed to drag them away from the boy in the tube, past a couple of tubes covered over with a tarpaulin.

'What's in there?' asked Liam.

Foster shook his head. 'Mis-growths. I'll need to flush them some time.'

'Mis-growths?'

'Ones that didn't turn out quite right. It happens from time to time.'

Sal started to lift the canvas and peek under, before Foster stepped forward and pulled the tarpaulin back down. 'Probably best if you *don't* look, Sal. Inside these tubes is the stuff of nightmares.'

'Oh,' muttered Sal.

'Here,' said Foster, 'this is your colleague.' He pointed towards the last tube. Like the others it was full of murky organic soup, but this time, through the floating clouds of debris, they could see a fully grown man.

'Gosh!' uttered Maddy. 'It's freaking . . .'

'Well built?'

She nodded. Liam studied the creature inside. He was easily six, maybe seven, feet tall, broad shouldered, every part of his stocky frame wrapped with well-defined, bulky muscles. Liam was reminded of a book by a woman called Mary Shelley. The story was about a monster raised from the dead by a mad old man called Frankenstein.

'It looks like some kind of superhero,' whispered Sal in awe.

'Uh . . . it looks very strong, so it does,' said Liam warily, guessing how much damage just one of those huge hands could do. 'Are you sure it'll behave itself, Mr Foster?'

The old man laughed. 'Oh, don't worry, Liam, you couldn't hope for a more reliable colleague.'

'Does this one have the brain of a mouse too?'

'Yes. But it also has a silicon neural net processor unit and a wafer-plex data storage unit inserted into its cranium.'

Liam looked at Foster, bemused by the gobbledegook. 'A silly-con new . . . what?'

'A computer in its head,' cut in Sal.

Liam, none the wiser, turned to Sal. 'A what?'

She sighed and cocked a dark eyebrow. 'You really are from 1912, aren't you?'

'It's a machine that lets the unit store information, Liam,' said Foster. 'Lots and lots of it. In that skull is a small block of circuitry that we can fit more facts into than a hundred libraries full of books.'

Liam's jaw dropped. 'How's that possible?'

Foster waved a dismissive hand. 'That'll have to come another time. The history of computers is another whole subject, and one we don't have time for right now.' He stepped towards a panel on the side of the tube. 'This unit's been full term for a while now – waiting its turn. So, let's not keep it waiting any longer, eh? Stand well back . . . This stuff really smells.'

He punched a button. The bottom of the perspex tube swivelled open, releasing a flood tide of the thick liquid on to the floor. It splattered and spread – a large viscous steaming pool of gunk that smelled appalling, like meat gone bad. The creature inside flopped out through the bottom on to the floor, loose and lifeless like a large twist of boiled tagliatelle.

'It's dead,' said Sal.

'No, it's *booting up*,' replied Foster. 'Give it a moment.'

They watched in silence as the warm foul-smelling liquid steamed on the floor. Liam noted with some relief that it was draining away through a grille in the middle of the floor.

Then the naked form twitched.

Maddy and Sal gasped.

'That's a good boy,' whispered Foster. 'Come on now.'

The muscles flexed and rippled down its back as it slowly stirred to life. After a few groggy seconds it pulled itself up on bulging arms, as thick as any normal person's thighs, until it kneeled on its hands and knees.

The creature's gaze slowly drew up from the floor and rested on them.

Liam could see in the thing's grey eyes the twinkling of something that looked like an awakening intelligence. The clone opened its mouth and vomited out a river of thick pink goo that splattered on to the floor.

Maddy made a face. 'Ewww.'

Sal curled her lip. 'Oh, that's totally jahully gross.'

'Has it just been sick?' asked Liam.

'No, it's emptying the liquid out of its lungs.'

It gurgled for a moment, the sort of sound a contented baby

might make after a feed. Finally, its mouth struggled slowly to form what appeared to be a clumsy and awkward version of a friendly smile.

'Ba-a . . . gagah . . . bub . . . glah . . .?' it uttered.

CHAPTER 18

2066, New York

Kramer finished erecting the wire cage, tightening the last of the bolts holding it together before standing back to look at it.

'This is it?' asked Haas. 'This really is the first ever time machine?'

Kramer nodded, admiring it silently.

It was little more than a metal grille box, the size of a shower cubicle. Sitting beside it on the floor was something that looked like a copper kettle and, next to it, a modest palmtop computer. A few feet away their portable generator chugged noisily, feeding a steady supply of power to Waldstein's machine.

'The displacement energy field is fed into the wire cage,' said Kramer. 'It's only big enough for us to go through one at a time. It's going to take us longer than I thought to get where we're going.'

Karl Haas looked at his watch. 'The deadline passed half an hour ago, sir. The police surely won't wait much longer.'

Kramer nodded. 'I know. We should get started.' He kneeled down beside the palmtop and started to tap the touch-screen with a stylus.

'It will be cold where we're going, Karl. The men will need to pull out their winter tunics.'

'I'll warn them. Should I call through the –?'

His question was interrupted by the sound of a muffled thud.

Kramer looked at him sharply. 'What's that?'

'They're coming in!' Karl straightened up. 'I'll have the men fall back from the main hall. We can hold them on the stairwell to the basement. It's a good choke-point.'

'Whatever you think best. Just buy me as much time as you can.'

Karl nodded and turned on his heel, running down the dark aisle and already on the radio to his men upstairs.

Kramer looked back at the screen and tapped in the time-stamp: a very specific time, a very specific place. He turned to two men standing nearby.

'Max, Stefan, we must start by sending the equipment through first, all right?'

Both men nodded and began dragging their boxes and canvas sacks into the cage.

Karl Haas reached the top of the basement stairs and stared out through the open double doors into the museum's dark main hall.

He thumbed his radio. 'Rudy, Pieter, what's your status?'

The earpiece crackled a reply. 'They're inside the building. They sent tear gas and flash-bangs down the left wing and they're moving our way.'

'Pull back to the main hall. And hold them there for as long as you can. We're setting up a defensive position on the basement stairwell.'

'Copy that.'

Karl squinted into the darkness of the main hall and realized, despite the slithers of blue flashing lights stealing in through the boarded-over windows, it was still too dark.

'OK, gentlemen,' he spoke quietly into his radio throat mic, 'it's show time. Everyone, go to night-vision.'

He reached up to the unit strapped around his crew-cut head and flipped the night-sight HUD down over his left eye.

Moments later he heard the first percussive rattle of a firearm echoing around the empty halls.

He turned to the man kneeling on the stairs beside him. 'You ready for a fight, Saul?'

The soldier nodded, even managed an edgy grin. 'Yes, sir.'

The men lifted in one last sack of equipment and closed the door to the wire cage.

'Stand clear,' said Kramer.

He looked down at the palmtop's small glowing screen. 'OK, then,' he said, crossing his fingers behind his back. He turned to Max and Stefan. 'This is where we get to see if this old machine actually works.'

He tapped an icon on the screen – PURGE.

Immediately sparks spurted from the wire cage, showering on to the equipment inside. For a moment Kramer worried the canvas sacks might smoulder and catch fire, causing the ammo clips inside to explode.

But the display of fireworks was short-lived. As the last glowing embers cascaded down, he realized the cage was already empty. He looked at his two men, wide eyed and grinning like fools. He laughed.

'And so it does.'

With no time to savour the moment, he ordered them to load up the cage again as he reset the transmission program on the palmtop.

At the back of Kramer's mind – although he realized now wasn't the time to voice it aloud – was: in what condition were those things arriving at their destination? Intact? Or in pieces? He could visualize too easily himself arriving in the past and only living long enough to see his body had been contorted into a steaming pile of inside-out organs.

He licked his lips anxiously.

You're not chickening out now, are you, Paul?

CHAPTER 19

2066, New York

Karl listened to the radio traffic coming in from his men. From their quick bursts of distorted cross-talk, it sounded as if they were doing a good job of keeping the police armed-response teams tied down. Both flanking teams had called in at least a dozen kills between them. The police were getting chewed-up out there from the snatched exchanges he could hear over his earpiece.

But already two of his men were dead.

Rudy had gone down early – took several rounds in the chest. Aden, one in the head: dead before he hit the ground.

His men were buying time all right, but they couldn't afford to lose too many. They couldn't afford to lose *any*, if truth be told. There were only two dozen of them. Twenty-four men . . . not exactly an army. Hardly enough to conquer history.

He tapped his throat mic. 'All units fall back to the basement stairwell. Immediately. Keep your heads down. I don't want any more casualties.'

'Doing our bloody best, Karl,' one of them called back. He recognized Pieter's voice. One of the other men laughed over the radio comms.

The intensity of chattering gunfire increased momentarily as both teams laid down suppressing fire before hastily abandoning their positions to fall back to the main hall.

Karl turned to Saul. 'Ready? They'll need covering fire.'

Kramer watched the fourth cageful of equipment vanish amid a shower of sparks. He just prayed to God that their invaluable equipment and his men were all going to end up in the same spot, rather than scattered throughout history.

He looked around. Most of the kit had gone through.

'So now,' he said, 'we need to start sending *people*.'

Max pulled his Arctic-camouflage jacket from his backpack. 'I'll go first, sir.'

'Good man, Max.'

He zipped up his jacket, unslung his pulse rifle and offered Kramer a crisp, clipped salute before stepping confidently into the cage.

'You ready?'

'Yes, sir. Ready to change history, sir.'

Kramer nodded. 'To change it to the way it *should* have been.'

'That's right, sir.'

Kramer saluted the man. He felt self-conscious making the gesture, having never been the military type – but it seemed like the right thing to do. 'I'll see you on the other side with the others, Max.'

'I'll see you too, sir.'

Kramer hit the PURGE icon.

The last of Karl's flanking men raced across the main hall towards where he and Saul were holding position in the open doorway to the stairwell.

Moments later several gas canisters rattled across the dusty marble floor of the hall and instantly spewed clouds of acrid smoke.

Karl's men squeezed past him, gasping and winded from their sprint.

'There're loads of 'em,' said someone. 'It's crawlin' with 'em out there!'

'Down the stairs!' Karl shouted. 'And set up a defence position below at the basement entrance! Go! Go!'

The men trampled downstairs, their heavy boots and equipment packs jangling noisily.

Karl aimed down the barrel of his automatic, his night-sight HUD of little use through the billowing smoke. He fired off a dozen rounds into it, more in the hope of forcing their heads down than in hitting a target.

The kill zone was too wide here for just the two of them to hold. They'd be better withdrawing with the others and holding the stairwell at the bottom. The police would be forced to bunch up on the stairs. A much better kill zone.

'Go, Saul, go!'

'Sir?'

'Down to the basement. Go!'

Saul followed the other men down, leaving him alone in the doorway. Karl pulled three manual-fuse anti-personnel grenades from his belt and set fuse times a minute apart. He tossed the first out into the hall, dropped the second at the top of the stairwell and turned round to scramble down the first two flights of stairs, where he placed the third grenade.

He raced down the third flight of stairs to the bottom of the stairwell.

'Hold your fire!' he called out in the dim light as he descended. 'It's me! It's Karl! . . . Hold your fire!' His voice echoed off the hard breeze-block walls.

His men were waiting, eighteen of them, tucked behind a barricade of boxes and crates hastily built across the open doorway leading to the museum's vast storage basement.

'Excellent work,' he said, slapping the shoulder of the nearest man as he clambered over to join them. 'There's a three-minute spread of grenades up there, which should slow them down.'

He looked around at his men. 'How many did we lose?'

'Another two,' said Saul. 'Dexter and Schwartz.'

His face tightened.

Not good.

'Karl? What about them?' asked one of his men, nodding at the museum's security guards huddled together a few yards away beside another stack of crates and boxes.

'Do we kill them?' he asked.

Karl bit his lip in thought for a moment. They were no threat. Old men, frightened men. He'd let them go up the stairs, but the chances were they'd be gunned down the moment they stepped out into the main hall.

'All right, Joseph, tell them they should go find a quiet corner and hide. Wait until the gunfight is over.'

'OK.'

'Oh, and tell them to make sure they call out to the police *first* before they show themselves. They'll be trigger-twitchy.'

Joseph grinned and nodded. He obviously shared the same opinion of the dunderheads upstairs.

Amateurs. Big boots, big guns and no brains.

The first charge went off in the hall with a dull thump.

Karl put a hand to his earpiece and nodded. He turned to his men. 'Ross, Pieter, Stefan, Joseph. Head down there,' he said, gesturing towards a narrow passageway between two tall storage racks on their left. 'Kramer is down there. He has the machine running now and is sending us back one at a time. You four are first.'

The men nodded and headed into the passage.

The second charge went off at the top of the stairs. Louder. Rubble and debris rattled down the steps.

This is it, Karl, he told himself. *The last holding position*.

CHAPTER 20

2066, New York

Kramer sent the man through and reset the co-ordinates for the next as the rattle of gunfire echoed down the passageway from the distant stairwell. He had lost count of how many of them he'd put through, perhaps a dozen, maybe fourteen.

Karl had radioed through a few minutes ago; they were down to the last five men holding position at the bottom of the stairs. Another man had gone down – Saul. Wounded badly.

Things were getting tight by the sound of it.

He tapped his throat mic. 'Karl, you need to come now!'

Haas's voice crackled back over the radio. 'Someone's got to hold them here, sir. If we *all* turn and run, they'll be on to us in seconds.'

Kramer cursed. Karl was right. Someone was going to have to be left behind to buy enough time for the last two or three to be sent through and for Kramer to sabotage the machine so they couldn't be followed. Already they'd lost five good men; to have to leave one or two behind to hold them off wasn't what he wanted to hear.

'Dammit,' he hissed.

If he'd managed to find the machine sooner, assemble it just a little more quickly . . . or if the police had taken a few more minutes to get organized before storming the museum they could have all been through into the past without any blood shed, without a single casualty.

'I'll hold them,' wheezed Saul.

Karl looked down at him; the front of his grey and white Arctic-camouflage tunic was almost entirely black with his own blood. Several unaimed shots sprayed over the top of the stair's handrail had found him, thudded into his chest and knocked him off his feet. The young lad was spraying thick gouts of blood with each laboured breath; a lung, or both, had been hit.

Karl didn't need a medic to tell him that the rest of this young man's life was now going to be measured in mere minutes, perhaps even seconds.

'Saul, I . . .'

'You have to go, sir.' The young man forced a ragged smile. 'You have to go . . . Change this world for a better one. Kramer's one.'

Karl nodded. 'We'll do it, Saul.'

'You better,' he gasped, a thick curl of congealed blood leaking from the side of his mouth. 'Go . . . now,' he whispered. 'I'll give you . . . as long as . . . I can.'

Karl nodded. Saul was fading fast.

He looked at the remaining men and gestured with a well-practised hand the signal for them to break cover and pull back to join Kramer. As they did so, Karl emptied a complete clip on to the stairs. Sparks and sprayed chips of concrete danced amid plumes of dust. The armed police, getting ready to storm the last flight of stairs, backed off, ducking their heads from the heavy fire.

The clip empty, he looked down at Saul quickly and squeezed his shoulder. 'Perhaps we'll see each other in another time.'

Saul grinned, then began firing at the stairwell with short

economic bursts that would conserve his ammo and hopefully buy his comrades the precious time they needed.

Karl turned and ran after his men, hearing their pounding footsteps ahead of him.

Kramer reset the machine once more. The last of the men with him had gone through and now he was waiting for Haas and whoever else was with him.

He could hear footsteps and, in the distance, short staccato bursts of gunfire.

'Hurry!' he called out.

Out of the darkness two men emerged. Ronan and Sigi.

'Quick!' he said, ushering the first of them into the wire cage. 'Where's Karl?'

'Coming just behind us, sir.'

'All right . . . good.'

He activated the machine, sparks showered and the darkness flickered alive with strobing light as Ronan vanished. Sigi stepped in just as Karl's pounding footsteps could be heard.

Kramer quickly reset and activated the machine.

The gunfire down the aisle suddenly ceased.

Damn . . . they're in.

Karl appeared. 'They're through!' he called out.

'I know, I know. Hurry up and get in,' he said, holding open the door of the wire cage.

Karl drew up and looked at him. 'Who will send *you* through?'

'Don't worry, I'll manage, Karl.'

He hesitated. 'No one gets left behind. Your words, remember?'

Kramer offered him a smile. 'No one left behind, I promise. I'll be right behind you, my friend.'

Kramer closed the door on him. 'I'll see you there, Karl.'

He replied with a salute. 'Yes, sir. I'll have the men ready to move out.'

Kramer nodded. 'Good . . . see you in a minute.' He activated the machine.

Once more the dark area of the storage basement lit up, throwing the wooden fascias of stacked crates into stark relief.

For a fleeting moment, as the sparks showered to the floor, it occurred to him that the contents of some of the crates and boxes down here in this dusty basement were about to be changed. History, recent history . . . the last hundred years to be precise, was soon going to be drastically rewritten.

No bad thing. History as it stood had led mankind here to this dark, poisoned, overcrowded, exhausted world.

No bad thing at all.

Over the noise of the portable generator he heard the thud of combat boots on hard concrete echoing down the passageway swiftly and voices calling out. The police were coming, and fast. He could see the dancing beams of their torches swinging from side to side in the distance.

He kneeled down beside the palmtop and set the co-ordinates one last time. Taking a deep breath, he set a five-second delay on the command, then hit the PURGE icon.

Quickly he stepped inside the cage, pulled a grenade from his pack, pulled the pin and placed it on the floor outside the cage. He shut the door and closed his eyes . . . hoping that the machine would have finished sending him into the past before the grenade detonated.

Come on!

He cracked open his eyes and winced at the sudden blinding shower of sparks cascading around him. Through the wire of the cage he thought he saw the approaching shapes of several armed police swiftly dropping to one knee and raising their guns to fire at him.

Come on! . . . Come on! . . . Come on! . . .

It would be the cruellest turn of fate for one of their bullets to find him a microsecond before he left this world for good. Kramer clamped his eyes shut, expecting any second to recoil from the impact of several lethal high-spread large-calibre rounds or to be blown to pieces by the grenade on the floor just outside the cage.

Then he felt it . . . a sensation like falling, as if the floor of the cage beneath his feet had been suddenly whipped away like the trapdoor of a hangman's scaffold.

CHAPTER 21

2001, New York

'Umm . . . that thing's a complete mong-head,' said Sal, studying the figure from the perspex tube pityingly.

Maddy regarded the creature with something approaching motherly sympathy. 'Are you sure it's meant to be like that?'

'Don't worry,' said Foster, 'the on-board computer is pre-loaded with a basic program of artificial intelligence: its adaptive learning code. It'll pick things up quickly enough, you'll see. The most important thing right now is that it *imprints* you people on its mind. Particularly you, Liam.'

He frowned. 'What do you mean by *imprints*?'

'Think of it as being a bit like a chick hatching from an egg and deciding the first thing it sees is its mother. To ensure the learning code embeds more efficiently, let it bond with you first, Liam. Go on . . . go say hello.'

Liam looked uncertainly at Foster.

'Go on, it's perfectly safe.'

He turned to look at the large muscle-bound form on the ground and imagined this thing could quite easily rip his arms out of their sockets and beat him over the head with them if it decided that might be a fun thing to do.

Warily, Liam took several steps forward, grimacing as his shoes slipped on the drying smelly gunk on the floor. He kneeled down beside the giant and studied it more closely.

'Glaf . . . bug . . . drah?' it gurgled in a deep voice that seemed to rumble up from its chest. The creature was entirely bald, not a single hair on its muscular body, its skin pale, almost milk-white. Liam offered the pitiful creature a friendly smile.

'Hello there.'

'Eh-oh,' it mimicked.

'My name is Liam,' he said, pointing at himself. 'Me . . . Liam.'

'Leee-hammm,' it repeated as it climbed to its feet and stretched out both big hands curiously towards Liam's face. He swallowed nervously as the thing's large hands cupped his face.

This thing's going to crush my head like a ripe melon.

With hands still wet from the sticky fluid, it curiously stroked Liam's cheek. 'Lee-aaamm?'

'Liam,' he corrected.

'Lii-aam.'

'And you are . . .?' Liam turned to Foster. 'Does it have a name?'

Foster shrugged. 'You can decide on the name you want to give it. Try not to think of something too stupid, though. The name's got to last.'

Sal suddenly giggled at the sight of the thing's genitalia.

Maddy turned to the old man. 'Foster, maybe the first thing we should do is give it something to wear? I mean . . . Sal's only thirteen, and I'm . . . well, I just don't want to be looking at *that* right now.'

'No, I'm sorry . . . *Patrick* is a completely dumb name for him,' said Maddy. She sipped her coffee as she studied the large muscular form across the floor while Foster finished putting some clothes on him. 'There was a stupid kid's toon called *SpongeBob Squarepants* that had a dumb starfish character called Patrick.'

Liam shrugged his shoulders. 'I had a big bruiser of a cousin called Patrick. The name seemed to fit.'

Maddy smiled. 'I've got the perfect name for him.'

They looked at her expectantly and her grin widened. 'Arnold! You know? After the *Terminator* guy?'

Liam looked confused.

'Arnie . . . Arnold Schwarzenegger!' she continued.

Sal looked surprised. 'Do you mean Schwarzenegger? The forty-fifth president of the United States?'

Maddy gawped at her. 'You've got to be kidding. *President?*'

'Of course! I remember now,' Sal continued. 'We studied him in American history; they amended their constitution to allow him to be a presidential candidate. Born in Europe somewhere, wasn't he?'

Maddy nodded.

'He started out life playing some kind of robot in a sci-fi movie once, didn't he? What was the movie called?'

'Duh . . .' Maddy rolled her eyes. '*The Terminator*?'

'Oh . . . yeah,' said Sal, 'that was it.'

'I love those *Terminator* movies. They were so cool.' Maddy ran her eyes over his hulking form and nodded approvingly at her suggestion. 'Arnie' was the perfect name.

Liam was about to ask what they were both talking about – *Terminators? Toons? Sigh-fies, Sponge-bobs?* The girls might as well have been talking in Mongolian as far as he was concerned.

'There was this funny bit in *Terminator 2*,' Maddy continued, 'when the hero, this kid called John Connor, introduces the terminator robot to this other guy as his Uncle Bob –'

'Uncle Bob?' cut in Liam. 'Bob. That's a good name. Nice and simple.'

Sal nodded thoughtfully. 'Yes . . . he looks like a Bob.'

Maddy stared at them. 'You don't want to call him Arnie?'

They shook their heads.

'Sounds like a daft name, so it does,' said Liam.

Maddy's shoulders sagged. 'All right, then, *Bob* it is. Nice and simple. At least it should be easy enough for dumb-nuts over there to say.'

Liam looked across at Foster and the large clone. The clone was dressed now in a crumpled blue boiler suit and Foster led him across by the hand, like a child, to join the others sitting around the table.

'Here we are.' Foster sat him down beside Liam. The armchair's tired springs creaked under his immense weight. 'The basic speech software should have fully installed by now. Give it a go and talk to him.'

Liam looked up at the large, hulking clone sitting beside him.

'Uh, hello again.'

The thing nodded and replied slowly in a deep voice that rumbled through the archway almost as loudly as one of the trains that routinely rattled over the bridge above them. 'Hell-o, Liam.'

Foster leaned forward and spoke slowly. 'His full name is Liam O'Connor. Let me introduce these other two. This is Madelaine Carter, and this is Saleena Vikram. But she prefers the name Sal.'

'Hell-o, Madelaine. Hell-o, Sal.'

'And you,' said Liam, pointing a finger towards him, 'we are going to call you *Bob*.'

His emotionless face considered that in silence for a moment. Then finally, with a sincere nod, he announced solemnly to them all, 'I am . . . Bob.'

Foster smiled encouragingly. 'Excellent! The name's registered in his memory; that's all the introductions done.'

'So, what happens next, Mr Foster?'

'You all get a good night's rest. It's been a long day for all of you. Tomorrow we're going to be very busy.'

'Doing what?' asked Sal.

'Training, of course.'

CHAPTER 22

2001, New York

Monday 2 (I think)

I found this exercise book in the archway. The front pages are all pulled out, so I guess someone from the previous team was using it before me. I'm going to use it as a diary. Maybe that's what they were using it for too, who knows?

So, it's weird. Like a dream. Like a strange movie. No school to go to. No busy streets thick with rickshaws and Mumbai smog. No having to wear an anti-choke airmask when I step out.

No Mum and Dad.

Jahulla. It's so weird.

The other two seem to be coping with this freakiness better. Maddy and Liam. I think I like them both. Maddy is eighteen. She's really über-smarts with technical things. She told me that she was a computer programmer back in 2010; she worked on computer games for a job. For a hobby she says she liked 'hacking' things. It's kind of strange, though. She's sort of from the same time as my parents . . . She even likes some of the same old-fashioned music as them. And yet she's just a few years older than me.

That's just so weird.

And Liam? How total-weird. Sixteen years old . . . or a hundred and five years old when you realize he was born in 1896. That makes him a really, really old man! But he's still cute. I like that he's from an oldy-fashioned time, when people dressed all smart in clothes with lots of buttons and said, 'How do you do?'

I feel so odd. I miss my parents. I miss our high apartment. I miss the tops of skyscrapers poking out of the street smog. I even miss watching the elektra-Bollywood show with Mum (even though the song and dance routines are totally jahully embarrassing).

But I'm sort of excited too. I'm here in New York! In the times before things turned bad. Before the global warm-up, the overcrowded cities, the food rationing, the terror bombs in the north, the oil shortages and all that nasty stuff.

And it's, like, so strange to think that in India right now my dad is about the same age as me, a fourteen-year-old boy living in Mumbai, and Mum's twelve and lives up in Delhi . . . and they won't even meet each other for another ten years!

I miss them, though. Sometimes, when the others aren't around I cry. But I don't let them see that. So far, I've kept cool.

Foster is taking me out of the field office this morning to begin my training as the team's 'observer'. I really don't understand yet what an 'observer' does, but I'm sure I will do very soon.

'OK, Sal,' said Foster, 'this is Monday morning, Monday the tenth of September, the day before disaster strikes.' He looked around at Times Square, the very centre of New York, the bustling heart of the city. It was just after 10 a.m., and 5th Avenue was teeming with life.

'Think of today as "normal" New York. This is how it *should* look. You understand?'

Sal nodded.

'You're the team's observer, Sal. The observer is like the nose of a dog – there to detect the very first scent of a reality shift in the timeline.'

'Because someone went and changed something in the past?'

'That's right.'

She gestured around at Times Square, busy and noisy with early-morning traffic. 'But how am I going to know when something is different here?'

He nodded, then thoughtfully stroked his chin. 'Perhaps I should explain why you in particular were recruited. What's so special about you. That might help to explain things.'

She shrugged. Perhaps it might. There was nothing she considered *particularly* special about herself. She preferred black clothes instead of the bright neon poly-silks all the other bolly-boppers liked to wear. She preferred dark-head rock music instead of boomtastic street hop. She preferred her own company and a good puzzle-ebook rather than hanging around some grimy street corner with a load of stupid ditto-heads choking behind their masks on street poison.

'Our archived records of 2026 zeroed in on you as an ideal candidate for recruitment for two reasons, Sal. Firstly, we knew *exactly* when and where you were going to die, which made it possible to locate and extract you.'

Sal nodded silently. She understood that now.

'But secondly you were a Mumbai regional under-12s champion for Pikodu.'

Pikodu was a picture-based puzzle game. It involved spotting repeated patterns in large, cleverly designed grids of random images.

Sal nodded. She was a champion, sort of . . . until she got bored of it. It was a fad, a craze that came in from Japan. For a few years it seemed everyone was into playing *Pikodu Training* on their Nintendo FlexiBoy, on the train, in the bath . . . on the toilet.

'The point is, Sal, it means we knew you'd make a perfect observer. Your ability to spot tiny details quickly – to notice things that others would easily miss, to see patterns in chaos – that makes you the perfect candidate.'

His hand swept out across the busy square.

'You'll witness this morning scene over and over. It'll always be the same and you'll become familiar with it. You'll learn that –' Foster glanced at his watch, then pointed across the square at a young mother who'd stopped pushing her buggy to pick up a soft toy tossed out by her child – 'at exactly ten fourteen a.m. the woman wearing red jeans over there will have to stop on a pedestrian crossing to retrieve a teddy bear for her baby.'

Foster looked around.

'That those two old men wearing smart suits will stop outside the McDonald's and light up cigarettes.'

Sal made a face. 'Ewww. Is that legal?'

'To smoke?'

She nodded, staring with wide-eyed amazement at both men as they casually sucked in then blew out clouds of blue smoke.

Foster laughed gently. 'Yes, Sal. It is still.' He pointed to a giant billboard high up the front of a building. 'You'll know that on this particular day the movie *Shrek* is showing.' He pointed to another billboard. 'That the movie *The Planet of the Apes* is opening soon.' And another. 'That Tommy Hilfiger shirts are the height of fashion.'

Sal curled her lips in disgust and realized that they really loved their naff clothes back in 2001.

He turned back to look down at her. 'Your eyes will register all these tiny details, your mind will remember them,' he said quietly, his eyes locked intently on hers, 'and then, one day soon, you'll know instantly when something's *different*.'

'A *shift*?'

His face creased with an approving smile. 'That's right, Sal, a shift – the very first sign that something has been changed in the past.'

She looked around and realized that, in a way, it was a bit like a very large game of Pikodu.

'You'll see this before either of the others will because, well . . . that's your special talent, Sal.'

'Because I once was a finalist in a jahully old puzzle competition?'

'Yes,' he laughed, 'because you once were a finalist in a *jahully old* competition. And because every Monday you will come out of the archway and take a walk across the Williamsburg Bridge from Brooklyn to Manhattan in this glorious sunshine and you'll get to know this day like no other person in the world.'

'Did the team before us have an observer?'

Foster hesitated a moment before answering. 'Yes, they did. Every team does.'

'Tell me about him . . . or was it a *her*?'

The smile slowly faded from his face. 'She . . . she didn't really have much time to learn her job before –' he sighed – 'before we accidentally trapped that seeker.'

She looked at him sombrely. 'Will there be other seekers?'

He shook his head. 'No . . . because we'll always be more careful in future. It's not a mistake I plan to repeat.'

'Where did it come from?'

He hesitated a moment before answering. 'Another dimension.' He turned to her. 'It's the dimension you travel *through* when you ride time.'

'That sounds . . . well, it doesn't sound safe.'

'It's chaos-space. We're merely travelling through it . . . *instantaneously*. You wouldn't really want to hang around there.' She sensed there was a lot more he could tell her about it, but for now he seemed keen to change the subject.

'Come on.' His face brightened. 'Let's see some more of the city. Did you visit Central Park when your dad took you to New York?'

She thought about that for a moment. She remembered a large open area in the middle of Manhattan in which rusting vehicles were stacked one on top of the other: a giant automobile junkyard.

'Is it the place where all the old cars were dumped when the oil ran out?'

Foster nodded sadly. 'Yes. But back in 2001 – now – it's still a beautiful park, with grass and trees and a lovely lake. Would you like to go see it?'

She smiled and nodded. 'I'd like that.'

CHAPTER 23

2001, New York

'You're kidding me, right? My job is an . . . an . . . *analyst*?'

Foster nodded.

She looked at him, her eyebrows arched with disbelief. 'You're telling me I've been plucked from a falling aeroplane and sent back in time to join a team of . . . of *time cops*, and my job ends up being exactly what I used to do?'

Foster shrugged. 'It's not *exactly* the same.'

She looked at the row of computer monitors on the bench in front of her. 'Great.'

'This computer is a cell-based tetra-gig mainframe, carefully transported back from the future and painstakingly assembled by our first team. Which means, Maddy, right now in New York 2001, you're looking at the most powerful computer system in the whole world. And guess what?' He grinned. 'It's all *yours* to play with.'

Maddy reached one hand out and stroked the slim casing of the computer on the bench. 'Mine, huh?'

'Yours.'

'OK . . . I guess that isn't so bad, then.'

'We know from our files,' Foster continued, 'that you worked for a computer-games company. You worked as a programmer on a hugely successful online role-playing game called *Second World*.'

Maddy clucked modestly. 'I guess it was quite popular.'

'You were listed in the credits as the database de-bugger.'

'Among other things,' she replied irritably. 'I also wrote the code for a bunch of decent AI combat stuff and coded some of the coolest parts of the user interface, but did I get credited? *Pffft*. Did I heck.'

Foster nodded. 'But it's the database work, the de-bugging, that makes you so incredibly valuable.'

'Because?'

'Because, Maddy, it's detective work, isn't it? Finding that tiny piece of computer code that's causing a computer game to crash or behave in an unpredictable way?'

'I suppose.'

Foster nodded towards Sal. 'You'll be working closely with Sal.'

Maddy turned to see her sitting on the far side of the arch at the wooden table with Liam and Bob. They both seemed to be teaching the lumbering oaf how to hold a knife and fork.

'As the observer, she'll be the first line of defence.'

Foster had explained Sal's role as observer. It seemed a tall order to her that a young girl's eyes would be better than a computer at identifying a shift.

'When she observes something that has altered, it'll be your lateral thinking, your programmer's mind, combined with the power of this system, linked into the web and countless historical databases around the world, to zero in on *where* and *when* history has actually been changed.'

Maddy shook her head. 'How am I freakin' well going to figure out stuff like that? I was crud at history in high school. I'm not sure I'm the right person to –'

'You'll do just fine,' he cut in. 'You don't need to know a lot of history; you just need a logical mind and a little common sense. I have faith in you, Maddy. You'll be this team's leader, the team's *strategist*.'

'Leader? *You're* the leader, aren't you?'

Foster's voice lowered ever so slightly, as if he was sharing with her something he didn't want the others to know. 'I'm not going to be here forever. Eventually, the three of you, and Bob, will be operating on your own.'

'What? Where are you going?'

'I . . . that's not important. The point is I'm here to get you ready as a team. To be able to function on your own.' He looked at her. 'And your team will be looking to *you* for leadership.'

She glanced across at the others, both giggling as Bob's large hands fumbled awkwardly with the knife and fork.

Me, a leader?

Up until now she'd considered herself more of a loner, happy to work in isolation with lines of code as her only company. Having those two – and that big ape – rely on *her* was bad enough, but having the history of mankind in her hands as well . . .

She shook her head. 'You've got the wrong person, Foster,' she replied. 'I can't do this.'

The old man reached for the keyboard and mouse on the bench, ignoring her. 'Let me show you just how powerful this computer system is. Did you know it's linked into *every* database in the world? From this keyboard you can, if you want to, hack into *any* other connected computer. Through any firewall or encrypted security system.'

'Uh . . . yeah, right.'

'You want to see what's in the President of America's email in-box right now?'

Maddy's jaw dropped. 'You can . . .?'

Foster chuckled. 'Shall we go and take a look at the words of wisdom George Bush has been tapping out this morning? Hmm?'

CHAPTER 24

1941, Bavarian woods, Germany

Falling . . . falling . . . falling.

Dr Paul Kramer opened his eyes and immediately winced in the brightness. He screwed his eyes shut.

'It's OK,' a voice spoke softly.

Kramer tried again, easing them open carefully. The first thing he registered was snow, a deep blanket of it, mostly smooth, with one or two tracks of footprints, and grooves where heavy things had been dragged.

Squatting beside him was a familiar face.

'Karl . . .'

'Just take a moment, sir. There's a minute of disorientation, dizziness. It'll pass.'

Kramer took a deep breath and puffed out a thick cloud in front of himself. There were too many questions he needed answered for him to wait. 'Tell me we have arrived at the right time?'

'It appears to be. Snow for April would seem right.'

'The right location?'

Karl nodded. 'The woods outside Obersalzberg.'

'The equipment?'

'Is right here. It was a little scattered, but the men have located everything that came through and hidden it in the woods.'

'The men all came through?'

Karl's hesitation was enough. Kramer looked up at him, hooding his eyes against the last faint glow of the dusk sky. 'Karl?'

'Tomas and Ethan . . . didn't make it.'

Kramer struggled up on to his legs and looked around at the men. All were kitted out in their Arctic-camouflage jackets, backpacks and webbing strapped on. Each held ready a state-of-the-art M29 pulse rifle; on their heads they wore Kevlar helmets complete with fold-down nightscope and heat-sensor eye-HUDs. An impressive sight that stirred in him a warm sense of pride.

But so few of them.

He counted just seventeen.

'What happened to Tomas and Ethan?'

Karl was reluctant to reply.

'Karl! Please . . .'

His second-in-command nodded reluctantly. 'I will show you.'

He stepped through his men across knee-deep snow that crunched beneath each step. Kramer followed him, pulling out his Arctic jacket, putting it on and zipping it up.

Karl led him into a thick copse of pine trees, branches drooping, heavily laden with snow.

'It appears something malfunctioned during their trip,' said Karl as they pushed through some branches, dislodging a small cascade of powder snow. 'Mercifully, neither of them lived for very long,' he continued, stepping to one side to reveal their bodies. 'They lasted no more than a couple of minutes,' he added sombrely.

Kramer stared at the twisted tangle of limbs and organs. It was unrecognizable as human . . . or, more to the point, two humans. Instead, it looked like some grotesque creature an insane God might construct from the parts left over from Creation – a pathetically corrupted thing with too many arms and legs and internal organs emerging into the open through distorted and bubbled skin that looked like melted plastic. One head, melded to the end of what looked like an impossibly long arm, Kramer recognized as Ethan. He spotted the face of Tomas emerging from a mass of flesh that could only be described as this thing's pelvis.

'My God,' was all he could whisper. 'They were still alive when you found them?'

Karl nodded, grim faced.

Kramer felt his stomach loosen, but he refused to vomit or retch in front of Karl. The man needed to see a confident and strong leader, not someone who doubled over at the first unpleasant sight.

'We knew this might happen,' said Kramer, 'that Waldstein's prototype might be prone to error.'

Put a brave face on it, Paul Kramer, he commanded himself.

'We were lucky to lose only two men, Karl. Only two.'

'Yes, sir.'

'Well, there'll be no more time travelling now; we're done with that. We're where we want to be.'

Karl nodded and managed a weak smile.

'Germany, fifteenth of April . . . 1941.' Kramer nodded at the crest of a nearby hill, now bathed in the cool, silver glow of moonlight. 'Destiny is waiting for us up there, Karl.'

Karl grinned eagerly. 'We will succeed, won't we?'

Kramer nodded. 'Yes . . . we will.'

CHAPTER 25

2001, New York

Maddy looked at Foster incredulously. 'We're going to do *what*?'

'I said, this morning we're going to *deliberately* change history.'

Liam, Sal and Maddy stared at him in silence over their bowls of Rice Krispies. Bob, sitting between Sal and Liam, observed them and Foster thoughtfully.

'Liam,' said Foster, 'today's going to be your first trip back into the past. You and Bob are both going together.'

Bob's thick lips managed a clumsy ill-practised smile that looked more like a camel chewing. 'Is good,' his deep voice rumbled.

'And you?' asked Liam.

'Yes, I'm coming along too.'

'Where are we going?'

The old man raised a finger. 'A-hah . . . now that's a secret. The point of this exercise will be to test Maddy and Sal's ability to find out exactly where we've gone, and what we might have changed.'

'But . . .' said Liam, looking confused, 'but I thought we're *not* allowed to change history, you know . . . at all.'

Bob nodded slowly. 'Changing history is bad.'

'It's what we call a test-bed location,' Foster replied. 'We use this little piece of history to test out new teams all the time. Don't worry. We'll be changing something for a short period of time only, then putting things back exactly as they were.'

'How long will you be gone?' asked Sal. 'Will it be dangerous?'

Foster smiled. 'Not at all. And we'll actually be in the past for a very short time. I've set the computer up to automatically open the return window, so all you two have to do is watch history and work out where we've gone.'

Liam looked across the archway towards the large perspex cylinder full of water. 'And we're going to be climbing into that?'

'Oh yes, I'm afraid so.'

Foster leaned forward and placed a hand on Liam's shoulder. 'Don't worry, we'll warm it up a bit. I'm not that keen on jumping into a test tube of freezing water either.'

Liam removed the last items of his clothing, leaving him wearing a pair of grubby underpants he realized he'd been wearing for far too long.

'You better not be peeking!'

He heard Maddy laugh from the other side of the archway where she was sitting at the breakfast table. 'What's to see?'

'Stop being an idiot, Liam, and get in!' snapped Foster.

Liam quickly scampered up a rung ladder, swung his legs over the side of the tube and into the water. He lowered himself down and found himself facing Bob and Foster, both treading water.

'Well now, this is fun,' he said sarcastically, holding on to the side of the cylinder nervously.

'Why is this fun, Liam O'Connor?' asked Bob earnestly.

Liam shrugged. 'It's not every day I climb into a large fish bowl with –'

'Be quiet and listen,' Foster interrupted. 'I set the computer to send us back in time automatically. We won't need Maddy to set any co-ordinates this time, but normally she would be in charge of co-ordinating this whole process.'

Liam nodded, glancing at her faint foggy form through the scuffed milky plastic of the cylinder. He wasn't sure how confident he was going to feel being zapped through history the first time she had her fingers on the buttons.

'For this exercise neither of the girls know where we're being sent. We'll be there for no more than an hour, then the computer will automatically bring us back. I have downloaded the relevant history data into the support unit's hard drive.'

'Into Bob's brain?'

'Yes . . . into Bob's brain.'

Liam looked at the muscular giant treading water beside him. 'How'd you get the information in?'

'Wireless. It's transmitted.' Foster turned to look at the muscular giant. 'What time are we heading back to, Bob?'

'Twenty-second of November 1963.'

'And where?'

'Dallas, Texas, America.'

'Good. How much time left before the displacement field activates, Bob?'

'Fifty-eight seconds until launch.'

'All right, then,' said Foster, 'any questions?'

'Mr Foster, why exactly are we in our underwear and floating in a pool of water?'

'Contamination protocol. We take as little as we can back with us. That's why. The water is a neutral buoyancy solution so that when the portal activates, we're *touching* absolutely nothing; we're floating. The water, and us, alone, will go back in time – nothing else.'

'I see.'

'Twenty seconds until launch,' said Bob.

'When we count down from five, Liam, I want you to take a deep breath and submerge yourself completely,' said Foster.

Liam swallowed nervously. The thought of letting go of the edge of the tube and allowing himself to sink beneath the surface sent his heart thundering.

'Uhh, Mr Foster, I suppose now's not a good time to mention I never actually learned to swim. I . . . uh . . . I never –'

'I know,' Foster sighed. 'Relax. You'll get used to it.'

Liam looked unhappily at the water. 'But I . . . I'll sink if I let go. Sink like a bloody stone, so I will. I –'

'Don't worry. You just need to hold your breath for ten, twenty seconds, and it'll all be over.'

'My head? My head actually . . . actually *beneath* the water?'

'Yes, head beneath the water.'

'What if . . . what if I'm not actually *completely* under? Would that sort of do, Mr Foster? If I could just keep my face –'

'No. You need to be entirely within the water. Every bit of you. The field scanner will detect if part of you is poking out and the launch will abort for safety reasons.'

'And?'

'And I'll be very annoyed and we'll have to try again.'

'Oh.'

'Information: ten seconds until launch,' announced Bob.

Liam felt his breathing coming out in short nervous gasps. 'I . . . I . . . I'm not sure I can go through with this. I really –'

'You just hold your breath and let go of the side, Liam. Nothing to it.'

'Information: five seconds until launch.'

'No, seriously, Mr Foster . . . I . . . I really –'

'Bob,' said Foster, 'pull Liam under.'

The clone reached out a big hand and a second later Liam

found himself beneath the surface with a mouthful of water, floundering and thrashing in a blind panic.

Sal's mobile phone vibrated.

She pulled it out of her pocket and grimaced at the sight of the old-fashioned handset, an ugly slab of shiny black plastic with the letters N-O-K-I-A stencilled at the top. Nothing like the cool *Earbud V3* mobile she used to own back in 2026. She felt embarrassed pulling this museum piece out of her pocket and self-conscious holding it up to her ear, until it occurred to her that everyone else's mobile phones in 2001 looked equally embarrassing.

She thumbed a button.

'Hello?'

'It's Maddy. They went into the past about a minute ago. Where are you now?'

Sal looked around. She was on Broadway, heading north, just passing the intersection with West 41st Street. 'I'm approaching Times Square, I think . . . yeah, I see it up ahead.'

'So you . . . uh . . . you see anything weird yet?'

She shrugged. 'Not really. It's just like it looked last time I walked over here. Same sunny day, same people, same traffic.'

'Hmm,' replied Maddy, 'not really sure what I'm meant to be doing back here. I'm looking at the Internet, the news pages and stuff. But I don't know what I'm looking for.'

Sal laughed nervously. 'Me neither. I'm just taking a nice walk in the sun, I suppose.'

'And I'm just sitting here like an idiot, looking at a bank of monitors. You OK, Sal?'

It was a busy Monday morning. With the morning rush over and the commuters all tucked away in their high-rise offices, it was mainly clusters of tourists, families and groups of friends taking in the sights of the Big Apple.

Sal sighed. Some company would've been nice. Last time she'd strolled this route a couple of *bubble*-days ago, Bob had been sent along with her to get some more experience at passing as human. With his lumbering seven-foot frame beside her, every inch racked with bulging muscle, she'd felt somewhat more self-assured, accompanied by her own pet superhero bodyguard.

'I guess I'm OK.'

CHAPTER 26

1963, Dallas, Texas

Liam landed heavily amid a tumbling cascade of water, splashing noisily as if a bath tub had been emptied from the top of a short ladder.

He looked up and saw Foster on one side and Bob on the other, both on their hands and knees in a large puddle that spread out swiftly. He looked around. He could see vehicles parked on a tarmac area. They looked less modern, more angular than the cars he was used to seeing every day in New York.

Bob was the first to his feet. He held out a hand each to Liam and Foster.

'I help you,' he rumbled.

Liam grabbed the hand and pulled himself up.

'We need clothes quickly,' said Foster, 'before we attract any attention to ourselves.'

Between a pick-up truck and a dusty-looking car there was a double door with a sign on it: BOOK DEPOSITORY – TRADE ENTRANCE ONLY.

'In there,' said Foster, 'is a locker room. We'll find some clothes on pegs.'

'You sure?'

Foster grinned. 'I've done this training trip a few times now.'

'What if there are people in there?' asked Liam, his hands hovering self-consciously to cover his soaking underpants.

'There aren't. They're all at the front of the building trying to get a glimpse of the president's limousine. It'll be arriving in a few minutes.'

Foster led the way across the parking area and pushed through the double doors. Inside, out of the bright morning sunlight, it was dim and smelled fusty from the stacks of school textbooks littering the floor in untidy piles.

'To your right,' said Foster.

They turned into a room lined with employee lockers and pegs on the wall opposite. At the end was a lost-property box stuffed with odds and sods left over the years. Between them they found enough items of clothing to dress all three of them – although the only items that came close to fitting Bob were a pair of sandals, which his large toes drooped over the end of, and a set of scruffy navy blue overalls.

'We look like three tramps,' said Liam.

'Perfect,' said Foster, 'no one'll think twice about us.'

'Mr Foster,' said Liam quietly, 'what's about to happen?'

Foster turned to the support unit. 'Tell Liam.'

Bob mentally extracted the relevant file from his recently installed database. 'Information: in precisely five minutes, thirty-two seconds, the thirty-fifth president of the United States of America, John F. Kennedy, will suffer a point-forty-one calibre projectile impact to the throat, and a second to the top of the cranium, ejecting approximately twenty-five per cent of his brain tissue.'

'The man's *killed*?'

Foster looked at him. 'Have a guess.'

'And what? We're going to *stop* this happening?'

Foster shrugged. 'More like . . . delay it.'

*

2001, New York

Sal looked around Times Square. This was probably the eleventh or twelfth time she'd taken a walk up from Brooklyn across the Williamsburg Bridge, along Broadway to the hub of the city teeming with endless life. There were so many things to observe in this place – so much going on. She honestly didn't understand how she was supposed to remember every little detail here, how she was supposed to know exactly what should happen in this thoroughfare from moment to moment at this time of day.

Her eyes scanned the major billboards. There was a giant display of a jolly green ogre and the title *SHREK* above his head, and another board with some hairy blue monster and a little green ball-like creature beside him entitled *Monsters Inc.* Further along she saw a poster for the stage performance of something called *Mamma Mia*.

Then, with something that felt like a reassuring stroke of déjà vu, Sal spotted the young mother in the red jeans pushing a buggy before her, across a pedestrian crossing.

Oh, that's right . . . she'll have to stop and pick up a soft toy.

A moment later she did, bending down irritably for it in the middle of the crossing and handing it back to a pair of chubby hands reaching out desperately from the buggy's seat.

That was a weird sensation.

She smiled.

'Wow,' she muttered, pleased with herself, 'I just predicted the future.'

★

'Up these stairs, one more flight to go,' Foster wheezed.

Liam looked across the stairwell, through an open office door. He could see desks and bookshelves and filing cabinets left deserted. Crowded around every front window was a crush of office ladies in floral print dresses, sporting beehive hairdos, eagerly peering out.

'What are we heading up these stairs for?'

Foster was too winded to answer. 'Bob, would you . . .?'

The support unit nodded obediently. 'Information: on the sixth floor of this building is a man called Lee Harvey Oswald. He will shoot at the thirty-fifth president of the United States of America in precisely one minute and twenty-seven seconds. Now, one minute and twenty-six seconds . . .'

'Uh . . . thanks, Bob,' said Liam.

The thing managed a cumbersome approximation of a smile. 'You are welcome, Liam O'Connor.'

As they reached the top of the stairs, Foster slowed down and put a finger to his lips. He pointed through an open door into what appeared to be a storage room.

'This is it,' he whispered. 'Through here, on the left, is a row of windows looking down on to Dealey Plaza. Oswald, right now, has his gun resting on the sill of the second window along. In about thirty seconds –'

'Thirty-nine seconds, precisely,' Bob cut in.

'Bob, be quiet.'

Bob nodded meekly.

'In about thirty seconds the president's car will swing round a corner and into view. The car will approach this building and when it's virtually beneath him Oswald will fire the first shot as it passes. But this first shot,' Foster continued quietly, 'we're actually going to prevent. Follow me.'

Foster walked through the door into the storeroom, Liam and Bob following cautiously. They stepped between stacks of school textbooks, precariously piled on top of each other, coated in a fine layer of dust.

Liam glimpsed, between teetering piles, the hairy tuft of the top of a head framed by a tall window. He turned to Foster and Foster nodded.

That's him.

They stepped across the floor quietly until they were standing over him.

'Excuse me,' said Foster.

Lee Harvey Oswald spun round. His eyes widened at the sight of three tramps calmly watching him. One huge and muscular, one looked very old and the third was little more than a boy.

His mouth flapped open.

The muscular man wrenched the rifle from his hands.

'Lee Harvey Oswald,' said the old man calmly, 'you'd better start running. Run as fast as you can,' he said, offering the slightest sympathetic smile. 'I suggest you head home.'

'Who . . . who are you?'

Foster smiled. 'Hmm, let's see. Oh, I know,' he said, grinning, 'we're the CIA. Anyway . . . you'd better get going or my man here will toss you out of the window head first.'

Oswald nodded uncertainly as he got to his feet, looking Bob up and down. He pushed past them and disappeared out of the storage room, casting one last frightened and puzzled glance at them as he descended the first flight of stairs, three steps at a time.

'Time violation,' cautioned Bob flatly. 'This timeline has now been altered.'

Liam shook his head. 'But . . . but have we not just done the thing we're *never* meant to do?'

Foster nodded. 'Correct. As we speak, time is already shifting, rippling forward through the years. The decades are adjusting themselves, making room for a new reality: that President Kennedy survived today.'

The old man looked out of the window and watched the open-top limousine, escorted by a string of motorbike cops, sweep sedately up the street towards an overpass . . . and a grassy hill.

CHAPTER 27

2001, New York

Sal was beginning to feel a little foolish now, standing at the intersection of Broadway and West 44th Street watching the world go by. A sweet old woman had stopped only moments ago to ask whether she'd lost her mommy and daddy and needed to be taken to a policeman.

Very embarrassing. I'm thirteen, for jahulla's sake!

She was about to head for somewhere a little less busy to stand, away from the steady flow of pedestrians, when she felt it . . . a passing moment of dizziness, disorientation, as if the world was a giant tablecloth and someone, somewhere, had just given the corner a very gentle tug. She reached out for a litter bin to steady herself. Then, recovering her balance, her eyes registered something very subtly different about Times Square long before her brain did.

Something was different.

Her eyes flickered around the busy triangular convergence of streets, thick with Monday-morning traffic.

'What is it?' she whispered. 'What is it?'

Then her shifting scrutiny rested on something that hadn't been there before . . . a new thing. Above the entrance to the PrimeTime cinema the billboard that had been announcing the arrival of *Planet of the Apes* had instead been replaced by a large flickering screen showing some kind of news programme.

There was text at the bottom: CNN: MISSION UPDATE – Day 346.

She watched a grainy image of several men in crumpled orange boiler suits holding clipboards and chatting amicably within the cramped confines of some sort of capsule . . .

Subtitles ticker-taped on to the screen: +++*Cmdr Jerry Hammond and crew celebrate Anton Puchov's thirty-fifth birthday*+++

Sal noticed that few, if any, of the pedestrians on the pavement around her seemed particularly interested in the broadcast, as if it was something commonplace – old news for them.

The image of the men manoeuvring awkwardly in the cramped interior changed to a picture of a rust-coloured sphere floating against an ink-black backdrop. A new ticker-tape subtitle appeared:

+++*Mission to Mars: 80 days to Mars orbit*+++

+++*CNN warmly wishes Anton a happy birthday*+++

'Oh my,' she gasped, and pulled the mobile phone out of her pocket.

The phone buzzed in Maddy's hand. 'Sal?'

'Did you feel it? The dizziness?'

'I felt sort of nauseous about a minute ago. Thought it was my asthma,' she said, glancing down at her inhaler.

'I think . . . I think . . . that was a . . . that was IT.'

Maddy sat up. 'What? . . . You mean a shift?'

Sal hesitated. 'Yeah . . . there's something else.'

'What?'

'On the big screen here . . .'

'What?'

'There's a rocket on its way to Mars . . . I think.'

Maddy nearly splashed some coffee on to the keyboard. 'You serious?'

'I'm watching it right now . . . on CNN.'

Maddy looked up at the row of monitors in front of her. At first glance none of them appeared to be showing anything out of the ordinary. One showed Fox News and some dull political story, the second was tuned into MSNBC and a weatherman promising a warm sunny day tomorrow, the next was tapped into the stock exchange, another showed BBC News 24 and was running a story about the Spice Girls' forthcoming world tour and the tickets selling out within an hour . . .

'Oh my God,' she wheezed, suddenly short of breath.

Didn't they split up in the nineties?

But here they were promoting their seventh album!

'You're right! Something's changed, Sal.'

She felt the burden of responsibility beginning to settle on her shoulders, remembering Foster's quiet pep talk, that it was down to her to pull the strings together, to make sense of the data . . .

. . . to locate the source of the change, Maddy . . . that's your job, to find where the shift is coming from.

She looked at the wall of screens in front of her and wondered where exactly she was supposed to make a start.

'Thanks, Sal. I'll call you back,' she said quickly, and snapped her phone shut. She tapped the keyboard and pulled up the CNN news feed. And there it was, a grainy image of the crew inside some cramped vehicle broadcast from God knows how many hundreds of thousands of miles away, and a computer graphic showing how far they'd gone, and how much further they'd yet to go.

A mission to Mars . . . that's got to be the biggest change here.

'Bigger than a freaking Spice Girls tour,' she muttered.

She did a Google search on the Mars mission, quickly reading the results before her. Not for the first time in recent days her jaw slackened and dropped open.

There was an *enormous* space programme in operation, co-operatively funded by the Chinese, the Russians and America. A small scientific outpost existed on the moon, a 'cartwheel' space station hung in geo-stationary orbit of Earth, a number of supply shuttles had already been landed on Mars ahead of the men en route there. The world – *this* world – seemed obsessed with space exploration, *driven* to reach out to neighbouring planets.

She dug deeper into the history of the programme.

Archived newspaper articles from 1983 described a conference of nations discussing the funding of a 'permanent lunar outpost', to build an 'orbiting mission platform' for 'future projects further afield'.

She found even older newspaper articles, dating from the 1970s, a meeting of minds between the Russian Premier Brezhnev and NASA's goodwill ambassador John F. Kennedy . . .

Kennedy?

She looked at the name again.

Not . . . that . . . *Kennedy? The one who got shot? The president?*

Her history wasn't great. But she'd seen enough movies and read enough books to be certain the guy died back in the sixties sometime.

She saw Kennedy's name suddenly flash up on the CNN ticker-tape feed. A moment later an old man appeared on the screen, a very old man, frail and snowy-haired.

'No way,' she whispered, 'that's not him . . . is it?'

+++Ex-president and goodwill ambassador John Kennedy extends his congratulations and best wishes to the Mars crew+++

Maddy stared at the old man on the screen. 'Hang on. You should be dead,' she said. 'You should've died ages ago.'

But when?

She was almost certain it had happened sometime in the

sixties. She vaguely recalled old news footage of an open-topped car, his wife wearing a pink dress in the back seat and Kennedy in a suit sitting beside her, both of them waving to crowds gathered at the roadside.

Where was that? When was that?

She remembered seeing old news footage from a shaky hand-held cine-camera . . .

The president's head snaps forward suddenly, then back. There's a puff of blood. The man slumps. The woman, his wife, panics. She's screaming. What's left of Kennedy's head is cradled in her lap. The woman looks around desperately for help. Men in dark suits clamber aboard the car. It speeds up. The crowd on the roadside look confused. Some are ducking to the ground. Some are screaming like the lady in pink . . . some seem to be crying . . .

The name of the place where this happened came to her out of the blue.

'Dallas, Texas,' she uttered.

She typed a search phrase into Google:

[+Kennedy +Dallas +assassination]

The search returned only one link that featured all three words. It was from a newspaper article dated 22 November 1963. It was an article about a 'suspected aborted attempt on the president's life'. She clicked the link and a newspaper article appeared on screen.

> . . . a .41 calibre rifle found abandoned on the sixth floor of the School Book Depository overlooking Dealey Plaza. The man suspected of owning the gun, a Mr Lee Oswald, was later arrested at his home. He claimed to have made plans to kill the president during his visit to Dallas, but said he changed his mind at the very last moment. The story is further complicated by sightings of three strangers in the same building

at the time the president's motorcade was passing, who staff described as 'being dressed like vagrants' and were certain had no reason to be in there . . .

Maddy slapped the bench and yelped. 'Yes!'

She knew exactly where and when Foster and the others had gone back to.

'Found you!' she screamed triumphantly.

1963, Dallas, Texas

The three of them watched the president's car slowly roll past them and up towards the overpass in the distance.

'Information: time contamination is increasing,' announced Bob in a calm emotionless voice. 'Mission priority: correct time violation.'

Liam looked at Bob. 'Um . . . how are we going to do that?'

'Recommendation: kill John F. Kennedy.'

'What?' gasped Liam. '*We've* got to kill the man now?'

Foster shook his head. 'Not this time, Liam. Relax.'

Bob's deep voice chimed again with an increasingly insistent tone. 'Recommendation: kill John F. Kennedy immediately.'

The old man watched the car drift slowly away from them. 'There'll be times, Liam,' he said wistfully, 'that you'll wish time could be changed, that things "down river" – in the future – could be made better than they've turned out.'

'But,' Liam replied, puzzled, 'we just *did* change things, didn't we?'

Foster nodded. 'Yes, but on this occasion, history corrects itself after about thirty seconds.'

'It does?' Liam cocked his head. 'How?'

They heard the distant crack of a rifle.

One shot, followed quickly by another.

Liam leaned forward, poking his head out of the window. He craned his neck to look down the road as the vehicle swung left and headed beneath the underpass. He saw a fading plume of smoke coming from a wooden picket fence at the top of a grassy slope. The president's limousine swerved. He saw the lady in the back seat, the lady in pink, scrambling over the seat to cradle her husband's head.

'In this training scenario, we've let history veer off track for less than a minute.' Foster sighed sadly. 'But, on this occasion, history does quite successfully manage to correct itself.' He turned to Liam. 'Many people believed it was Oswald *on his own* who killed Kennedy. But there were other men . . . hired contract killers ready to fire in case he missed or chickened out at the last moment.'

'Information: time violation has been corrected,' Bob announced formally. 'Mission priority: return without causing further contamination.'

Liam watched the chaotic scene down below. The panic among the gathered crowd, the president's bodyguards clustering around the car.

'Was he a good man? A good president?'

Foster shrugged. 'If he'd been given more time, from what I've read in history books, perhaps he might have been a *great* president.'

Liam nodded. 'Pity.'

'Yes.'

'Information: extraction window approaching,' said Bob, closing his eyes and retrieving data from his embedded computer. 'In exactly fifty-nine seconds.'

'We're going to leave now,' said Foster. 'Soon every building along this road will be crawling with police and federal agents.

Bob,' he said, turning to the support unit, 'place the gun on the floor.'

He did so.

The old man led them away from the window of the sixth floor.

'So, how do we get back, Mr Foster?' asked Liam.

'Any second now.'

'Nine seconds to be precise,' offered Bob.

Liam looked about, but couldn't see any large cylinders of water for them to climb into. Then, all of a sudden, he felt a puff of displaced air on his face. A yard ahead of him he could just about make out a shimmering circular outline.

'Automated return window is now activated,' said Bob.

'Say goodbye to 1963, Liam.'

Liam looked around at the storage room, the dusty stacks of school books, and heard the tearful commotion of women's voices coming from the floor below.

'Goodbye, 1963,' he uttered obediently, and then followed the other two into the shimmering air, holding his nose and his breath as he stepped forward.

2001, New York

Liam felt that horrendous familiar falling sensation. Worse still, he anticipated finding himself floundering around submerged underwater.

But instead he found himself standing in the middle of their field office, his feet on hard cold concrete.

'Uh? . . . I thought we . . .?' he blurted.

Foster slapped his back gently. 'We go out wet, we come back dry. I'll explain why some other time.'

Liam spotted the girls sitting at the breakfast table, both holding red and white cans of a fizzy sugary drink called Dr Pepper that they seemed to like drinking copious amounts of. Spontaneously they clinked their cans together and cheered the return of the boys.

'We know exactly where you went, fellas!' shouted Maddy. 'Being the pair of complete freakin' geniuses we are.'

Foster spread his hands. 'And?'

She grinned triumphantly. 'So, how was Dallas?'

'Well done.' He smiled.

'I'm guessing you interfered in some way with the assassination of John F. Kennedy. You saved him maybe? But then you must have put it all right again.' Her face dropped a little. 'Unfortunately. I'd have liked us to have a mission to Mars on the go.'

Sal cocked her head curiously. 'You managed to stop an assassination attempt and then made it happen again . . . and also found some really disgusting clothes to wear . . . and you did *all* that in just under an hour?'

Foster opened his mouth to answer.

'An hour?' cut in Liam. 'We've not been gone that long, have we? Ten minutes at the most maybe –'

Foster chuckled. 'Time travel isn't *symmetrical*, Liam. I could send you to one time location and arrange a return window for fifty years later. As far as you'd be concerned, fifty years would have passed . . . a whole lifetime. And yet to someone standing here you'd have disappeared as a young lad and returned again just moments later as an old man.'

Liam shook his head and grinned. 'Jay-zus, this timeriding thing is making my head hurt, so it is.'

CHAPTER 28

1941, Bavarian woods, Germany

Kramer watched Karl with admiration. The man was a professional soldier, had served with some of the world's elite special forces and thereafter been a highly recommended and highly paid mercenary. In the troubled world of 2066, there was plenty of work for men like him.

Karl had been one of the first to be won over by Kramer's dream of a better world. He'd spoken on Kramer's behalf to other mercenaries he knew and trusted, men he knew who also longed for a better place, a better time.

The world they'd left behind was a place that was dying, choked by pollution, strangled by dwindling resources, a world horrendously over-populated and ultimately doomed.

Who wouldn't want to leave that behind?

It had been easy for Karl to recruit two dozen men he could trust for this mission. Every single man he'd approached had been ready to jump at the chance of leaving the twenty-first century for a chance to rewrite the twentieth century. And good men they were, all of them. Very experienced, very disciplined. They all spoke at least two languages, English being their shared language. Most of these men quietly stepping through the snowy woods with well-practised stealth were German, some were Dutch, a few were Norwegian, a couple of them British.

But . . . only seventeen of them now. Kramer shook his head.

We lost seven men just getting here.

Suddenly up ahead Karl silently raised his hand and made a fist. The men understood the signal and squatted down amid the snow-covered foliage. In their mottled white and grey Arctic-camouflage tunics and waiting perfectly still, they were almost undetectable in the dark.

Karl turned round and beckoned Kramer forward. He crunched lightly across the snow and squatted down beside him.

Karl pointed through the trees ahead. 'Is that it, sir?'

Kramer craned his neck to get a better look. Up a winding track he could make out a couple of sandbagged machine-gun posts either side of a gravel track and a sentry hut bathed in the light of twin floodlights.

'This is it, Karl.' He smiled. 'This is it! Hitler's winter retreat!'

'*Der Kehlsteinhaus*. The Eagle's Nest. It does not appear that heavily guarded.'

'It's up this one road, perched on the side of a steep hill,' said Kramer. 'The building itself is defended by several dozen of Hitler's personal bodyguards, the *Leibstandarte SS*. A little further up the hillside, only a few hundred yards away, is an SS garrison housing four or five hundred of them.' He turned to Karl. 'They will happily die to defend their leader. Your men will have to be very fast, Karl. The moment the first shot is fired, the alarm will be raised and the garrison alerted.'

Karl looked back at his men, perfectly still in the snow, weapons ready and waiting for an order. They were expertly trained and well equipped with modern weapons and nightscopes.

He smiled. 'My men will get to him. Don't worry.'

Kramer wished he shared the man's confidence.

Just seventeen of them. If Karl's men were unable to complete their objective before the regiment-strength SS garrison descended upon the Führer's retreat, then it would be all over.

Seventeen against five hundred?

Even with the advantage of combat technology from 2066, he wondered for a moment if he was asking too much of these men.

CHAPTER 29

2001, New York

'Why have you brought us here?' asked Maddy, looking around the entrance hall of the Museum of Natural History. It was crowded mostly, it seemed to her, with Japanese tourists.

'Because, Madelaine, this building, these exhibits, are what we're all about.' He gestured with his hand at the giant skeletal frame of a brachiosaurus looming over them and all but filling the grand entrance hall.

'This is the history that was *meant to be*. This is the history that you – just like the other field teams – are tasked with defending.' His eyes drifted down from the giant skull above to rest on them.

'Madelaine – the analyst. Sal – the observer. Liam – the operative . . . and Bob – the support unit. You're a team now. And everybody alive today and alive tomorrow is depending on *you* to keep an eye on the time. This museum records how history *is* . . . and it cannot be allowed to change.'

Foster's voice carried a little further across the grand hall than perhaps he'd intended, but since no one else here seemed to speak English Maddy thought it probably didn't matter too much.

'So, this afternoon, I want you to explore the museum. To reach out and really *feel* the history you're defending. I'll leave you to make your own way around and then we'll meet back here in the entrance hall at five sharp.'

They nodded in silence.

'Then I'm taking you guys out to the best ribs and burger place I know. A celebration . . . Think of it as a sort of graduation party.'

Liam found the display of dinosaurs breathtaking and was unable to tear himself away from the giant skeletons and the animatronic dioramas. He was soon left alone as the girls and Bob wandered off to view the other exhibits.

Before he knew it, several hours had passed and he decided to make his way back to the entrance hall to await the others.

He watched the busy area, full of snapping cameras and quietly whispered family conversations, overexcited children and mewling babies. Not for the first time, he felt a warm glow of gratitude to Foster for plucking him from the bowels of the stricken *Titanic*, saving him from the worst possible death he could imagine.

In the last dozen or so days – he'd lost track of how long they'd been here – he realized he was the luckiest person *born in the nineteenth century* for the things he'd been privileged to see almost a hundred years into his future, and all the amazing things he was *yet* to see. He grinned like a fool, like a child promised every Christmas present he could wish for.

His gaze drifted across to a milling crowd beside the large entrance doors. People seemed to be hesitating there on their way out. Curious, he crossed the hall.

On a podium, a large leather-bound book lay open beneath the glow of a brass reading lamp. Beside it an old security guard with a ruddy face, topped with thick bushy eyebrows and an odd heart-shaped mole poking out from one of them, stood to attention.

'Guest book,' growled the guard, noticing Liam's curious

gaze. 'Feel free to sign and add a comment if you wish, sir,' he added reluctantly. 'And keep it clean.'

Liam looked down and noticed the scrawled messages of hundreds of visitors, so many different names, so many languages.

'Keep it clean?'

The guard cleared his throat. 'I know what you damn teenagers are like.'

Liam felt a tap on his shoulder and turned round. It was Maddy.

'Guest book,' said Liam.

'Oh yeah . . . I know. I came here on a school trip once and left a dirty poem,' she giggled.

The guard scowled disapprovingly, his bushy old eyebrows knotted together, as if he actually recalled the very words she'd written.

'You still archive them?' Maddy asked the guard.

'We do,' he replied stiffly. 'We keep every guest book, down in the basement. We've done that since before the beginning of the last century. A hundred years of comments,' he said proudly. 'Not all of them *dirty poems*, neither.'

Maddy cringed guiltily. 'Sorry.'

But the guard was already busy directing a visitor to where the toilets were.

'Go on, Liam. Why don't you sign it?'

He looked at her. 'Uh . . . will I not change history, or something?'

'I can't see how you would.'

He gingerly picked up the pen, attached by a chain to the podium.

Liam O'Connor, 10 September 2001 – I loved the dinosaurs a lot.

'That it?' asked Maddy.

He shrugged. 'Don't want to push me luck now.'

She shook her head and snorted. 'Ah . . . there are the others.'

Liam followed her across the hall, casting one last glance back at the book.

There, I left me mark on history.

If he died tomorrow for whatever reason, at least there'd be a scribbled line on a page of a book somewhere that showed he'd once existed.

'Well done,' said Foster, clinking his glass tankard of beer against Liam's, and Maddy's and Sal's glasses of Dr Pepper.

Bob observed the ritual with a curious expression on his face, picking up an empty glass and tapping it against another.

'You all did very well,' added Foster, before slurping a large frothy mouthful of ice-cold beer. He wiped his lips and, cautiously glancing around at the busy restaurant, he lowered his voice. 'You've all seen how it works now. You all understand the part you have to play in the team?'

Maddy and Sal nodded.

Liam shrugged. 'But I didn't actually do very much, Mr Foster.'

'No . . . not this time. But you will. The agency uses the Kennedy incident as a standard training mission. It's a little piece of history that corrects itself. But when you go back on a *proper* mission it'll be down to you and of course the support unit –' he looked across at Bob, studiously examining a steak knife – 'to make things right.'

'But how will I know what to do?'

'You'll know, Liam. Because you're a very bright young man, quick on your feet.' Foster placed a fatherly hand on his shoulder. 'Initiative . . . that's what you've got. You're a smart lad. No amount of training can give a person that.'

'Uh . . . thanks.'

'What do you think, Bob?'

The clone looked up from the steak knife. 'Mission Operative Liam O'Connor is . . . good.'

'There. I think he likes you.'

Liam smiled. 'Thanks, Bob.'

Foster turned to Maddy and Sal. 'And you two . . . you did very well.'

They grinned, both very pleased with themselves.

'But this exercise is just the beginning.'

A waitress arrived with a tray full of plates. She prepared to deal them out like playing cards. 'Who's havin' the rack of ribs?'

Liam raised a hand. 'I'm starving,' he said.

'The salad?'

Sal raised her hand.

'The burgers?'

Foster and Maddy nodded.

The waitress looked at Bob, confused. 'I'm sorry, sir. What did you order?'

Bob glanced up at her with his piercing grey eyes. 'I do not eat human food unless it is a necessary mission requirement,' he explained dryly.

The waitress cocked her head. 'Excuse me?'

'Oh, don't worry about him,' said Foster. 'He's just not allowed to eat on duty.'

She smiled coyly at Bob, admiring his physique. 'So . . . are you, like, some kind of undercover cop, then?'

Bob turned to Liam. 'Liam O'Connor, explain the term "cop", please.'

Liam shrugged and made a face. 'You're asking me?'

'A "cop",' explained Foster, 'is a slang term for a law-enforcement officer.'

'I understand.' Bob nodded slowly and closed his eyes. 'I am filing the term for future use.'

The waitress looked from Bob to Foster, bemused.

'You guys ain't from around here, are you?'

Maddy finished chewing her first mouthful of burger. 'Oh, you can forget about them – they're Canadian.'

CHAPTER 30

1941, Berghof – Hitler's winter retreat

Kramer cowered behind a small oak bureau in the hallway. Shards of wood stung his face as a dozen rounds slammed into the far side and sharp slithers splintered off.

He rattled a stream of curses out under his breath as the corridor filled with the deafening crack of machine-gun fire.

At the end of the hallway several SS Leibstandarte were dug into covered positions, defending the double doors to *die Große Halle*, the main room of Hitler's mountain retreat.

Karl and several of his men returned fire, their shots peppering the overturned marble table ahead of them behind which the SS were putting up a valiant defence. Showers of powdered marble erupted from the once mirror-smooth table surface, now pockmarked with cracks and bullet craters.

'We have to move, Karl! They'll have reinforcements here any second!'

Karl nodded. He understood the situation all too well.

The attack had started out smoothly. He and his men had quietly slipped past the machine-gun posts either side of the winding road and made their way up the steep rise towards Hitler's hillside chalet. But the game was up when a guard spotted them at the last moment approaching the building's main entrance. He'd managed to fire off a single shot from his gun before Dieter had slipped a blade into his throat.

Hitler's hand-picked guards had been surprisingly swift to react, bustling their leader to safety behind the thick double doors of the main hall and setting up a defensive position outside it. The rest of the SS guard detachment in the building had been quickly and ruthlessly picked off by Karl's men.

It was just these stubborn guards at the end of the hall now. The problem was, though, that their attack had been stalled right here and time was rapidly working against them. Outside the chalet a distant klaxon was sounding and the regiment garrisoned nearby was undoubtedly already scrambling into their boots and on their way over.

Karl's five-man rearguard covering the front entrance of the chalet had as much chance of holding their position as they'd had holding the ground floor of the museum – they were certain to be quickly overwhelmed.

Kramer was no soldier, but he could see that this last hurdle could be the one that finished them. If they remained in this stalemate a minute or two longer, then it was going to be all over. The numbers were quickly going to mount against them, and having modern pulse rifles and elite training wasn't going to make a blind bit of difference.

We're going to die if we don't take those men.

He looked across the hallway to where Karl was crouched. Their eyes met. The man nodded, knowing what Kramer was thinking. A faint smile slipped across his face as he slapped in a fresh cartridge and racked his pulse rifle ready for action.

The other men around Karl took his lead, quickly reloading their weapons and then readying themselves to burst out into the open and sprint the length of the hallway under fire.

Silently Karl mouthed a countdown, turning back to his men, encouraging them with a final devil-may-care grin that told the mercenaries they were going to succeed or die heroes.

Five . . . four . . . three . . . two . . . one . . .

They emerged from their covered positions as one, laying down a withering barrage of rapid-fire high-impact shots that filled the air around the table with a blizzard of chipped fragments and marble powder.

They ran forward, still firing, ten yards . . . five yards . . .

Kramer followed in their wake. He found himself screaming like a banshee.

Karl was the first to reach the overturned table, crashing heavily into it. He swiftly poked his rifle over the top and sprayed the SS guards sheltering behind it point blank with a sustained burst until his pulse rifle clacked like a woodpecker, exhausted of ammo.

Rudy and Sven joined him, emptying their clips blindly over the top of the table into the space behind it.

Then all of a sudden it was as silent as a graveyard.

The smoke and dust cleared around them and Kramer, gingerly lifting his head to look over the top, saw the men dead on the floor, an unpleasant mash of flayed flesh, splintered bone and tattered black ceremonial uniforms.

In the distance, muted through the thick stone walls of the chalet, he could hear the rapid tap of gunfire from the front of the building.

The garrison's here already. We're out of time.

Karl clambered over the table and aimed a swift, hard kick at the oakwood double doors. They rattled heavily and swung inwards.

Karl led the way in.

As he stepped through, a single pistol shot echoed across the grand room and a solitary shard of wood flung off the oak door beside his head.

Rudy, stepping in beside him, swung his weapon round and

emptied half a dozen shots into a portly looking Wehrmacht general with braids on his shoulders, throwing him back across a grand banqueting table covered with maps and scattered typed pages of intelligence notes and field deployments. The general rolled off the side of the table and thudded heavily on to the floor.

Kramer stepped into the room, slowly scanning the sweat-soaked faces cowering behind armchairs and coffee tables. Generals and field marshals – so much gold braiding, so many medals pinned to their chests – and yet here they were looking very much like a class of startled children. His eyes finally rested on a trembling man in a tan-coloured tunic with a dark fringe drooping over one eye, and his distinct toothbrush moustache.

Unmistakably . . . it was the very man they were after.

Hitler was crouching on the floor holding an ineffective-looking pistol in his shaking hand. As the sound of the distant gunfight around the Berghof's entrance grew more insistent, Kramer took a step forward.

'Adolf Hitler,' he said in fluent German, 'your plans to attack Russia in the next few weeks will result in you losing this war.'

Hitler's eyes widened, his lips flickered and tensed, but he said nothing.

'Now, if you want to win this war, if you want detailed intelligence of what your enemies are doing right now, if you want weapons technology that will make you invincible –' he nodded back down the hallway, at the growing cacophony of approaching gunfire – 'then I suggest you call off those men outside and listen *very closely* to what I have to tell you.'

CHAPTER 31

2001, New York

Maddy walked alongside Foster as they crossed the Williamsburg Bridge back over the East River to Brooklyn. In the darkness, the lights of the city danced on the water magically.

'It really is a beautiful city,' she said.

Foster nodded. 'Tonight is special,' he said. 'I always think of this evening as the last one of the "old" New York. Tomorrow, when those two planes arrive, it'll change.'

They walked in silence for a while, watching the others ahead. Sal and Liam seemed to be teasing Bob, laughing at the stiff, unnatural way he talked. There's no harm in that, she supposed. Bob needed to sound a lot more like a human if he was going to blend in, particularly if he was going to be sent alongside Liam on assignments back into the past.

She noticed the old man was looking a little frailer than he had when he'd pulled her out of that plane. He rarely seemed to sleep. Almost every night, after they'd all tucked themselves up into their cots, she heard the archway's door creak open.

'Where do you go at night?'

He looked at her.

She shrugged. 'I hear you sneaking out.'

'I walk around Brooklyn.' He smiled. 'I clear my head. The fresh air does me some good.'

She studied him silently for a moment. 'Are you OK, Foster?' she asked.

Foster took his time replying. 'You've noticed, then?' he said eventually.

'I'm not sure what you mean.'

'That I'm dying,' he said quietly.

'What?'

He looked at her. 'I figured you would've worked it out soon enough.'

'Actually, I was just thinking you weren't looking too well . . . that's all.'

He smiled again. 'That's kind of you. But, in fact, I'm dying . . . very quickly as it happens.'

'What's . . . what's wrong? Do you need a doctor?'

'No, it wouldn't help,' he said, shaking his head. 'This is something *you* need to know, Maddy,' he said, grasping her forearm. 'You can't tell the others right now. Particularly not Liam.'

'What?'

Foster took a deep breath. 'It kills you, eventually.'

'What does?'

'Timeriding,' he replied, 'going into the past. It only has a gradual effect at first – so gradual he won't notice to begin with. But the more he does it, the further back he goes, the greater the harm he'll be doing to his body. The process will gradually corrupt the cells in his body, prematurely ageing him.'

She looked at him, alarmed.

'Yes . . . *ageing* him. At first it won't be apparent. But towards the end, when the corruption has reached a certain level, he will suddenly age fast.'

A thought occurred to her – a question she didn't want to ask, but knew she had to. 'So, Foster, could I ask you –?'

'You want to know how old I really am?'

She nodded.

He shook his head sadly and she thought she saw the glisten of a tear nestling in the deep wrinkled fold beneath one eye.

'I was pretty young when I made my first trip.'

'And now?'

'If I add up all the Mondays and Tuesdays I've served in that field office,' he said, running a hand through his fine snow-white hair, 'I suppose I'd be about twenty-seven now.'

Maddy covered her gasp with a hand. 'Oh God . . .'

He managed a wry smile. 'About ten years older than you. Although inside I still feel young, I've become an old man,' he said, his voice tapering off with the sound of regret, even bitterness in there somewhere. 'He can't know, Maddy,' he added. 'Not yet . . . He's not ready.'

'But it's unfair that he doesn't know what this is doing to his body!'

Foster raised a finger to his lips. Even above the noise of traffic rumbling past them over the busy bridge, her voice might just carry enough for him to hear.

'He has no choice, Madelaine. Either he does this or he has to return to the *Titanic*. At least this way he gets another seven or eight years of life.'

'What if he left? What if he decided to walk away right now, and never came back?'

'He can't do that. It would cause problems.'

'This seems . . .' She felt her voice thicken. 'This seems so unfair.'

He shrugged sadly. 'Life is unfair. You make the best of what life deals you, Maddy. In Liam's case, he's been given a few more years of life that he wouldn't have had otherwise. And think of all the incredible things he's going to see in those years. What about all the incredible things he's seen already? He's a young man who was born in 1896, and yet just now he's enjoyed a cheeseburger, fries and an ice-cold soda whilst gazing out on twenty-first century New York. What do you think Jules Verne or H. G. Wells would have given to trade places with Liam? Just for five minutes? Just for a glimpse of this world?'

'But it's not right that he isn't allowed to know,' she replied.

'Perhaps the kinder thing would be to keep this truth from him as long as you possibly can,' said Foster. He looked at her. 'That'll be your call, Madelaine, when I eventually go and leave you in charge as the team leader. It'll be *your* decision how and when you break this to Liam.'

She bit her lip unhappily and looked at the others again, still giggling and goofing about at Bob's expense.

Oh, Liam . . . poor Liam.

'I mean you both sound so . . . *wrong*,' said Sal, pulling her hood up over her head. 'Real freak show. Like characters out of an old black and white movie.'

Liam scowled. 'What do you mean? Do I not sound enough like everyone else around here?'

She shook her head and laughed. 'No. That funny Irish way you talk –'

'I'm from Cork – that's how we talk there,' he replied defensively. 'Anyway your Indian accent sounds funny to me too. Sort of like Welsh.'

She laughed. 'Bob,' she said, jabbing the support unit lightly in the ribs, 'do your impersonation of Liam.'

'You wish me to replicate Liam O'Connor's speech patterns?'

'Go on.'

Bob's eyelids momentarily fluttered and ticked as he retrieved data stored somewhere in his tiny computer mind.

'*Oi'm Liam O'Connor, so Oi am . . . and Oi come from Cork in Oireland, so Oi do*,' uttered Bob with an expressionless face.

Sal giggled. 'Perfect.'

'Argghh! Don't be taking the mickey like that, Sal. Hang on . . .' Liam's eyes narrowed suspiciously. 'You've not been training him to do that, have you?'

She nodded, clamping her lips tightly.

'Affirmative,' said Bob dryly. 'Sal Vikram assisted me in replicating your speech pattern, Liam O'Connor.'

Liam shook his head with a show of good-natured disgust. 'Well, at least I don't dress like some sort of carnival street beggar, all ripped clothes and messy orange paint splashed over me front.'

'Uh?' Sal looked down at the neon logo on her hoodie. 'Oh, that . . . It's the logo for a rock band. Ess-Zed.'

'Rock band?'

'Bangra rock . . . my parents really hate it. Think it's too western, too American.'

'Oh,' said Liam, nodding politely but not really understanding what she was talking about.

'But it's ten times better than American stuff . . . much darker, with, like, hip-hop dance loops and scream-rap.'

Liam frowned. *Hip-hop dance loops?*

He looked at her. '*Dance* . . . ahhh! So is it a kind of *music* we're talking about?'

Sal looked at him, her face half smile, half bemusement.

He shrugged and grinned. 'Hey, I like music too. I like the brass bands. Marching bands as well. I tell you, you can skip merrily along to that, so you can. And then there's the folk tunes where I come from. Would you have heard of "The Galway Races"? "Molly Malone"? . . . "The Jolly Beggarman"?'

She stared at him in silence.

'No? I guess not.' Liam shrugged. 'Ah well . . . those are ditties you can really dance a sweat to. And then there's . . .'

Sal listened to him chattering on about the dance halls back in Cork, secretly delighting in the fact that he sounded like a walking antique – an old-fashioned young gentleman from another century, all manners and quaint charm – and so unlike the boys from her time. She loved the curious sound of his accent, despite teasing him.

Sal smiled. *What a strange little group we make.*

Like some kind of odd family.

For the first time since she'd 'died', since she'd been plucked away from the life she knew, she felt almost . . . almost *happy*. In a strange way, this felt like it could be a new home to her, a new life she could get used to.

She looked out at the glittering lights of Manhattan, pleased that their field office was here . . . and now in this time, pleased that she was privileged enough to be seeing New York City at its prime before the world started to change – the global crash, the depression – before it all began the long slide downhill.

The night sky above her was thick with churning clouds, bathed in amber light from the city below.

Red sky at night . . . shepherd's delight.

It looked like it was going to rain this evening.

A gentle breeze tossed hair into her eyes and touched the bare skin of her forearms, a murmuring breeze that seemed to quietly whisper in her ear a promise of more than just a little rain.

A storm's coming, Sal . . . Can you feel it yet?

CHAPTER 32

2001, New York

<u>Tuesday 12 or 13</u> (I'm losing count)
It's a Tuesday morning. The Tuesdays I think of as the 'sad' days. The Mondays are the 'happy' days. I hate the Tuesdays, full of grief, those smoking Twin Towers, the crying and fear . . . that terrifying rumbling as they come down, and the air full of dust and scraps of paper.

I'd prefer not to go out into them, prefer to stay in the arch. But Foster says it's important I'm equally familiar with both versions of New York, the 'before' and the 'after'.

It's early right now, 7 a.m. I always seem to be the first to wake. The others are all fast asleep. Maddy snores in the bunk below. Liam whimpers like a puppy.

Sal looked up. All was still in the archway. Foster was asleep on an old sofa beside the kitchen alcove, stirring restlessly beneath a quilt. And Bob . . . Bob rested in one of the birthing tubes in the back room. She wondered what he dreamed about, if anything.

She closed her diary, sat up and pulled on some clothes under her blanket and then climbed down quietly. She grabbed a bin bag full of dirty clothes lying beside the bottom bunk and walked across to the breakfast table.

One duty – collectively agreed – was that every other Tuesday would be a good day to take their meagre supply of clothes down to the laundromat in the morning to collect in the evening.

She checked their small fridge.

No milk.

She sighed. One of the others had finished the last of it without saying. She shook her head and clucked like a mother hen.

They'd starve if it wasn't for me.

She decided to stop off at the 24/7 store on the way back to pick up some half-fat milk, some bagels and some more Rice Krispies since Liam had discovered a passion for them and seemed to devour bowl after bowl of the stuff.

She punched the red button and the shutter whirred up, quietly rattling and letting in the cool morning air of the city. She breathed in deep and looked up at the clear blue sky. It was going to start out as a lovely sunny day today . . . as always.

Sal dropped off the laundry with the sweet old Chinese lady who worked at the laundromat. She was a chatty old thing whom Sal was beginning to get to know well, always talking proudly – sometimes in broken English, sometimes in Cantonese – about her nephew whom she announced with pleasure '*alway wear 'spensive smart soo' to go for his work*'. Of course, it was exactly the same greeting every time she stepped into the shop, as if she was setting eyes on Sal for the very first time.

Which, of course, she was. But Sal decided to politely steer their brief chit-chatty conversation in different directions with every visit . . . gradually learning a little bit more about her and her family each time.

She headed across the bridge into Manhattan, enjoying the warm sun and watching the city streets grow steadily busier. The air was thick with smells both pleasant and not so, but nothing quite as bad as she remembered in downtown Mumbai

– particularly on the smog-heavy days. Entering Manhattan's lower east side, her nose picked out the acrid smell of exhaust fumes mixed with the delightful odour of freshly brewed coffee and oven-baked bagels billowing from the various coffee shops and fast-food restaurants she passed on the way across to Broadway and up to Times Square.

Tuesday starts so well, she noted sadly. Right now, in the early morning, it was as fine a day as one could ask for. She looked at her watch.

8.32 a.m.

The day would continue to be lovely for another thirteen minutes. She sighed sadly. Then it would turn into the nightmare of nine-eleven. She entered the busy nexus of Times Square and took a seat on a bench – her regular bench – beside a litter bin. She watched the stop-start traffic at a busy intersection and the pavements filled with people on their way to work: men already hot with their jackets over one arm and their ties loosened, women in smart summer blouses and light linen trouser suits.

8.34 a.m. Eleven minutes to go.

The large green face of Shrek, looking equally bemused and irritated by Donkey, hung above the square – as always. She studied the movie billboard and the others dotted around, beginning to find them all very familiar, like bedroom posters long past their time to be taken down and replaced with something else.

8.37 a.m. Eight minutes to go.

A homeless man approached the bench – as he always did at 8.37 a.m. – pushing a shopping trolley in front of him, piled high with cardboard boxes and an old tarpaulin. He smiled politely at her – as he always did – before rummaging through the litter bin and finding a half-eaten sausage McMuffin.

He sat down beside her, his lined and pockmarked face creased with quite possibly the last smile New York would see today and opened his mouth to say the same thing he always said.

'Hey, lucky me . . . it's still warm!' He eagerly tucked into his rescued sandwich.

Sal politely returned his smile.

'I'm glad,' she said. And she genuinely was. She was familiar enough with the next few hours to know this was the last fleeting moment of contentment left in the day, a homeless tramp, chewing gratefully on a discarded sausage in a bun.

8.43 a.m. Two minutes to go.

She looked up at the skyline, seeing in the distance the very tops of the two World Trade Center towers, glistening like polished silver in the morning light. Proud structures that confidently seemed to reach up to the blue sky and actually touch it. And inside . . . so many thousands of people, sitting down to start a regular day at work, opening their email in-boxes, peeling the lid off their Starbucks coffee, unwrapping their salt-beef and mustard bagels.

8.44 a.m. One minute left.

The tramp finished his breakfast and sighed with contentment.

He turned to Sal and sucked in his breath to say what he always said at this time. 'Gonna be a helluva day, ain't it?'

'Yes.' She nodded. 'It is.'

The tramp got up off the bench and pushed his trolley away from her, whistling cheerfully as he went.

8.45 a.m. Now only seconds to go.

Sal hated this final countdown. Beginning with the distant drone of an engine in the sky and ending with cries of disbelief from the pedestrians around her, and a moment later the boom and rumble of the plane's impact.

She'd sat through this at least a dozen times now. And God knows how many more times she'd have to – hundreds?

Thousands? Sal wondered if it would get any easier for her, counting down those last few seconds.

She closed her eyes. Foster probably wouldn't approve of that if he knew, but there were only so many times she could bring herself to watch.

She could hear the plane now.

And then she felt it: a dizzying sense of losing balance, of falling, as if just for a moment the ground beneath her had been whipped away.

She opened her eyes, looked up . . . and gasped at what she saw.

Maddy studied the screens before her, steaming mug of coffee in hand – black coffee because *someone* had used the last of the milk and not left any for breakfast – and waited for the first ticker-tape newsflash to report 'some kind of explosion' at the World Trade Center.

She checked the clock on the computer. It was 8.45 a.m.

It was due.

The clock display now flickered to indicate 8.46 a.m.

OK, it's now past due.

'Hmm,' she grunted. She looked around for the others. Liam was drowsily slumped on his cot, reading a *National Geographic* magazine he'd found lying around the archway. Foster, who looked frailer and ill this morning, remained fast asleep on his couch. Bob was still in his tube, being nourished intravenously with some horrible-looking gunk.

'Er . . .' was the best Maddy could come up with right now.

Sal stared dumbstruck at a very different world around her. Shrek and Donkey were gone, so were the posters for *Mamma Mia* and *Planet of the Apes*. She noticed some of the more recent buildings looked a little different too.

But, most importantly, the Twin Towers were gone and in their place, not quite so high but easily as grand, stood a giant marble column from which an enormous red pennant proudly flapped.

Her eyes dropped to street level. It looked so much less chaotic: fewer billboards adorned the sides of buildings; the shopfronts looked somehow tidier, more reserved, more upmarket; the streets were far less clogged with vehicles, which themselves looked strangely old-fashioned, reminding her of some of the odd-looking automobiles she had once seen in a transport museum.

The pedestrians, many more of them than there were a few moments ago, eyed her tatty clothes curiously. She looked down and realized her hoodie with *Ess-Zed* splashed brightly across it, the ripped and patched drainpipe jeans stood out in stark contrast to the sombre and characterless grey suits everywhere. And something else: virtually everyone was wearing a red armband that featured a white circle and some small black design on it. It reminded her of the old war films; the bad guys used to wear those red armbands . . .

What were those bad guys called? Oh yeah . . . Nazis.

She turned to look for the homeless man who'd been sitting on the bench beside her, but he was gone, along with his supermarket trolley. Feeling dozens of curious eyes begin to fix on her, she got up off the bench and quickly hurried across the busy pavement to the mouth of a quiet backstreet. She pulled out her mobile and dialled the field office.

The display showed two words. *No signal.*

Confused for a moment, she quickly realized she could see no one else talking into a mobile phone either. In fact, she could see no one even holding one, nor any adverts for top-up cards or service providers or deals with free texts, nor stalls selling novelty phone covers . . . *nothing* at all to do with mobile phones.

*

Maddy looked up at Foster.

'The plane impact just *didn't* happen,' she said. 'And a moment later most of the news-feed screens went blank,' she added, pointing to the row of monitors now all synchronously blinking an error message.

Foster, looking bleary-eyed from being woken, and far too pale for her liking, nodded thoughtfully over her shoulder. 'We're in trouble . . . this looks like a big shift,' he said quietly. 'Normally they come in waves, subtle ones at first that bring very minor changes, then the bigger ones come later if events up the timeline aren't corrected.'

One computer screen still seemed to be functioning; beneath a prominent red banner with a logo on it were the headlines of the day's news.

'What is that?' queried Liam, pointing to the logo on the banner.

'Reminds me a bit of the Nazi swastika,' she replied, 'but it isn't.'

'What's a *swastika*?' asked Liam.

Foster waved a hand. 'Sorry, Liam . . . I'll bring you up to speed later.' He looked more closely at it. 'It looks like a black eel or snake or something, biting its own tail.'

'Yeah.' Maddy nodded.

Liam spotted something the other two hadn't yet. 'I wonder if you noticed the news is in two languages?' He pointed to the lower half of the screen where the same headlines had been duplicated in another language.

'German and English,' said Maddy, 'that's all I can see. No other language options.'

Foster turned to them and gathered his thoughts. 'OK, well it doesn't take a genius to work out that history's been shifted to incorporate a pretty significant alteration.'

'Er . . . the Germans *won* the Second World War?' suggested Maddy.

'More than that, Madelaine; it looks like they went and conquered America.'

Liam looked at both of their ashen faces. 'That really isn't good, is it?'

CHAPTER 33

2001, New York

The archway's shutter rattled gently as it whirred up. All three of them spun round anxiously. A pair of Doc Martens boots and skinny legs quickly reassured them.

'Sal!' cried Maddy. 'I was getting worried about you.'

Sal stepped in smartly and lowered the shutter. 'It's all . . . different . . . out there,' she said, gasping for breath. 'I . . . ran . . . back . . . all the way. I was frightened . . . My phone wasn't working.'

Foster turned to Maddy. 'Yes, of course. In this new history maybe they don't have things such as telecommunications satellites in orbit.'

'Or mobile-phone masts,' she added. 'If this is, like, some Nazi-styled government, maybe they're not so keen on letting people communicate with each other so easily.'

'That's true,' he replied, hands clasped thoughtfully.

'And this,' said Maddy, gesturing at the screen, 'this looks like some kind of online government-approved news site.'

He made a face. 'Which means we can't entirely trust it as a source of information.'

'But it's all we've got,' Maddy pointed out.

He nodded. 'This is true.'

Liam beckoned Sal over. 'Come and sit down,' he said, patting an empty seat beside the old man. 'Let me get you a drink of water or something.'

'Thank you,' she panted.

He reached out and touched her lightly on the shoulder. 'You all right there, Sal?'

She nodded. 'I was so . . . Jahulla! It was so frightening. It's like another world.'

He headed towards the kitchen alcove and ran a glass of water from the tap.

'Is there an archive section on this page?' asked Foster.

Maddy moved a cursor across the screen. 'Yeah.' She clicked a button on an info tab.

[HISTORY/GESCHICHTE]

The screen paused and flickered before presenting them with a surprisingly limited menu.

'Not a lot of info listed here,' sneered Maddy derisively.

Foster studied the meagre list of menu items. 'There, click on Timeline . . . *Zeitlinie*.'

She did so and a moment later they were presented with the graphic of a time bar with the significant events of the last fifty years laid out along it.

'My God . . . look,' she said, pointing at the screen, '1997: end of war with China. 1989: the Führer's hundredth birthday. 1979: the first man in space . . .'

'But look at the beginning of the timeline,' said Foster.

Maddy frowned. 'It starts in 1956. Why nothing before?'

'I don't know.'

She clicked on a button beside the beginning year and was answered with a red warning dialogue box:

Frühgeschichtenfrugen erfordern Korrekte Ermächtigung.
Access To Earlier History Requires Authorization.

Maddy shook her head. 'It seems history before that date is out of bounds for everyone. It all starts with 1956.' She checked the historical marker for that particular year. '1956: America celebrates joining the Greater Reich.'

Maddy clicked on the tab and a small article appeared. A grainy black and white photo showed some city street lined with cheering people and a motorcade of vehicles proceeding down it. She read the words aloud.

'September, 1956: Vice-president Truman reluctantly concedes defeat and signs the terms for an unconditional surrender in the presence of the Führer's highest ranking field officer, Reichsmarschall Haas. The American nation is now a part of the Greater Reich. The Führer is greeted on the streets of Washington by hundreds of thousands of enthusiastic supporters heartened by his promise to rescue their nation from years of poverty and hardship.' She shook her head. 'I can't believe that! I can't believe the American people would roll over and *welcome* Adolf Hitler in as their ruler. That's just crazy!'

Foster nodded. 'Well, I agree it's odd. But whether they did or they didn't, history has gone off track . . . wildly off track.'

He turned to Liam. 'I'm sorry, lad. I feel like I'm throwing you in at the deep end. We need to send someone back to check things out.'

'Uh . . . all right,' replied Liam unhappily.

'This time, though,' said Foster, 'I'm afraid, this time, I can't go.'

Liam swallowed anxiously. 'I'm . . . I'm going back *alone*?'

'No, Bob will go along with you.'

'I . . . er, I'm not sure I –'

'I'm sorry, lad, but there are no choices here. You have to go back and find out what's going on.'

'But why aren't *you* coming?'

Foster's eyes met Maddy's briefly. 'It's too far back in time for me.'

'But, but did you not go back to 1912 to get me?'

'Yes . . . yes, I did, but this time . . . I'm sorry, I'm going to have to sit this one out.'

'Oh.'

'We haven't another moment to lose.' He turned to Sal. 'Revive Bob from his birthing tube.'

She nodded and headed off to the back room.

'Madelaine?'

'Yes?'

'We need to prepare a data download for Bob. He needs all of this alternative history downloaded into his brain. Also, he needs to have a complete understanding of the German language and I'd download, from our on-site files, everything we have on Hitler, the Nazi high command, the Second World War. I guess that should do it for now.'

'What about me?' asked Liam.

Foster shrugged. 'Sorry, Liam . . . It's come sooner than I expected. I'd hoped to take you through a couple more training trips, but it looks like we've run out of time.'

'Oh boy,' whispered Liam.

Foster pointed towards the cylinder. 'You'd better start filling up the tube with water.'

CHAPTER 34

2001, New York

Liam clung desperately to the side of the perspex tube with both hands, unhappily kicking at the warm liquid beneath him. Bob floated beside him, calmly treading water.

'OK, Liam, you're going to be there for two hours exactly. We've set the co-ordinates for the first of September 1956. We're sending you to the grounds of the White House – the president's Washington office. All you and Bob are going to do is observe, OK? Just observe. Do you understand?'

Liam nodded. 'Y-yes.'

Foster patted his hand. 'Relax, Liam. You'll do just fine.' He looked at the support unit treading water. 'And you must trust Bob. In that silicon brain of his is everything you'll need for this quick trip. He's going to be your walking encyclopedia . . . aren't you, Bob?'

'*Ja. Ich habe alle benötigten Daten, Herr Foster.*'

'English for now please, Bob.'

Bob nodded sternly. 'I have all the required data, Mr Foster.'

'Good.'

Liam looked up at the old man. 'I . . . I've got to admit I'm a little scared.'

'I know,' he replied softly. 'First time alone is always a bit daunting.' He smiled. 'I've been there before myself. You'll be fine.'

With a little effort Liam managed a cavalier grin.

'Just go there, lad, look around, see what you can see . . . and come back to the same spot a couple of hours later.'

'What if we're late?'

'If you miss that window, we'll open the window again exactly an hour later, for just a few minutes. If you miss that, then we open it exactly twenty-four hours later. That's the standard missed-rendezvous procedure. Don't worry, Bob knows all about that and will keep you on schedule.'

'But if we miss all the windows?'

'Just make sure you don't.'

Liam swallowed anxiously. 'But . . . but if we do miss every one of them windows . . . is there not a way to arrange another one?'

'If it comes to that, there is a way for us to talk to you, but it's one-way only. You'll not be able to talk to us.' He patted Liam on the arm. 'Just make sure you stick to the schedule.'

'I . . . I'll try me best, Mr Foster, so I will.'

'I know you will, lad.'

Foster got to his feet and took the steps down the side of the cylinder on to the concrete floor of the arch. 'OK, Madelaine, begin the launch procedure.'

'Launching in one minute.'

The displacement machinery attached to the water tube began to hum deeply.

Sal stepped forward, staring at their foggy outlines inside the tube. 'Good luck, Liam!' she called out. 'Be careful!'

He let go of the side with one hand and quickly waved. 'I'll be all right there, Sal. Don't you worry about me now.'

The lights in the arch dimmed and flickered as power diverted to the tube.

'Forty seconds to go until launch!' announced Maddy.

'Remember, Liam,' shouted Foster as the hum grew more intense, 'you're just going for a *look* . . . Don't get involved in anything.'

'Right you are!' cried Liam, his voice rattling nervously.

'Thirty seconds, fellas!'

Liam's legs kicked in the water, sending cascades of bubbles up the tube. The hum of the generator increased in volume and pitch.

'Twenty seconds!' Maddy called out, her voice almost lost in the deafening whir of charging-up machinery.

'OK, Liam,' shouted Foster, 'time to let go and go under!'

Liam nodded, sucking in one deep breath after another.

'Fifteen seconds!'

'Come on, lad . . . you've got to let go!'

Liam nodded, still sucking and blowing air, hyperventilating, his legs thrashing in the water beneath him.

'Ten seconds!'

'Come on, Liam, you've got to let go now!'

Taking one last gasp of air, he did so, quickly sinking under the water. Through the scuffed and foggy plastic, Foster, Maddy and Sal watched him flail in panic as he sank slowly to the bottom. Bob ducked down effortlessly beside him . . . and touchingly – so Sal thought – reached out and held Liam's hand.

It seemed to calm him, just a little.

'Three . . . two . . . one . . .'

With a *pop* the water and both occupants vanished.

CHAPTER 35

1956, Washington DC

They landed amid a small copse of mature cedar trees with a heavy, wet splash.

'Arghh!' yelped Liam. 'I hate that goldfish-bowl thing!'

'Information: the device is called a displacement cylinder,' said Bob, crouching beside him, already alert and assessing their surroundings.

Liam picked himself up and squatted beside the support unit amid the foliage. Beyond the low-hanging branches, out on the well-trimmed acre of lawn in front of the White House, he could see soldiers gathering.

'Who are they?'

Bob's eyes slowly panned across the scene in front of them. 'The insignia and uniforms indicate that they are a mixture of American marines, rangers and airborne,' he replied. 'Recommendation: we must have clothes.'

'Yes, clothes would be really nice.'

Bob stood up and announced, 'I shall acquire clothes,' before disappearing through the trees and foliage.

Liam continued watching the soldiers. They looked like they had already seen some fighting; many were wounded, some being dragged by their colleagues. All of them looked exhausted and battle-shocked; their grimy faces had defeat written across them.

He noticed a large olive-green vehicle with tracks instead of wheels, and a turret with what appeared to be a long, slender barrel protruding from it. It lurched across the grass amid a plume of dark smoke. It looked dented and scorched as if it too had seen some action. The vehicle reversed across the lawn, kicking up divots of soil and leaving deep tracks in its wake, backing up against a large white building – the White House.

To his untrained eye this looked very much like the ragged assemblage of some kind of a last stand around the building – perhaps it was all that was left of the United States army.

'Blimey,' he muttered.

He heard a deep rumble coming from above and glanced up through the leafy branches. The sky was overcast, thick with grey low-hanging clouds that promised an imminent downpour. The rumbling was deep, so powerful he could feel it vibrate against his chest. It was coming from somewhere *above* the clouds.

The American soldiers, like him, were watching the sky anxiously – all eyes trained upwards, waiting for something to appear.

Liam craned his neck to get a better view.

What's up there?

Behind him he heard a heavy footfall and turned to see Bob holding out clothes and boots. 'The owner of these clothes is dead,' he explained without any trace of emotion. 'He will not be needing them.'

Liam took them and looked at the damp stains of blood. 'You didn't kill someone to get these clothes for me, did you?'

Bob shook his head. 'No killing was required.'

Liam grimaced at the thought of stepping into another man's clothes. On the other hand, standing undressed in the middle of a war zone struck him as the worse alternative. He pulled them on as quickly as he could.

'It looks like those soldiers are setting themselves up for a last-ditch defence.'

'Correct,' said Bob, his eyes smoothly scanning across the lawn.

'And I guess whatever's coming –' Liam looked up again at the darkening sky from where that deep rumble was issuing – 'is coming from right up there.'

'Possibly an airborne weapon system.' Bob's eyes flickered shut. 'I have data files on the advanced aeroplane prototypes that were being developed by the Germans at the end of the Second World War.'

'They actually used *aeroplanes* during the . . . the Second World War?'

'Affirmative.'

The rumbling grew even louder and Liam found himself having to shout to be heard. 'Big ones?'

'Jet propulsion, delta-wing designs, VTOL systems,' replied Bob, raising his flat-toned voice to compete with the deafening drone from above.

'Well, that means nothing to me,' shouted Liam. 'What the hell are those?'

Bob cocked his head for a moment. 'I am able to provide detailed schematic blueprints if I can locate a drawing implement –'

Suddenly, the tumbling dark clouds above them momentarily spread thin enough for Liam to see what was approaching.

'Bob! *You see that?*'

Above them, descending through the clouds, was a giant dull-grey disc-shaped vessel, easily a quarter of a mile in diameter. It almost seemed to fill the sky above the White House as it slowly pushed its way down through the billowing clouds. He could now make out dozens of spinning rotors slung beneath the craft, giant propeller blades whisking the air beneath the belly of the enormous disc, projecting a powerful downdraught that set the cedar trees around them rustling and swaying.

Liam noticed the emblem he'd seen earlier on Maddy's screens, stencilled across a hundred feet of the vehicle's immense hull.

'What the hell is that thing?' he yelled.

'Information: it appears to be a circular dirigible,' replied Bob. He seemed to recognize the bemused and panicked shrug returned by Liam as an indication that he hadn't a clue what one of those was. 'It is a disc-shaped airship – a reinforced aluminium hull containing many large cells filled with buoyancy gas.'

Some of the marines on the lawn, frozen into a motionless stupor by the sight, raised their firearms and began to shoot pointlessly at it.

A black square slowly appeared in the dark underbelly of the craft, then another, and another.

'Er . . . now that's not good, is it?' cried Liam.

Bob nodded in agreement. 'Is not good.'

Liam saw something dark emerging from the squares, dots that quickly grew in size as a shower of *somethings* rapidly appeared to be descending towards them.

A canister the size of a Thermos flask thudded into the grass thirty yards from them among a group of haggard-looking marines. The marines backed away from it as it started to spew out a yellow smoke. Several more canisters landed heavily and started billowing smoke across the lawn.

'Tactical smokescreen,' offered Bob.

The air was soon thick with a mustard-coloured mist. Through it Liam could just about make out the nearby silhouettes of the American soldiers on the lawn, drawing fearfully back across the clipped grass towards the steps and the grand portico at the front of the White House.

Now he could see more dark shapes descending through the mist from above – dozens, perhaps hundreds, of them. Bigger than the canisters this time.

They heard something crash heavily through the cedar trees behind them, accompanied by a shrill hissing sound. They spun round to see a man tangled awkwardly amid thick branches; he wore a loose black rubber boiler suit that reminded Liam of the bin bags that seemed to line every backstreet in New York. Covering his face was a dark rubber mask with two glass plates where the eyes should be. His head was kinked at an impossible angle and Liam realized the neck had been snapped on the way down through the tree's branches.

Twin cylinders strapped to his back continued to discharge high-velocity geysers of gas noisily, which lasted only half a dozen seconds more before finally fizzing to a silence.

'Aerosol-based fast-descent system,' announced Bob calmly.

Above them Liam could hear that same hiss multiplied through the air as other men in rubber suits began to land nearby.

'Sod this! We can't stay here!'

The support unit nodded. 'Recommendation: it will be tactically correct to go inside the building known as the White House.'

'Yeah . . . OK,' Liam said, stepping out from the cover of the small copse and on to the open lawn.

'Please wait!' barked Bob. He stepped across to the body dangling from the branches and, with a hard tug, pulled it to the ground. He effortlessly flipped the body over and withdrew a weapon from the man's backpack. His calm eyes appraised its effectiveness and how to use it within seconds. He shouldered the weapon and nodded approvingly.

'Rapid-fire pulse carbine.' His grey eyes locked on Liam's. 'Weapon technology from the middle of the twenty-first century.'

'Well, that's interesting . . . but can we go now?'

'Affirmative. Please follow me, Liam O'Connor.'

Liam nodded. 'Uh . . . sure, all right, you go first.'

Bob pushed out through the foliage beneath the trees and into the open, striding forward with the carbine held at his hip.

The yellow murky air was now filled with the sound of hissing canisters and the thud of boots making a heavy landing on the lawn. Liam could see the smudged outlines of men all around them; mask-muffled voices barked orders in German.

Oh, I'm so-o-o very going to die.

One of the moving outlines took a step too many towards them and suddenly called out a sharp challenge.

Bob was frighteningly fast – lashing out with the edge of his free hand and chopping at the man's throat. Liam heard a dull crack above all the other noise.

'Follow,' said Bob.

CHAPTER 36

1956, Washington DC

They moved quickly across the lawn until Liam realized they were now among the retreating marines backing up the alabaster steps and firing sporadically out into the mist in front of them.

Rapid bursts of fire lanced back at them out of the smoke, exploding showers of dust and plaster from the steps and the columns of the palisade. A marine standing beside Liam pin-wheeled from the impact of a shot and collapsed to the ground, a gaping hole blown out of his torso.

'Follow,' said Bob again, leading Liam through the marines returning fire towards a glass-panelled double door. A wounded soldier slouched by the doorway halted their progress.

'Hey! Where the hell you two goin'? We're holdin' the line right here, goddammit!'

Bob calmly twisted his arm and pushed him aside without any apparent effort. They stepped through the doors and into the White House.

The carpeted entrance hall was thick with the stretched-out bodies of wounded soldiers, one trembling, harried army medic moving among them and tending them with little more than mercifully lethal shots of morphine. Ahead was a double doorway leading further into the building and the west wing. Holding position behind a hastily assembled blockade of furniture were a dozen more soldiers, grim faced and clearly ready to go down defending their president to the last.

'My God, Bob,' uttered Liam, 'this is the president's last stand!'

Bob scanned the hall, the blockade, the marines ready to die.

'Correct. The president called Eisenhower must be in this building.'

'What do we do? Save him?'

Bob turned to Liam. '*You* are the mission operative. Tactical decisions can only be made by the operative, not the support unit.'

'What?'

'You are in charge, Liam O'Connor.'

'I . . . I . . . I don't know what we should do.'

He looked out through the glass doors. Through the mist he could see little, but he could imagine hundreds more faceless soldiers hidden behind gas masks forming up on the lawn in front of the grand steps and the portico and readying themselves for a final devastating assault on the building.

We're here to observe, that's all. Here to learn what happened. Nothing more.

Well, he'd already guessed that the American people hadn't politely invited these Nazis to come on over and run their affairs. But they needed more details, details that would help them pinpoint the moment further back in the past where history had taken a turn in this direction.

'We need to find out how things got like this.' He turned to Bob. 'Right?'

'Correct. Mission priority one: obtain information.'

'OK,' he replied, looking around the hall. 'So we need to grab someone and ask questions?'

'Correct.'

Liam stepped forward through the dead and the dying. To their left was a doorway that led to a communications room. He could see soldiers on field radios, civilians on telephones, typists and telephonists all making hurried calls, situation reports or, more than likely, final messages to loved ones.

To the right was a room full of desks and filing cabinets. It looked less busy. Liam stepped across the carpet of bodies into the room. Some of the smoke from outside had leaked in through several shattered windows and the air was tinged with a fine yellow mist.

He spotted a man in a smart blue suit sitting on the floor between two filing cabinets, his face covered in dust and dry-caked blood from a head wound.

The man stared into space in front of him. 'This is it,' he muttered, his voice cracked and tired. 'It's all over. They're coming for us . . . coming to get us . . . to get us . . .'

Liam squatted down in front of him. 'The Germans? Nazis?'

The man didn't seem to hear the question, his eyes unfocused. 'We should've known . . . should've prepared . . . should've realized this was going to happen eventually.'

Bob mimicked Liam's posture and stooped down in front of the man. 'Information request: please tell us everything about your divergent history timeline.'

'Bob?'

'Yes, Liam?'

'Let me try first, eh?'

He nodded. 'You are the mission operative.'

Liam reached a hand out to the man and rested it on his shoulder.

'Hello? Mister?'

The man's eyes focused on him.

'There isn't much time,' said Liam. 'Listen to me, things *can* be changed. This isn't how it was meant to be. We're here to put this –'

'No . . .' replied the man, shaking his head. 'No, you're *goddamn* right this isn't how it should be! They surprised us, just like them Japs did back in '41.'

Liam looked at Bob questioningly.

'Information: in the twentieth century, the Japanese launched a surprise attack on the US naval base at Pearl Harbor. This act effectively brought America into the Second World –'

Liam held a hand up to hush him. 'Tell me what's been happening.'

'What? Where on earth have you been?' the man asked.

He shrugged. 'At sea . . . for a long time.'

'The Nazis launched an assault on the beaches of New England a couple of months ago. Overwhelmed our Atlantic defences like they were nothing, took New York inside of a week. We mustered everything we had to hold 'em outside Washington. But . . . but they crushed our boys, swiped 'em aside. Their *Führer* offered terms,' he snorted. 'Our president and his cabinet and chiefs of staff to be handed over as prisoners – or they'd come in and get 'em.'

The man suddenly looked up at Bob then back at Liam. 'Wait! You said this isn't how it should be. What's going on? Who are you guys? SOE? Secret Service guys?'

'This may sound incredibly strange,' said Liam, 'but you need to believe what I'm about to say.'

'What?' The man shook his head. 'What is it?'

'We're from the future. From the year 2001. And right now is a bit of history that shouldn't be happening.'

The man's face hardened. 'This ain't a time to play the fool, son. I –'

'He is correct,' said Bob.

'We're sort of *agents* sent from the future to gather information on what's going on here,' said Liam. 'We need to find out what's been happening.'

The man stared at them both in silence. 'You're crazy.'

Liam shrugged. 'I wish I could show you something to prove what I'm saying. But I can't.'

'Mission parameter: we have nothing on us from the future. This is an observation-only mission.'

Through the shattered windows they heard movement going on outside above the drone coming from the sky: men barking orders, the jangle of equipment belts, the cocking of weapons.

'Oh Jesus, we're dead men,' cried the man. 'There are rumours their Führer wants to completely wipe clean America's government: the president, Congress, the Senate, all the top-level civil servants. They'll kill every last person they find in the White House.'

'Listen,' said Liam, 'we're going to change this. We're going to stop this Hiffler from doing what –'

The man looked up at him. 'Hiffler? What the heck you talking about, son? You talking 'bout *Adolf Hitler*?'

'Yes, that's it, *Hitler*. That's the correct name, right?' He looked at Bob for confirmation. 'Did I say it right?'

'Correct. Adolf Hitler, the Führer, leader of the Nazi Party and the Third Reich.'

'But that guy, *Hitler*, died about ten years ago. You guys gonna try telling me you don't know *that*?'

Liam and Bob stared at each other. 'Assessment: history diverged at least ten years earlier than this time.'

'1946 instead of '56?' Liam spoke under his breath. 'We have to go back *another* ten years?'

'That is correct.'

The man studied them both suspiciously. 'Dammit, who are

you guys, really? You Secret Service guys? Some kind of special forces or something? Tell me you got some secret plan . . . some kinda super weapon we can use back on 'em Nazis. Right?'

The sound of gunfire around the front entrance suddenly intensified.

'They are coming now,' said Bob. 'We must leave. The portal is due to open in exactly one hour and thirty-three minutes.'

'Right . . . but we know now that we've got to go back again . . . but *further* back next time?'

'Correct.'

The man in the suit reached out and grasped Liam. 'Have we got something secret hidden away? Some weapon we gonna fight back with?'

Bob answered. 'There is nothing. In this timeline you and all the people in this building have a high probability of dying in less than five minutes.' Bob mimicked Liam's attempt to calm the man and rested a large palm on his trembling shoulder. 'But be reassured, citizen, this timeline will be completely eradicated once we have corrected the time contamination.'

Liam shook his head as the hapless man stared at him in bewildered silence.

Yes, very reassuring, Bob.

The support unit turned to Liam. 'We must leave now.'

CHAPTER 37

2001, New York

'There must be some way to hack past their security and access the rest of the online history database,' said Maddy.

'Maybe there isn't any more?' asked Foster. 'Maybe the rulers of this time consider history before this date, before the conquering of America, as irrelevant. One way they could have chosen to keep control of the American people is to delete records of their national history, maybe even world history.'

Maddy shrugged. 'But these are the Nazis, right? Surely they'd want to keep records of Hitler's rise to power, the Second World War and how in this screwed-up history they actually *won* it? I'm sure Adolf Hitler would want all his subjects to know how brilliant he was and how hard a struggle he had as a younger man . . . and all that rags-to-riches rubbish.'

Foster sighed. 'It doesn't make sense. I don't know why all that's not there, Madelaine. I really don't. Perhaps, for these Nazis, the day they took control of America is all that counts. Everything before that was of no importance?'

Sal coughed politely and the other two turned to face her.

'Maybe,' she said, 'maybe the Hitler guy died and the one who took over from him, you know, didn't like him or something? Decided to remove Hitler from the records?'

Foster nodded. 'Sal might be right. We've been assuming *Der Führer* is Hitler.'

Maddy's eyes widened. She looked for a search function on the main page and after a minute of trying various buttons labelled in German gave up.

'God, these Nazis really suck at laying out a web page.'

'Perhaps in this version of the year 2001 the Internet is a brand-new thing.'

She gave up on the idea of doing a search on the name 'Hitler'. Instead she clicked through the various article tabs along the timeline chart – scanning each article for the name.

Five minutes later she shook her head.

'No mention at all of Adolf. It's like he never existed.'

'But plenty of mentions of *Der Führer* . . . the leader,' added Foster.

Maddy ground her teeth with frustration. 'So *who* exactly is *Der Führer*?' She accessed the computer's on-site database, a vast encyclopedia of *correct* history, and pulled up files on Hitler's high command, his inner cabinet . . . the men most likely to succeed him. 'Heinrich Himmler? Hermann Göring? Martin Bormann? Joseph Goebbels?' She turned to Foster and Sal. 'One of them maybe?'

Foster splayed his hands. 'It could be *any* of them.'

Sal spoke quietly. 'Or perhaps *none* of them?'

1956, Washington DC

Splinters of plaster erupted around Liam's head.

'Oh God help us!' he yelped, ducking down behind a desk. 'They're in the entrance hall!'

The air was thick with the percussive rattle of machine-gun fire, and the throaty burr of the invaders' pulse rifles.

Bob pointed down to the far end of the room. 'Recommendation: go to the end and take cover.'

'What about you?'

'I shall secure tactical advantage.'

'What's that supposed to mean?'

Bob shoved him. 'Please go now,' he said calmly as bullets from the entrance hall sprayed in through the open door and noisily shredded the typewriter and telephone on the desk they were crouching behind.

'What about me?' asked the man in the suit.

Liam half smiled. 'Come with us for now, but we can't take you back with us.'

'Jeez . . . I'll be happy staying alive just a little while longer.'

'You must go now,' insisted Bob.

Liam pulled himself to his feet, poked his head round the desk and stole a glance through the open door into the entrance hall. He could see a couple of dozen black-suited men firing on the marines' blockaded position. The staccato chatter of the marines' guns was lessening against the incessant snatched purr of the pulse rifles.

Liam realized the Germans had whittled down the defenders to one or two marines. The fight was all but over.

We have to move now.

He pulled himself out and sprinted down an aisle between two rows of desks, away from the open door and the one-sided battle. He came up against a wooden-panelled door at the far end.

The man in the suit was right behind him.

'Where does this door lead?'

'A hallway. If we turn right there's an exterior door that leads us out to the rose gardens.'

Liam looked back the way they'd come. At the far end where they'd been hiding was the mustard-coloured mist. He could only just make out a dark blob that might have been Bob.

'Your friend coming?' asked the man.

'I hope so.'

The dark shape moved suddenly, lunging out from behind the desk, and then it was gone through the doorway and into the main hall. A moment later Liam heard a renewed and intense burst of gunfire: pulse rifles. He heard cries of alarm and panic, muffled voices barking hasty commands in German. He heard several loud screams that ended abruptly, the sound of a ferocious struggle, something toppling over and shattering.

'What in the heck is happening back there?'

It's Bob happening.

For the briefest moment, as he imagined what those powerful arms could do to mere flesh and bone, he almost felt sorry for them.

A moment later, emerging through the mist, he saw something lunging like a charging bull down the aisle towards them. Bob emerged from the smoke, his face and chest spattered with blood, none of which appeared to be his own.

'I have acquired a tactical advantage.'

Hands slick with fresh blood, he held out a gas mask and a black rubber hood. 'Suggestion: Liam O'Connor, you wear the mask and hood. You will appear to be one of them from distances greater than ten feet.'

'What about me?' asked the man.

Bob regarded him dispassionately. 'You are not a mission priority.'

Liam took the hood, wet with blood. 'You killed one of them?'

'Incorrect. Seven enemy units were killed.'

'*With just your hands?*'

Bob looked sternly at both of them. 'There is insufficient time for this conversation.'

Liam noticed several ragged fleshy wounds across Bob's hip and waist. 'Jay-zus! Bob, you've been shot! More than once it looks like.'

'The wounds will heal in no more than three days. The blood is already coagulating. This is not a priority.'

The support unit then turned swiftly to the man.

'Question: do you have detailed information on the floor plans of this structure?'

The man looked at Liam. 'Uh?'

'I think he's asking if you know of another way out.'

'Oh . . . yeah, it's just up ahead.'

Bob nodded. 'This is good.'

'Hey,' said Liam. 'I think I've got a better idea how we might get back across the gardens to those trees.'

'Please explain now,' said Bob.

CHAPTER 38

1956, Washington DC

Liam and the man in the suit stepped out through the door into the rose garden, their hands raised. The smokescreen was still relatively thick out here and through the wafting mist he could see squads of soldiers fanning out across the lawn, rounding up able-bodied prisoners and shooting those marines too wounded to get to their feet.

Inside the building, sporadic gunfire could still be heard as the men in dark rubber hoods and suits moved from one room to another, finishing off the last few pockets of resistance.

As they stepped through the decorative maze of bushes towards the main lawn, Liam looked up at the sky and saw that the giant saucer had moved along, slowly drifting across towards downtown Washington DC, spraying out occasional jets of black dots from the dark trapdoors in its underbelly; squads of men dropped swiftly down to the ground, no doubt with key objectives in mind, to hastily secure administrative buildings, critical utilities and intersections.

Behind them Bob marched stiffly, a pulse rifle levelled at their backs, the bloodied hood and mask stretched over his thick skull.

A soldier nearby, unhooded and unmasked, called out to them across the waist-high rose bushes.

Bob replied in German.

'What did he say?' hissed Liam out of the side of his mouth.

'I told the man you were being taken for questioning.'

'That's very good, Bob,' whispered Liam almost proudly. 'Very good thinking.'

'I am programmed to mimic human traits such as lying and also duplicate –'

'Shhh, save it for later, Bob,' muttered Liam.

They walked through the garden and diagonally across the White House's north lawn towards the copse of trees they'd first arrived in. Liam stared wide-eyed at the corpses littering the ground. He had seen only a couple of German bodies, but was now staring at no less than a hundred dead marines. Clearly, while they'd been inside, many more American soldiers had bravely converged on the White House in a vain attempt to defend their president.

The smokescreen had hidden a massacre out here before the building, those pulse rifles mowing them down as they charged pointlessly into the mist to save their commander-in-chief.

He looked for the copse of cedar trees amid the clearing smoke and finally found it. His heart sank as he spotted a platoon of German soldiers resting in and around the small stand of cedars. They had removed their hoods and masks and chatted animatedly, many lighting up cigarettes.

'Dammit! They're covering our way home!'

'Way home?' The man looked askance at him. 'It's just a bunch of trees!'

'Our exit window will appear there,' said Bob beneath his hood. He accessed his internal mission clock. 'The window will open in precisely one hour and seventeen minutes and thirty-four seconds.'

'What the flippin' heck do we do?' whimpered Liam under his breath.

'I have no tactical suggestions at this moment.'

'Great.'

He looked around. A fresh autumnal breeze was blowing away the last wisps of the smokescreen and he could see that the few prisoners taken alive inside the building were being ushered towards the centre of the lawn where half a dozen Germans were standing in a circle watching the defeated, dispirited civilians and soldiers already slumped to the ground.

He felt a cold stab of fear and desperation run down his spine. *They'll expect Bob to herd us over there. And once I'm dumped with the others I'm going to be stuck.*

As if overhearing his thoughts, a German officer, his black rubber jumpsuit rolled down and tied round his waist, revealing his grey Wehrmacht uniform, pointed to the prisoners and gave Bob an order.

Bob nodded, replied and steered them towards the holding area.

'I have been instructed to leave you there,' the support unit uttered quietly. 'What are my orders, Liam O'Connor?'

'I really don't know. What do you suggest?'

'Suggestion: I can attempt an attack on the soldiers among the trees. But I estimate a point-five per cent chance of success in taking and holding the position until our extraction window arrives.'

They were running out of time and options. The gathered prisoners sat in a cluster only a few dozen yards away, and no matter how slowly the three of them walked towards it, that's where they were headed.

'Suggestion: I leave you here and attempt a rescue when the percentage chance of success exceeds ten per cent.'

Liam gritted his teeth.

No, both he and Bob would be riddled with rapid-fire high-calibre rounds before he could get them both halfway across the lawn to the trees. Bob might well be able to survive several more shots on target, but Liam didn't fancy he'd survive one . . . given the ragged wounds he'd seen the pulse carbines inflict.

'There's nothing we can do right now, Bob. It looks like we're going to miss this window,' he hissed out of the side of his mouth. 'And I don't fancy having my head blown off trying to make it. How long now?'

'In one hour and fifteen minutes, precisely.'

'But there'll be another, right?'

'Correct, an hour later. And twenty-four hours after that.'

'So,' said Liam, now just a few yards away from the seated prisoners and the nearest guards, 'leave me here. If you see an opportunity to get me, take it. But, for Chrissakes, don't get us both killed doing it.'

'What percentage chance do you authorize me to take, Liam O'Connor?'

'I dunno!' he uttered under his breath. 'Just take your best shot.'

One of the German guards called out something and pointed at Liam and the man with him.

'I am being told to leave you here,' said Bob quietly. Liam thought he detected the slightest note of anxiety in the unit's deep flat-toned voice.

'Then do it. If they take us from here, then follow me . . . wait for a chance and get me out of this fix, all right?'

'Mission priority: primary duty is to observe and report back.'

'What? You are *not* leaving me here, Bob! Do you understand?' Liam snarled under his breath. 'That's an order!'

A guard stepped forward and roughly grabbed Liam by the shoulder.

'Be quiet!' he snapped in accented English. 'Join the others!'

Liam staggered forward and then slumped to his knees among the group of prisoners. He watched as Bob stood perfectly still, face still hidden by the mask and hood, and looked helplessly on.

An officer called out to Bob from across the lawn to help with dragging and stacking the bodies for disposal.

The unit turned hesitantly.

Behind the glass plates of the gas mask, a complex computer loaded with AI that was still in the process of learning, still almost childlike, was desperately juggling mission priorities and variables, calculating a million different ways to proceed.

Liam watched the lumbering figure move away.

Oh blimey. What kind of a mess am I stuck in now?

CHAPTER 39

2001, New York

'How long until the return window, Madelaine?' asked Foster.

Maddy looked up at a screen. 'We're counting down the last two minutes,' she replied.

'All right, then. We'll find out what the boys have seen and work it out from there.' He smiled thinly.

The sudden erasure of history *before* 1956 made it almost impossible to identify exactly *when* and *where* things had begun to change – and to zero in on that. While the wiping out of historical records may well have been on the whim of some insane Nazi dictator, to appease his ego no doubt, it also had the additional effect of completely hiding the tracks of whomever had instigated this time shift. If that's what some time traveller had intended, then he was being very, very clever. Leaving no trace, no tracks . . . nothing for them to identify the moment they'd arrived in the past.

Very clever.

Maddy interrupted Foster's train of thought. 'Uhh, Foster . . . a warning dialogue box has come up.'

He looked at it.

```
LOCATION POINT PHASE INTERRUPTION
ABORT OR CONTINUE?
```

'The computer's picking up varying density packets in the pick-up window.'

'Meaning?'

'The computer monitors the area inside the target window for the minute *before* we're due to send back our operatives. If there's a lot of unexpected movement through it, we can assume there are unwary people or perhaps an animal walking across it. If it's persistent enough, the computer flags a warning.'

'What do we do?'

'Wait and see if it continues,' he replied, pointing to a graphic display on the screen. 'There's a density packet spike. Someone or something walked through about ten seconds ago.'

'We aren't going to leave them?' asked Sal, her voice brittle with worry.

Foster shook his head. 'That won't happen,' he reassured her. 'If we need to abort this window, we'll try again in an hour.'

He looked at the display. There were no more density spikes.

'It looks like a one-off,' he said. 'Could easily have been a bird flying through, or rubbish blown across. It happens quite often.'

Sal managed a wan smile. 'OK.'

'Thirty seconds,' said Maddy. 'We aborting or continuing?'

The display looked flat. Whatever had passed through didn't look like it was coming back. In all likelihood it was Liam accidentally stepping in too early. The support unit had probably advised him to stand clear and now they were both waiting patiently to come home.

'Continue,' said Foster.

Maddy clicked the mouse and the dialogue box winked off screen.

'Ten seconds.'

Sal turned towards the middle of the archway's floor, ready to welcome them both back.

'Keep well clear, Sal,' said Foster, pointing at a faint circle of yellow chalk on the concrete, scuffed and in need of a refresh. It marked out the dimension of the return window. You really didn't want to be standing there when it opened.

'Five seconds.'

The generator hummed, the lights momentarily flickered and dimmed. Foster looked at the graphic display, expecting to see the graph spike as Liam and Bob stepped in together. But it remained flat.

Come on, boys . . . stop messing around.

'And three . . . and two . . .'

The graph suddenly spiked.

The lights went out completely.

As they flickered back on, he was about to turn round and give them both a telling-off for cutting it so fine when he heard Sal's scream.

A young man stood there, staring at them, eyes widened with fear and incomprehension – a young soldier, perhaps no more than a couple of years older than Liam, blond hair cropped short, his pale choir-boy cheeks smudged with dirt and flecks of dried blood. He wore a black rubber boiler suit, rolled down to his waist. Beneath it was a grey army tunic with oak leaves on the collar and an eagle emblem on the chest.

His eyes darted from Sal, to Maddy, to Foster . . . and then to someone else's dismembered leg and arm lying at his feet amid a scattering of dried leaves, twigs and a circular tuft of blood-spattered grass and soil.

'*Was –? . . . Was ist das?*' He looked down at the severed limbs on the ground, oozing blood on to the concrete floor. '*Was geschieht? Wo bin ich?*'

His mouth fluttered in fear, his voice broken, shrill, like a child suddenly finding himself lost in a crowded mall.

Maddy reacted first. She stood up and slowly approached him, hands raised. 'It's OK,' she cooed softly. 'Everything's all right . . . We're not going to hurt you.'

The young man gathered his wits enough to unsling his gun and swivel the barrel down to point at her.

'*Halt, stehen bleiben! Wer sind Sie? Wo bin ich?*'

Maddy shook her head. 'I don't . . . I don't do German, sorry,' she said, offering him a friendly smile.

'Keep him talking,' said Foster quietly.

Maddy pointed to herself. 'My . . . name . . . is Maddy. And you?'

The young German stared silently at her, his breath rasping in and out, fluttering with fear.

'What's your name?' she asked in her best motherly voice. 'This,' she said, pointing to Sal, 'this is Sal.'

'Hi,' said Sal, smiling sweetly and slowly offering him a small hand to shake.

He glanced from one girl to the other.

'*Ich . . . Ich bin Feldwebel Lohaans.*'

Maddy guessed she was hearing his rank and surname.

'But what's your *first* name? Hmm?' she asked, taking another step forward.

The young man racked his gun nervously. '*Stehen bleiben! . . . Stay!*' he barked, licking his dry lips.

Maddy stopped dead and shook her head apologetically. 'Sorry. I'll stay right where I am. I won't hurt you.'

He nodded, seeming to understand that. He took another deep breath. 'You . . . *Amerikaner*?'

She smiled. 'Yes.'

'This . . .?' he said, and shrugged, lacking the words in English to complete the question.

'This place is in America. In New York, actually.'

The man's eyes widened. 'This . . . *New York*?'

She nodded.

He snorted nervously. 'Washington . . . *zehn* –' he made a whooshing noise – '*New York*?'

'That's right,' she replied. '*Whoosh* . . . and now you're right here. Crazy, huh?'

That seemed to be one of the three or four English words he knew. He nodded and managed a bemused grin. '*Ja . . . craz-ee*.'

The generator suddenly hummed, the lights winked and a moment later the young soldier, the arm, leg and most of the tuft of grass and soil were gone.

'What happened?'

'I initiated an emergency dump,' replied Foster. 'He's back where he came from. Although he's . . .'

'What?'

'It doesn't matter now,' he replied. He looked at Maddy and Sal. 'That . . . that was a German soldier who looked like he'd just been sucked out of a fight, right off the lawn of the White House, no less.'

'An invasion?'

He nodded. 'Day one of recorded, or should I say *approved*, history, it would seem, begins the day that America was successfully conquered by the Germans. Just like we were saying.'

'Oh, no,' whispered Maddy, 'then we dropped Liam and Bob right into the middle of a battle.'

Sal's face paled.

'We can get them back, though, right?'

'We'll try again in an hour. But only if we don't see any other odd density packets at the last moment. I don't want to bring back another Nazi, or a part of one, if I can help it.'

'But if we can't bring him back? Is that it? Is he stuck there?'

'There's another scheduled for twenty-four hours later.'

'And if he misses that too?'

'Madelaine, he's a resourceful lad. He has Bob with him. They'll do just fine where they are. And, as I said, there *is* a way we can communicate with them. We can let them know a where-and-when for another extraction window.' He turned to both the girls. 'What's of more importance to us right now is whether there are any more shifts due, whether the world has stabilized as it is, or whether it'll get worse.'

'Is there anything we *can* do?'

'All we can do right now is try to work out where history was altered, see if we can narrow things down a bit. My guess is something must have happened during the Second World War, something that changed the balance.'

Maddy nodded. 'Yeah . . . maybe.'

'So,' continued Foster, 'what we'll do is work with what we have. We'll have to explore the New York out there. Perhaps there'll be clues as to what happened prior to the invasion of America. OK?'

She nodded.

'OK, Sal?'

She looked at him, tears rolling down her pale cheeks. 'Poor Liam,' she whimpered. 'I hope he's all right.'

Foster got up tiredly and walked over to her. He stooped down in front of her. 'Don't worry, Sal . . . He'll be fine. With Bob right beside him, he'll be just fine, I promise you.'

'What now?'

'We need more information. Sal, I want you to head out to Times Square again. Just find a seat somewhere and observe all you can. See if you can pick out any visual clues . . . anything at all that hints at events prior to 1956. And, Madelaine?'

She nodded.

'We need to trawl their historical database. If you can find a way to hack through their security measures, perhaps we can learn a bit more. And then we'll get ready to activate the back-up rendezvous.' He sucked in air through gritted teeth. 'Hopefully, second time round it won't be cluttered with German troops, eh?'

CHAPTER 40

1956, Washington DC

Bob observed the hive of activity going on around him. His cold eyes locked on and studied the giant disc floating gracefully above the city and intermittently spewing out troops. He could hear the distant rattle of gunfire, the muffled thud of explosions.

Somewhere in the city, small pockets of American soldiers were still holding out, unaware that the struggle was all over, that their leader, President Eisenhower, had gone down fighting, and even now his body was being carried out and laid across the steps in front of the building along with the rest of his cabinet and chiefs of staff.

An officer standing nearby adjusting his tunic and Wehrmacht peaked cap, no longer encumbered with a drop suit, was hurriedly directing activity on the ground.

'You!' He pointed at Bob. 'You can remove the mask. The air's clear.'

Bob silently removed the gas mask. His hair – only a fortnight's worth of growth, still just coarse bristles – and his hard emotionless face made him look no different from the other storm-troopers around him.

'When we've tidied up the mess out here, then you can take a rest,' the officer said. 'Now, get a move on, man.'

Bob's eyes narrowed as he made a millisecond calculation on whether he should continue to pretend being an enemy unit or sprint a dozen paces across the rutted grass and effortlessly rip this man's arms from their sockets.

[Attack: tactically *incorrect* at this moment]

He turned away and reached down for the body of a marine, flinging the ragged remains over his shoulder and carrying it across to where a pile of corpses was slowly growing. As he did so, Bob's inexperienced silicon mind worked on a bigger issue, more important than any immediate tactical assessments. He had a strategic command decision to make . . .

Tactical Options:

1. Rescue Operative Liam O'Connor

2. Return to field office with gathered intelligence

3. Prevent further contamination – self-terminate

Bob's AI routines worked more efficiently with smaller numbers of options on each branch of its decision tree – two or three was the ideal number. Any larger an array of choices slowed down the risk-assessment processing exponentially.

He scanned the prisoners clustered together and identified Liam crouched miserably among them and looking back at him. If Bob had had a little more time to become more familiar with human facial expressions and muscle tics, he might have been able to recognize the mixture of fear, anger and betrayal written across the young man's face.

His eyes suddenly registered a growing commotion among the cedar trees; the place where the time window had been due to open. Soldiers were gathering round *something* on the ground – something unpleasant enough for one or two of them to double over and dry-heave.

Whatever was going on it was becoming too busy to clear the area, too busy to consider it a viable extraction point, for now, at least. He decided the option that best satisfied the mission's parameters was the first option: to rescue Liam.

Option 2 left Liam stuck in the past where he might potentially be tortured and expose dangerously revealing details of the future.

Option 3, to trigger his computer brain to fry itself, achieved absolutely nothing useful at this moment in time.

He cocked his head.

Option 1 had the highest mission-relevance rating. He closed his eyes for a moment.

Option 1 Solution Assessment:

1. **AWAIT 2nd extraction window – 57.30 minutes' time**
2. **IF success of extracting Liam is greater than 25%, THEN proceed**
3. **ELSE . . . Await 3rd extraction window in 24 hours**

Bob opened his eyes and tossed the corpse he'd been carrying on to the pile. The solution was an acceptable one, even though it amounted to little more than *wait and see*. He was not going to leave nor was he going to terminate himself; instead he was going to wait for a better opportunity to rescue Liam to present itself.

But, he realized, something else had been factored into the decision, something to which he couldn't assign a recognizable label.

For now he decided to give it the name *indefinable factor*.

This *indefinable factor* wasn't coming from his database or his AI code; it was coming from the small part of his brain that was organic, the tiny nub of wrinkled flesh in his skull linked by a myriad hair-thin wires to his on-board silicon wafer-cell computer. And all this indefinable factor could do was whisper a very illogical and impractical message into his logical computer, an awkward message that was beginning to cause a little confusion amid his carefully ordered AI code.

Liam O'Connor is my friend.

CHAPTER 41

1956, command ship over Washington DC

Oberleutnant Ralf Hoffman stepped on to the freight platform with two other men who were hefting a heavy body bag between them. They let it down gently and, like him, looked up in awe at the dark sky above them, at the giant grey underbelly of *Der Führer's* command ship.

Hoffman had been billeted aboard the ship with the men of his unit, the 23rd Fallschirmjäger Assault Corps. He was familiar with the inside of the air vessel – but, viewing it from outside, the truly immense size of the thing came home to him.

The freight platform, a square alloy plinth large enough to fit one truck at a time, slowly began to winch upwards. Beneath them the grounds of the White House and proud boulevards of Washington DC gradually receded.

Hoffman watched the waning light of the afternoon fade as dusk rapidly toned the smoke-smudged sky over the city. There were no street lights on, no lights on in any of the buildings. The city's power stations had been taken out in the first wave of the assault. Only sporadic fires burning here and there illuminated Washington DC, along with the occasional stabbing flicker of gunfire in the streets.

He took a deep breath.

Nerves.

He was on his way up to *Das Mutterschiff*... 'the mother ship', the nickname his men had for the giant airship. More specifically, he was on his way to the upper deck of the mother ship, where a long line of broad windows looked out on to the world below – *Der Führer's* viewing deck.

Hoffman had never been invited up there. Few men, other than the Führer's high command and senior chiefs of staff, had. It was more than the great man's command and control point – it was his campaign home. A very special place.

The platform continued to winch them up with a dull motorized clacking from above. He looked up to see the trapdoor yawning open in the vessel's belly.

All of a sudden, floodlights kicked in and powerful columns of light speared down into the gathering twilight, panning across the city below. Hoffman winced and shaded his eyes. Gazing up just as the damned things had been switched on, he was surprised he hadn't been blinded.

Ralf... you may actually meet him. It's a distinct possibility. Prepare yourself.

The thought sent an unwelcome shudder of fear and excitement down his spine. He didn't want to appear foolishly nervous in front of the Führer. He so wanted to impress the man, to appear calm and professional as an officer of the elite Fallschirmjäger should. The two men with him, on the other hand, were grinning like excited children on their way to meet Father Christmas.

'You two,' he snapped irritably, 'you look like fools. Smarten yourselves up and stop gurning like a pair of monkeys.'

The men obediently tidied their appearance and stowed their smiles away beneath solemn parade-ground faces.

Hoffman looked down at the body bag. The order had come

directly from the Führer's senior field officer, Reichsmarschall Haas to Hoffman's commanding officer. *Der Führer* had asked to inspect this curious body for himself . . . and to ask the men who'd seen what happened to explain directly to him what they'd witnessed.

The clattering from above had grown much louder. He looked up, carefully shading his eyes, to see the yawning loading bay was now only twenty or thirty feet above them.

The freight platform finally jerked to a halt inside the bay where Hoffman saw a couple of SS Leibstandarte guards standing to attention, dressed crisply in ceremonial black.

For an unhappy moment he thought they were going to take possession of the body bag and send Hoffman and his two men back down. But, with a perfunctory nod from one of them, they beckoned Hoffman and the others to follow.

A stairwell guarded by two more men took them to the upper deck. The battleship-grey walls that Hoffman and his men had grown used to on the way over – living like battery chickens on the lower decks as *Das Mutterschiff* sailed gracefully south from the conquered area around New York – now gave way to dark oak panels. The floor no longer metal grilles but a soft maroon carpet that whispered beneath his muddied combat boots.

Ahead of them, double doors guarded by two more SS Leibstandarte standing to attention.

'Oberleutnant Hoffman, to see the Führer,' announced one of the guards who'd escorted them up from the bay.

One of the two standing guard announced their arrival into an intercom. A moment later a young smartly dressed adjutant appeared from a side office.

'Ah, good.' He smiled. 'I'll see you in.'

Hoffman felt his heart pounding in his chest as the young man pushed the double doors open. His first glimpse of the

Führer's grand chamber was almost too much for him to bear.

Remember, professional, calm. Look good for the Führer.

The adjutant spoke softly with someone before turning round to them.

'Come on in.' He smiled smartly and waved them forward.

Hoffman stepped through the doors, his two men behind him lifting the body bag between them. His first impression was of one long wall of broad windows slowly curving around, like the stern of an eighteenth-century tall ship, and the brilliant glow of the floodlights outside pouring in, bathing the ornate decorated ceiling of the large room. Through the glass he could see an outline of the dark city and, above, the turbulent rolling thunderous clouds of the September sky, framed together like a large oil painting.

Standing behind a generous conference table spread with maps of the east coast of America and dotted with flagged tokens representing the invading German forces, stood the Führer, every bit as tall, slim and charismatic as all the posters and billboards made him out to be.

To one side, a few feet away, stood the Reichsmarschall: stern faced, fit and alert, as his reputation portrayed him. It was well known that Haas and the Führer went back a long way, more than a decade. It was said they'd first met while serving together during the Second World War. Before that time, of course, there was nothing known about them.

Two very enigmatic men.

The Führer smiled generously at Hoffman.

'You led the attack?'

'Yes, m-my Führer,' Hoffman stammered awkwardly.

He waved a dismissive hand and laughed. 'Relax, Oberleutnant . . . I don't bite. You led the assault on the White House?'

'Yes, my Führer.'

'Congratulations. A very well-done job.'

Hoffman's chest swelled with pride.

'So . . . I believe you have brought something to show me?' said Paul Kramer.

CHAPTER 42

1956, Washington DC

'Where . . . w-where are we going?' asked Liam.

The rear of the army truck dropped down, presenting them with a ramp. The German soldiers ushered them up, waving their guns.

'Re-education camp,' said the suited man Liam and Bob had interrogated earlier in the White House.

'What?'

'I heard that's what happened to all the people in New York when the Germans took it. That's where everyone's headed.'

'Re-education camp?'

'Prison camps, that's what they really are . . . that's where we're headed,' the man sighed. 'If we're lucky.'

Liam turned to look at him. 'Uh . . . what if we're *unlucky*?'

'They'll just take us somewhere quiet and shoot us.'

Liam felt his mouth suddenly dry and his skin prickle. He looked across the heads of his fellow prisoners, searching once more for any sign of Bob. If the support unit was going to actually *support* him, he'd better get a move on and do something.

In the gathering dusk it was getting harder to pick anything out. But he thought he could just about detect the distinct outline of a particularly tall and muscular German soldier, standing perfectly still a hundred yards away, looking intently back at him.

Bob?

'Oh Jay-zus . . . come on, Bob! Get me the hell out of here!' he whimpered under his breath.

The man in the suit looked at him curiously. 'Hey, kid. You and that big friend of yours . . . you said some weird thing about the future back in the –'

'Yes,' Liam replied distractedly, 'I don't suppose it matters now *where* we said we came from.' He craned his neck to catch sight of Bob one last time, but the lone figure, standing motionless, had disappeared.

God help me.

A soldier barked irritably at Liam to get a move on up the ramp and into the truck, grabbing his arm and pushing him roughly forward.

'Do as they say,' muttered the man beside Liam. 'Be glad they didn't just shoot us all right here on the lawn.'

Liam stepped up and inside, finding a wooden bench in the darkness to sit down on. It was dark enough, he hoped, to ensure the man wouldn't see the twin tracks of tears rolling down his dirt-smudged cheeks.

Bob watched the last of the prisoners climb aboard and the truck's engine rattle to life, billowing out a cloud of exhaust fumes.

[Chance of success 0.5%]

It made no practical sense to attempt a rescue of Liam O'Connor now. Even if his body could survive dozens of bullet wounds . . . Liam's wouldn't. He watched as the truck rolled away across the lawn, through a fence and bounced across a pavement and on to the hard tarmac of a broad avenue.

The highest priority at this moment in time was for him to return to the future with what little intelligence they had managed to gather. The missed-window protocol meant the field office would try one last scheduled window amid the cedar trees in precisely twenty-two hours.

Until then Bob calculated his best course of action was to find somewhere to lie low and undetected. More importantly, his body had sustained several bullet wounds around his torso. No critical organs had been damaged and the blood had clotted, preventing further loss, but the wounds would need cleaning, disinfecting and dressing. His software informed him that failure to do so soon would result in an eighty-three per cent chance of a spreading bacterial infection and eventual systemic failure of his organic body.

He would die . . . just like a human.

He walked away from the other soldiers, some of whom had begun to glance suspiciously at his unfamiliar face. He strode swiftly across the grounds of the White House, passing unnoticed amid the flurry of activity going on – appearing in the gathering dusk as if he was just another trooper given an important errand to perform with all haste.

CHAPTER 43

1956, command ship above Washington DC

Kramer turned round to look out of his sweeping observation windows down at Washington, a dark, still city. He had expected far stiffer resistance around the capital. Washington DC had fallen in just two days. The major battle had taken place just north of the suburbs on the first day. The American tanks, the lightly armoured and cumbersome Sherman MkIIs, had been outmanoeuvred and out-gunned by their Blitz Raptor MkVIs from the very first moment; the Raptors' agile hovercraft weapons platforms had made pitifully short work of them.

Their hastily assembled and dug-out defences, running east to west above the city, had been so easily bypassed. The American battle line fell to pieces in the early hours of this morning, the second day of the battle for Washington. When Kramer's highly trained Fallschirmjäger, equipped with gas-propellant landing packs and their recently upgraded pulse rifles, had dropped behind the Americans' crumbling line, further panic and disorder had soon spread among them.

Today had mostly been a mopping-up exercise.

The Americans had managed to muster together a few defensive clusters. His intelligence corps informed him a brigade-strength force of American marines was holding a strong position around one of the southern suburbs of the city, and there were pockets here and there within Washington DC. But the Americans had not had enough time to set up anything more than a shambolic line of battle-weary troops around the White House itself.

Kramer shook his head. President Eisenhower's last stand had been pitiful and undignified. He'd hoped for a much more dramatic conclusion to the campaign. America had surrendered with a whimper instead of a bang.

The complete surprise with which they'd caught the Americans had left them scrambling from the very beginning. It had taken little more than eight weeks from the first massed amphibious assault on the beaches of New England . . . to today.

It was of course better for the civilians this way, better than a long drawn-out campaign stretching into the autumn and winter, with innocent people dying unnecessarily. He genuinely felt no ill will towards the people of America. In fact, his mother had been American – a woman born in Minneapolis – and he himself had once had an American passport. He smiled at the absurd complexity of things. His mother, Sally-Anne Gardiner, all-American girl, wasn't due to be born for another forty-five years, wasn't due to meet and marry his father, Boris Kramer, for another sixty-five. And yet here was her son, leader of the German nation, the European states . . . and now also the United States.

Such is the absurdity of time travel, Paul . . . eh?

Background details, of course, known only to the few men he trusted around him: Karl Haas and the three other men who'd come through the time machine and survived to this day. Storming Hitler's Bavarian retreat had proven costly. Just the five of them left by the time Hitler ordered his men to stand down.

The people of Germany adored Kramer, their Führer – the one who led them to victory, the leader who'd replaced that confused anti-Semitic old fool, Adolf Hitler. They believed him to be German, they cared not that there was no record of his childhood, no record of a mother or a father, no trace of his existence in this world . . . until the spring of 1941. All they cared was that he had emerged from nowhere, like a guardian angel falling from heaven, and led them to victory. He'd united Europe under one proud banner, not that idiotic symbol, the *swastika*, but a banner of his very own design, the uroboros – the serpent eating its own tale – a symbol of infinity.

What comes around . . . goes around.

Europe, and now America, had at last been united – the combined muscle he needed to eventually bring the rest of the world to heel.

And it was going to be a much better world. A world where no one starved. A world whose population could be responsibly controlled to not exceed what this earth could feed. A world whose resources would be carefully used and not squandered by disgustingly rich and self-serving politicians. A world not poisoned by vehicle exhausts or coal fumes. A world not dying because mankind could not control its greed.

But more importantly . . .

It will be your world, Paul. All yours.

The quiet voice of his ambition made him stir uneasily.

You've conquered more than any leader in history.

Kramer knew he should be feeling elated, proud of what he'd achieved so far. But he wasn't. And the reason for that was lying on the floor in front of him, brought up by the oberleutnant and his two men: a hideously deformed *thing* that once might have been a young German soldier, but was now a twisted mix of two, maybe three, young men.

It lay in front of him in an unzipped body bag. Kramer had seen something like this only once before, over a decade ago in the snowy woods of Obersalzberg. He remembered he'd nearly vomited then, just as he felt like doing now.

Karl squatted down beside the body and inspected it closely. 'This *could* be the result of an incendiary weapon. The intense heat could have fused these poor men together.'

Kramer nodded, tight-lipped, stroking his chin. It could well be that . . . or the result of one of their pulse bombs, designed to pulverize soft tissue with its shock wave. His modern weapon designs had a habit of producing unpleasant-looking casualties like this.

Or it might be something else?

That voice again. He bid it be silent.

'Yes, Karl . . . it's a possibility.'

CHAPTER 44

1956, outside Washington DC

Liam looked out of the back of the truck as it rumbled noisily along a road away from DC lined with German troops on patrol, civilian refugees herded at gunpoint and pitiful lines of beaten American soldiers in their khaki greens, many of them wounded.

'I'm Wallace, by the way,' said the man in the suit. 'Daniel Wallace. I work in the White House press corps. Well,' he sighed wearily, 'at least I did.'

Liam held out a limp hand. He wasn't sure what 'press corps' did, but he guessed it was to do with newspapers. 'Liam O'Connor, from Cork, Ireland.'

Wallace nodded. 'You're a long way from home, son.'

'Tell me about it,' he replied with a lacklustre smile.

Wallace spoke quietly. 'I'm still puzzled about you and your friend. You said you were . . .' Wallace looked around at the other prisoners; many of them were either in shock, or had retired into themselves, shutting out this grim reality.

'Look, why don't we forget what I said?' Liam replied. 'It's not like it matters now, does it? I'm right here in the same boat as everyone else.'

'What about the man you were with?'

'What about him?'

'I . . . I swear I saw him take gunshot wounds that . . . that he shouldn't have survived.'

Liam said nothing and Wallace let it go for now, turning to listen to a couple of other prisoners in the back of the truck talking quietly, a silver-haired army colonel and a naval officer.

'. . . were all strung out, shell-shocked. I can't believe two months ago the big story was Eisenhower meeting Kramer on neutral ground to discuss peace – an end to the growing tension between us and them.'

'And all the while,' cut in the navy officer, 'Kramer was putting the final preparations together for his invasion of America.' The colonel ran a hand over his buzz-cut hair. 'We never even saw it coming, Bill . . . We were just kidding ourselves that they wanted peace and would leave us alone.'

Liam gazed out of the back of the truck, his mind a million miles away.

My first trip . . . and it's already over for me.

The last few weeks of his life felt like a crazy dream. A little over three weeks ago, he'd been a junior steward on the *Titanic*, tending to rich, pampered passengers, looking forward to arriving in the land of opportunity, America. The plan had been to quit his job the moment the ship docked and begin a new life of adventure and discovery. He'd read so much about America and knew this was the place for him, the country in which he would make his fortune.

Then a chunk of bloody ice at sea had changed everything.

And with it came Foster . . . saving him from the sort of death he'd always had nightmares about – drowning. The old man had opened an incredible door for him. A stunning world of the future, a world of chrome and glass buildings, of neon lights and flashing screens of colour, of excitement, of movement, of technology that seemed out of this world. But also a world of the past, of any time he wished, for Foster assured him he would see so many wonderful things, wonderful moments, that in a way . . . no, definitely . . . he was the *luckiest* young man alive.

Now here he was. Stuck. What he faced now along with everyone else in this truck was a frightening and uncertain future. They were going to be shot and, if not, then most probably put to work as prisoners of war.

Some small voice inside tried to reassure him that at least he was alive instead of crushed and rotting fish-food at the bottom of the Atlantic Ocean. It did little to cheer him. He was stuck here. There was no way for him to return to that third and final extraction window. And, without any way at all to communicate with Foster, Maddy and Sal . . . that was it for him.

Might as well forget those names, he told himself. *I'm never going to see them again*.

The truck rattled past a picket fence plastered with photographs of all shapes and sizes, the smiling faces of those missing printed on *Have you seen them?* posters placed by worried husbands and wives, mothers and fathers. Along the bottom of the fence were piled posies of flowers, fresh and old, crosses, mementoes, teddy bears and dolls. It was a shrine to those who had vanished amid the whirlwind carnage of recent weeks.

Several of the other people in the back of the truck watched the fence pass by, a painfully endless display of hope and sadness. A woman opposite him sobbed at the sight of it.

So many dead and missing.

A soldier in the truck ground his teeth. 'Never even stood a goddamn chance 'gainst them Nazis.'

Perhaps the only comfort, Liam considered, was that the war had been so short, that it was already over.

CHAPTER 45

1956, command ship above Washington DC

Kramer watched the nervous young Fallschirmjäger officer and his two men leave the room.

He had a million and one things to attend to, a steady stream of command decisions waiting to be made, not only to do with this recently conquered country, but also with affairs of state back home in Europe.

But his mind was now on this one thing, the report he'd just heard from the young officer, the report of a shimmering window of air among the White House trees. There had been eye-witness statements that one man was 'swallowed' by it, only to be returned a minute later, his body appearing and instantly merging with that of another man who had accidentally stepped into the shimmering air.

These were eye-witness statements made in the immediate aftermath of a battle; the men's blood was up, adrenaline flushing through their veins. Soldiers, after the rush of combat, have always been prone to seeing things. Military history is filled with the stories of soldiers who saw armies of angels coming to their rescue. Kramer might have dismissed this as the overexcited rambling of young soldiers, except the officer had brought them this . . .

His eyes drifted across the twisted, mutated thing in the body bag between them.

Karl looked up at his leader. 'You think this might have been the result of another time traveller?'

Kramer said nothing in response.

How could someone else travel through time?

Waldstein's carefully hidden prototype had been the *only* time machine. International law had come down hard and unanimously, and thoroughly closed the door on this technology. Any nation, any corporation, any individual caught developing it was subject to the ultimate punishment: complete obliteration. No warning. No arguments. No mitigating factors. Even in the chaotic troubled world of the mid-twenty-first century there was an accepted understanding that, for better or worse, time could not be allowed to change.

'That machine *was* the only machine, wasn't it?' asked Karl. 'Paul . . .?'

Only Karl was allowed that privilege now – using his *first* name, and then only when it was just the two of them.

'Yes, Karl . . . it *was* the only one.'

By destroying Waldstein's prototype behind him, Kramer had been certain that *no one* could follow them back in time and their efforts to change the world for the better be undone.

But what if there was another machine?

The thought sent a chill down his neck.

And someone determined to come back after us?

If this twisted body on the floor was the result of a time window opening, then *someone* from the future had chosen to zero in on today. Someone from the future was trying to correct history and assumed today, 5 September 1956, was the day history was changed.

But it wasn't today.

History had in fact been changed fifteen years earlier, the day Kramer and his men had fought their way through SS guards to have an audience with Hitler. The day Kramer had explained that

Hitler's impending attack on Russia would be the beginning of the end of his dreams, an end that would come four years later in a bunker beneath Berlin with a bullet in his temple and a cyanide capsule crushed between his teeth.

Kramer looked up from the corpse, out through the panoramic viewing windows. 'Karl, we must completely *erase* history.'

'What?'

'Everything before today . . . particularly everything since we arrived in 1941.'

'Covering our tracks?'

'Yes. But we should present this to the people as a symbolic gesture.'

'I don't understand.'

'This day will be known as *Day One*, a new beginning for all of mankind. We will announce that after so many thousand years of bloodstained history – countries, kings, popes, emperors fighting each other for land or money, or faith – that *all war* is over.'

'No more wars, yes.' Karl nodded. 'It would be a popular message.'

Kramer pointed towards the city skyline through the broad window. 'America *was* our biggest threat, and now it's part of our Reich. We can't be challenged any more. We're now looking at the chance that every person in this world can finally be united under one banner.'

'The Russian and Chinese states still remain.'

Kramer shrugged. 'Their time will come.' He turned to Karl. 'I think now is the perfect time, anyway, to make this sort of a sweeping gesture.'

He turned away from the smouldering body, glad the young officer and his two men were gone and that he could turn his pale face from the awful sight.

'But, Karl, you and I must never forget that we're strangers in this time. Even though it's been fifteen years since we time-travelled, we must be ever vigilant of covering our tracks.'

'I understand.'

'By declaring today as the first day of a new era, we'll be wiping the last fifteen years clean, Karl. Leaving absolutely nothing. No clues for anybody in the future to close in on. But, more than that, we'll erase all of history. And why not? Isn't this also the reason we came back? To wipe the slate clean . . . A new beginning. A new order?'

Karl nodded.

'I will make an announcement over state television and radio. We shall decree a day of celebration across all the nations of the Greater Reich – a unity day of –'

'*Unity Day* . . . it is a good name for it, Paul.'

'Yes . . . yes it is. We'll call it that, then. As well as this celebration, we'll begin a systemic purging of history books, documents, relics. It all has to go. It all has to be burned.'

Karl nodded. 'Yes, sir.'

'And we'll tell the people of America that there's nothing to be afraid of. They will *not* be enslaved, but instead will be invited to join the Germans, the French, the British and all the other citizens of the Greater Reich.'

'I will have a speech drafted for you,' said Karl.

'Thank you, old friend. This . . .' he said, pointing at the body on the floor, 'is nothing for us to be alarmed at, do you understand? *We* control history now, Karl . . . you and I . . . it's clay in our hands to be moulded exactly as we want. There will be no way for anyone from the future to find our entry point.'

'If this body was the result of an attempt by somebody to find us –' Karl looked at Kramer – 'the fact that they tried *today* and not back in the spring of 1941 . . . this proves . . .?'

'Yes.' Kramer smiled. 'That they have no idea what date we

went back to originally.' He patted Karl affectionately on the shoulder. 'I think this shows that we're safe.'

'Yes, sir.'

Karl crisply saluted. 'I shall see to your speech.'

'Thank you.'

Kramer watched Karl go, closing the grand double doors behind him, and then turned once more to look out of the panoramic windows.

Will that be enough, though . . . erasing history?

It would be a sensible precautionary measure, but Kramer still felt a chill of unease. Half an hour ago he'd been certain that Waldstein's prototype had been the world's one and only time machine.

Is it possible I'm wrong?

In the sky he watched a squadron of Messerschmitt Jetlanders swoop down from a higher altitude and hover just above the deserted streets below, sweeping them with their searchlights.

What was left of the world to conquer would present even less of an obstacle than America had. His Reich was now unassailable, unbeatable, all powerful. The remaining countries would fall one by one. Russia and China, two large but backward nations, were isolated, blockaded on all fronts. Sooner or later he could finish them off and be done with war.

Nonetheless, it was an unsettling prospect that someone somewhere out there in the future could – if they got very lucky – find a way to get to him.

Or it might be something far worse, Paul. Do you remember what the old man Waldstein once told you?

Kramer cursed, glancing at the body. He ordered his guards standing outside to take the thing away and dispose of it. He'd seen enough bloodshed for one day . . . and there was much to attend to now that the United States had officially surrendered.

CHAPTER 46

1956, Washington DC

It was dark and wet. Bob's eyes had adjusted hours ago to the dimness down here in the sewers. Pallid tendrils of light lanced through the grating in the pavement above. It was a grey, overcast afternoon in Washington DC, the day after America had been defeated by its invaders.

The support unit sat motionless on a damp concrete sill, his legs dangling in the foul-smelling water that trickled past.

From above, he could hear the occasional movement of vehicles, the tramping of boots and every now and then the rattle-dash of distant gunfire. Over the last twenty hours, thousands of people, potential trouble-makers – those who might try their hand at rallying the people: senators, congressmen, judges, lawyers, journalists – had been rounded up and put on convoys of trucks heading out of the city. The rest of the city's population cowered in their homes and could only wonder at what Kramer and his invasion force would do with them all now.

It was quiet at the moment, save for the persistent echo of water dripping from the sewer's curved brick ceiling and the languid trickling of stinking sewage.

Bob sat motionless. Absent-mindedly a finger flicked the safety catch of the pulse carbine held in his hands. On and off, off and on, the metallic click echoing loudly down the sewer.

Waiting patiently. Counting down on his internal clock.

Bob closed his eyes.

[Information: final window due in 23 minutes]

He was only ten minutes from the White House, a mile as the crow flies, and half that distance he could cover underground along the network of sewage tunnels, emerging from a manhole along Pennsylvania Avenue. He would have to run the rest of the way in plain view. His black rubber suit and mask might disguise him for a short few moments. But since all the other enemy soldiers had discarded those and were now wearing their grey Wehrmacht uniforms, he'd most probably attract attention the instant he was above ground.

However, if he timed things correctly, and was lucky, he stood a fair chance of managing to fight his way quickly to the space beneath that copse of cedar trees just as the air began to shimmer and the window appeared. Yet it was quite probable that his body would suffer too much combat damage to recover itself.

But that was of little importance.

The small wafer of silicon in his head was all that mattered; getting that through the window and sent back to the future in one piece was the *only* consideration. Even if the best he could do was poke his head into the portal as it activated, leaving his headless corpse behind, then that would satisfy his primary mission objective. The gathered intelligence would be back with the field office, precisely where it needed to be.

Bob stirred. It was nearly time for him to make his move.

But something in his small organic mind urged him to reassess his mission priorities, like a small child's nagging voice. A whimpering plea that travelled down thin internal wires.

Don't leave him behind.

Bob's head twitched uneasily as his AI attempted to deal with conflicting assertions. There was an authoritative, emotionless silicon reply to that child's voice.

[Mission objective: gather and return information]

But . . . there was so little information to relay, so very little that they'd managed to gather. Bob could return to the field office – alive or dead – and they could download from his head what he'd seen and heard. But the vast majority of this data was just smoke and gunfire; there was little they'd learned that could be of use. Not enough to fix on a precise point of origin for this time contamination. More information was needed, much more. Specifically – knowledge of the events that had come *before* this invasion. Located here in 1956 he had a far better chance of uncovering the recent past than back in the altered world of 2001.

His head convulsed anxiously, his finger thumbed the safety catch with increasingly distracted vigour.

[Mission parameters require *reprioritization*]

The unit was out of his comfort zone now. His AI could deal with detailed and speedy situation analysis, but *decision-making* was something far better dealt with by a human mind. His on-board memory recalled Foster's words from a few days ago.

'. . . *And that's the reason the agency sends a human operative back as well as the support unit. A robot can't make intuitive judgements, Liam . . . not nearly as well as a human can . . .*'

The tiny nodule of wrinkled flesh in Bob's skull – the undeveloped brain – understood this all too well. It understood help was needed while the hard-wired computer code continued to argue the case that mission orders were orders to be obeyed at all costs.

Must Find Him.

[Recommendation: update mission parameters]

Bob's finger froze; his body remained rigid, utterly still. His internal computer focused now on one thing alone, every micro-volt of computing power devoted to one end.

Re-ordering his mission priorities.

Making a decision.

[Mission updated: locate and rescue Operative Liam O'Connor]

CHAPTER 47

2001, New York

Foster and Maddy watched the countdown on the computer screen. 'Thirty seconds,' he announced.

Maddy nodded; she could see the display too. 'And what if they miss this window as well?'

'We'll deal with that when – *if* – it comes to it.'

Maddy looked over her shoulder at the floor, an area cleared of cables and detritus with the faint circle of chalk inscribed in the middle where Liam and Bob were – hopefully – going to materialize very soon. She was glad Foster had sent Sal out to sit in Times Square and observe. If she was here, she'd be worrying, interrupting, agitating . . . distracting. Foster already looked stressed enough as it was, without having to constantly assure her Liam and Bob were going to be fine.

And what if they came back, Liam wounded . . . or worse?

Better that Sal was elsewhere right now.

'Since they missed the other back-ups,' she said, 'something must have happened to them. Right?'

'We don't know that for sure. Quite often I've missed a scheduled window or two on the missions I've been on,' said Foster. 'The unforeseen happens – that's why we have several back-ups.'

'But if they *do* miss this one . . .?'

He looked at the display.

Ten seconds.

'If they miss this one, then we need to communicate a new rendezvous point to them.'

She looked at him. 'Communicate? How?'

'It's complicated. I'll talk you through that later.'

She let out a breath. 'So it's not the end of the world, then? I thought . . . you know . . . I thought we'd lost them forever.'

Foster checked the phase interruption indicator; no sign of any shifting packets of density where the extraction portal was due to open. That was good. The soldiers must have gone.

'All right . . . here we go,' he said.

The displacement machinery began to hum and the lights in the archway dimmed as all power diverted towards it. Then, across the floor from them a large sphere suddenly began to shimmer, and through the undulating air Maddy thought she could make out the dancing, twisting form of tree trunks.

'Come on, Liam,' whispered Maddy. 'Move your butt.'

Foster swallowed anxiously. 'Yes, get a move on.'

If they were there, they should step through immediately. Keeping a portal open unnecessarily wasn't wise; a window on to chaotic dimensions in which *anything* could lurk . . . The sooner it was closed the better.

'Come on!' he uttered impatiently.

The sphere hovered, shimmered, glowing a soft blue in the flickering dimness of the archway. Foster glanced at the computer screen. The portal had been open ten seconds and a red caution message had already begun flashing on the screen.

'I have to close it,' said Foster. 'Any longer and we risk attracting a seeker. They're not there.'

'No!' cried Maddy. 'Let it stay open just a bit –'

'They've failed the rendezvous,' snapped Foster. He hit the ABORT button on the screen and instantly the sphere vanished, the hum of surging power diminished and the dimmed flickering ceiling lights grew bright once more.

'Dammit, Foster, they might just have been running a bit late!'

'There's no *running late*, Madelaine. You're either there or you're not. The window opens, and either they step through or they don't. I'm afraid there's no leaving it open just to wait and see.'

They sat in silence for a moment, staring out across the floor at the chalk circle, as if hoping both Liam and Bob might still magically appear, Liam with a guilty expression on his face for their rather late arrival.

'So . . . OK. It's not the end of the world, then,' said Maddy, forcing herself to be businesslike. 'You mentioned something about sending a message?'

Foster nodded. 'That's right. We need to send them details on a new time-stamp . . . and perhaps we need to pick another location. Not too far away from the first location, but somewhere more discreet, less busy, I think would be better.'

Maddy pursed her lips. 'And how exactly will they get this message?'

'Tachyon transmission,' he replied. 'I'll give you the technical explanation later . . . It's complicated.'

She shrugged. 'I can wait.'

CHAPTER 48

1956, command ship above Washington DC

Kramer dined alone. He wasn't in the mood to celebrate the victory with Reichsmarschall Karl Haas, the senior divisional commanders and their aides. Several days since the surrender, and despite a few minor skirmishes as several individual US states in the west fought on bitterly, America was now a part of the Greater Reich.

His high command was celebrating right now, no doubt solemnly toasting their absent Führer in smart dress uniforms, then sitting down together in the White House's state hall to discuss the administrative business of running America. He trusted Karl to keep all those ambitious generals and Gauleiters in line; he suspected they feared him almost as much as they did their Führer.

No, tonight he wanted to be alone. Things were troubling him.

That body, *that damned body* . . . the unsettling questions it raised. Despite what Karl had said, that was no corpse twisted by a mere incendiary grenade. He'd seen what a time portal could do to a human body once before. He'd never forget the twisted flesh, organs turned inside out and still somehow managing to function . . . for a while.

'Someone from the future's after us,' he muttered to himself.

He could almost feel that *someone* probing the past, finding their way slowly towards him, stalking him. At any moment the air could shimmer beside the table and an assassin appear, a gun raised and ready to execute him. It was something Kramer constantly feared. The recurring nightmare had troubled him almost every night for the last fifteen years – awakening in his bed in the dark stillness of night to see an assassin leaning over him and announcing his immediate execution for travelling through time.

The body . . . *that* body . . . had made his nightmares a thousand-fold worse, and now he spent every waking hour fearing what might be out there. It was a struggle to keep this torment from Karl, to keep his composure in front of the man. He wondered sometimes if there was an easier way out.

A soft voice whispered quietly in his head.

There is a way out for you, you know.

Suicide?

No, another way.

He looked out of the window at a dark city punctuated with sporadic smouldering fires and speared with the sweeping, searching floodlights coming from his command ship.

Think on it.

His quiet voice. The voice that was always there, had always been with him as long as he could remember. The voice of . . . ambition . . . daring him on, pushing him to do those things he wouldn't normally have the resolve to do. As a child it had helped him achieve academic success, as a young man driven him to earn a doctorate in quantum physics, to become a research fellow at the Waldstein Institute. It had given him the confidence to finally put together his audacious plan to go back into history and make it his.

You could destroy this world, couldn't you, Paul? After all, it's your world now. All yours to do with as you wish.

'That's madness,' he replied, putting down his fork suddenly. It clattered noisily on the plate, filling his large, stately quarters with a diminishing echo.

Madness, is it?

Since going through time, convincing Hitler to accept him into his inner circle and finally becoming the Führer himself, the voice had become quiet, unneeded by him. Like a child brooding, sulking. But now – since that body, in fact – it seemed to have found a new energy.

Madness, is it? What would happen if a traveller from the future were to appear right here and put a bullet through your brain?

Kramer closed his eyes. The thought had him trembling. The answer was obvious. This history he had worked so hard to create would change.

And what if a traveller learned the exact time and place that you entered history? Those woods, 1941? And killed you there? Before you met Hitler?

'The world would be as it was,' he replied aloud. 'The future would once again be the dark and dying one we left behind.'

That's right. A dying world. Choking on toxic fumes. The seas poisoned. People slowly starving. In a way, it would be kinder to end it now. Would it not?

Kinder? Kramer hadn't thought about the world they'd left behind in a long time. Global warming had become an uncontrollable force. By 2050 the ice-caps had finally vanished. The entire African continent was as sun-blasted and lifeless as the surface of Mars. And people, nine billion of them, crowded into the few tolerable regions of the earth left, most of them starving migrants living in dust-blown shanty towns outside the few mega-cities. Like almost every other species on earth, Kramer wondered whether one day mankind would also eventually become extinct.

'Kinder,' he said eventually. 'Perhaps it would.'

Much kinder.

He had no appetite for his meal now.

You trust me, Paul, don't you?

He'd always trusted his inner voice, his instinct. It had guided him far better in his life than any tutor or mentor, any father-figure or friend. 'If you can't trust your own instinct,' someone had once told him, 'then you're a lost man.'

Don't you see? Someone or something is out there. And it will find you, whatever you do, however much you decide to erase history and disguise your tracks. It will eventually find you. The body was a warning.

Deep down he knew there was truth in that. Perhaps he'd known that from the moment he and Karl had been presented with that cruelly twisted corpse, but he'd been unable to bring himself to admit it.

I think you realize now . . . your run of luck has finally come to an end.

'Fifteen years,' he said.

That's right, fifteen years. Twelve of them as the world's greatest ruler. And in that time you've achieved so very much. But your time has finally run out. Someone has come to get you.

'A time traveller?'

Possibly. Or worse.

'Worse?'

You've meddled with time. You've crossed dimensions. You've stepped through chaos itself. There's no knowing for sure what seeks you out.

Kramer felt his guts twist with anxiety, a churning unease eating away inside.

An agent of the future could take this world from you with an assassin's bullet. But it could be far worse. Something we can never hope to understand could come for you . . . could be out there in that dark city right now . . .

He felt his scalp prickle, his skin turn cold.

But you could prevent that.

'By destroying this world?'

Yes, Paul . . . by destroying this world.

He pushed his chair back. Oddly, there was some growing comfort in that notion. This world rendered still, silent, lifeless and unchanging. An everlasting monument to the world created by Paul Kramer. All life ended with a sudden flash, instead of the protracted misery that would exist in the future. And there was a way – a doomsday device he'd considered in his idle moments.

We both knew this might happen one day. Didn't we? Perhaps it was always going to be your destiny.

Kramer narrowed his eyes, almost sensing the inevitable subtle shifting of destiny ahead of him, future histories adjusting, rewriting, as he felt his decision being firmly made.

'Then it has to be so.'

His voice, his instinct, seemed appeased by that.

A fitting end to things, Paul. Mankind was always destined to destroy itself. It's in our nature to destroy all that we create. And you will be the one who does it.

Isn't that just a little bit like being God?

CHAPTER 49

2001, New York

'Sal will be all right out there, won't she?' asked Maddy.

Foster was scrolling through their history database. 'She'll be just fine.'

They'd found her a plain dark-blue T-shirt and grey jeans. They belonged to a member of the previous team and were large on her, almost swamped her. But she stood out far less than she did wearing her favourite emo clothes.

'No one will notice a little girl,' he added. 'She's just a harmless child.'

Maddy shuddered. 'It looks so grim, so grey and *ordered* out there.'

She had stepped out with Sal briefly to get a glimpse of this alternate New York. The city looked tidy and drab. The only colour amid the uniformly monotone towers was the stabs of bright red from unfurled banners and pennants that dotted the city skyline.

Foster nodded. 'It is grim. But, for an innocent child just walking around, perhaps walking home from school or an errand to a shop, it's probably a great deal safer right now than it would be otherwise.'

'What do you mean?'

He looked up from the screens. 'I don't imagine they have a crime problem, hmm? This is a fascist state. I think it's a safe bet that muggers don't get away with a slapped wrist and a behaviour order in this version of New York.'

Maddy nodded. 'I guess not.'

'Anyway, back to business,' he said. 'I suggest we pick a return window within the vicinity of the White House, not too far away but safely beyond any security perimeter. We need to see whether they have a map of Washington in this new Nazi version. The city may be different, sections rebuilt.'

'OK.'

'So that's the *where*. We need to now consider the *when*. I have a suggestion for that. We set it for the last possible time for their mission. Bob's maximum mission durati–'

Maddy felt it. Light-headed, as if she was losing her balance.

The screens went blank and a moment later the fizzing strip light above them winked out, leaving them in pitch black.

'What the –?'

'That was a time shift.' Foster's voice emerged from the dark beside her. 'A big one. I felt it as well.'

'We've lost power,' whispered Maddy. 'That's not good, is it?'

'It means that whatever the world is like outside our *field bubble*, we're no longer able to tap electricity from it.' Foster balled his fists with frustration. 'In fact, the field generator's down as well. That means there's no forty-eight-hour flip-back. We're well and truly stuck *in* this world's timeline . . . whatever it is.'

'I'm not sure I like the sound of that.'

'We should take a look,' he said quietly.

She heard his chair scrape on the concrete. 'Come on.'

She stood up, her hands spread out in front of her.

'This way.'

She followed his voice across the floor.

'Keep coming.'

A moment later her fingers brushed the crumbling brick wall.

Foster cursed under his breath. 'I hate winching this wretched thing up.'

'I'll give you a hand,' said Maddy. She felt her way along the wall until her fingers brushed the winch box. She found a space on the handle beside Foster's frail old hand.

'Let's get to it, then,' he said quietly.

They pulled on the handle and it creaked round. The shutter door began to crank up slowly and noisily.

A faint afternoon light eased into the room, pushing back the absolute darkness behind them.

'Looks like another grey day in Manhattan,' laughed Maddy skittishly.

The shutter inched up until it was waist height.

'That'll do, Madelaine,' said Foster. 'Duck down, will you, and take a look?'

She nodded. 'Sure.'

She stooped down and peered outside. The backstreet was littered with rubble and twisted spars of rusted metal that looked like they had tumbled down from the bridge above many, many years ago. A tangle of coarse dry weeds emerged through it all and laid claim to the ground, nature clawing its way back.

Maddy slid under the shutter and stood up on the other side.

'What do you see?'

She glanced up at the bridge above them, the one that had majestically crossed the East River only moments ago. It was now little more than a creaking ruined web of rusted metal stretching across the river. In the distance the tall slab-like buildings of the Nazi-Manhattan she'd observed a short while ago as she'd let Sal out now looked like the crumbling stubs of rotten teeth. Bare skeletons of iron sprang from collapsed ruins across the river. The sun hung low and heavy like a bloodshot eye peeking through scudding brown clouds that looked threatening and toxic.

New York was utterly dead. An apocalyptic wasteland.

Something dreadful had happened here. It had happened decades ago from the look of the sparse and withered plant life that emerged here and there among the crumbling ruins.

'My God, Foster . . . it's . . . it's the end of the world,' she said, hearing her own voice catch, falter and die in her throat.

The end of the world.

CHAPTER 50

2001, New York

Sal was afraid. Very afraid.

She looked up at the dark, silent, blasted structures around her. Tall ruins that creaked and groaned while skeins of dust chased like fleeting ghosts through them.

Times Square was no longer Times Square – it was a tomb, the crumbling relic of a long-dead civilization. She couldn't begin to imagine what must have happened. The breeze moaned through open windows, a haunting cry like some tormented spirit warning her to leave now and not delay a moment longer.

She decided that was probably good advice and turned to head back to the field office, wondering for a moment if the bridge and the archway beneath it, their little backstreet . . . was actually still there.

As she turned, she saw something move.

The faintest flash of something pale flitting from one dark window to another.

Just a bit of rubbish . . . that's all.

She picked her way quickly across the rubble, kicking stones that clacked and clattered noisily in the silence. Again she thought she spotted another flash of movement from within the darkened bowels of one of the buildings.

A pale oval . . . with two dark holes that studied her intently for the briefest moment, then disappeared into the gloomy interior.

I'm not alone.

She picked up her pace, not wanting to run in case it encouraged whatever was inside to come out after her in pursuit, but too frightened to just walk.

She hummed a tune. A stupid over-cheerful plastic Bollywood song from her mum's childhood. One of those tunes you can never get out of your head once it gets in.

She clattered her way across Times Square, her humming echoing off dark scorched and blasted walls. She was passing the rusting skeleton of a vehicle, on to what had once been Broadway, when a creature emerged several dozen yards in front of her.

It stopped and stared at her with deep, dark, soulless eyes set in a pallid ash-grey bald head.

She stopped humming.

It reminded her of a creature she'd once seen in an old movie from way back, a movie with elves and dwarves and magical rings. One of the creatures she remembered in particular, though, was called *Gollum*. The thing standing in front of her reminded her of that. It stared at her, motionless. Its mouth finally opened to reveal bloody gums and one or two ragged teeth.

And it screamed.

The scream echoed off the tall ruins and was soon joined by other shrill voices joining in.

Sal looked desperately around and saw other pale oval faces, each with dark eyes and toothless bleeding mouths, emerging from hundreds of windows, like termites stirring from a disturbed nest.

And she screamed along with them.

Foster joined Maddy outside, surveying the broken and blasted city. 'Complete devastation,' he whispered. 'Something happened here a long time ago. And if it happened here, I can well imagine it's happened everywhere.' He looked at Maddy. 'Perhaps some sort of a nuclear war?'

She nodded. 'Oh God, what is it with mankind? Never happy unless it's blowing someone up.'

'I'm afraid that's us as a species.'

Isn't it just, she mused. Sometimes she felt disgusted to be human.

'Sal's out there,' said Foster quietly.

She looked at him. 'She'll be terrified. And she may have difficulty finding her way back. That's a very different-looking landscape out there.'

'I'll just grab some things,' he said, ducking back under the shutter.

A few minutes later he emerged from beneath the shutter door with a couple of flashlights, a bottle of water and a shotgun in the crook of his arm.

Her eyes widened at the sight of it. 'You think we're going to need it?'

'Best to be prepared, eh?'

She swallowed nervously then nodded. 'OK. Let's go find her.'

CHAPTER 51

2001, New York

Sal was running as fast as she could amid the rubble and blocks of crumbling masonry, long ago collapsed across forgotten streets. She kept stumbling, losing her footing, barking her shins, scraping and cutting her hands.

Behind her the creatures – there seemed to be dozens now – kept pace with her easily. There was surprising agility in those frail and pallid bodies. They were small like undernourished children, but with faces that were lined with age . . . or grief. They followed her, keeping a wary distance, not closing, not falling behind . . . just intensely curious.

For now.

She glanced up at the street ahead, little more than an undulating bed of shattered blocks of concrete and protruding spars of rusted metal. The frames of buildings either side were the only visual clue that this had once been a street.

If this was Broadway . . . once, then she knew she needed to turn left at some point, left on to East 14th Street. That would take her east towards the river and the Williamsburg Bridge.

If it's still standing.

Another glance over her shoulder and she saw one of them had closed the distance between them and was right behind her, a long pale hand reaching out ahead of it, its bald head cocked to one side, eyes curiously regarding her long black hair.

'Oh God!' she screamed. 'Leave me alone!'

She suddenly stopped dead in her tracks and spun round to face it.

The creature drew up short of her, the others coming to a halt behind it. They fanned out either side, all of them studying her silently with eyes wide, a burning curiosity written on all of their faces.

Sal reached down for a length of rusty metal piping. Lifting it up, flakes of rust crumbled away. She wasn't entirely sure the thing wouldn't crumble to dust the first time she swung it at something, but all the same it felt good in her hand.

'Stay back!' she snarled, her voice shrill and high.

The creature closest to her stayed its distance, standing low, crouching almost like a primate. The silence was filled with her ragged breath and the mournful wind; she had time to look at it more closely.

A pair of expressive eyes. Clearly a human. But it seemed such a pitiful-looking human. If she wasn't so terrified, she could almost imagine feeling sorry for it.

The creature nearest her took a careful, measured step forward, extending one hand towards her.

'No! You stay back!' she barked, brandishing the crumbling pipe.

She heard the thing whine, a keening sound, like some pitiful dog behind bars in a rescue compound. The pale skin – stretched across lean arms and legs, stretched across ribs and a pelvic bone that protruded unpleasantly – was so ghostly white it was almost translucent. She could see the faint lines of violet arteries beneath. Its mouth, eyes and nose oozed a bloody mucus.

The thing wanted desperately to come closer to her. The hand stretching further forward, wanting to make contact.

'No! I'll hit you!' she screamed again.

It cocked its head again. The almost completely toothless mouth opened and closed with a wet snapping sound.

'Oh! Ahhh-iiitttt-oooooo,' it uttered.

It was attempting to mimic her.

'You . . . you . . . you can speak?' she managed in response.

'Ooo . . . ooo . . . ooo-annng-zbikkkkk?' it gargled.

She noticed something in its face. Intelligence. Perhaps a long-faded memory stirring behind those milky boiled-fish eyes. This thing was human, or at least it had once been human, she was sure of that.

'My . . . my n-name is Sal,' she said loudly, for the benefit of the others behind it, gesturing at herself. When she had introduced herself for the first time to Bob, he had cocked his head curiously, his lips trying crudely to repeat her name. These creatures, on the other hand, cowered at the sound of her voice. Their dead eyes seemed less curious than Bob's. They mewled and whined among themselves.

Is that their language? The whining noise?

'Sal,' she said again, encouraged that her talking seemed to be holding them at bay for the moment. 'I'm Sal.'

'Annng-aahhhh.'

'That's right.' She smiled. 'Sal.'

The hand, still reaching towards her, was now only a few inches away. She wondered whether to swing her pipe at it or let it touch her. There was no way of knowing whether these things wanted to communicate in some way or were just attempting to test how much of a threat she posed to them.

If I hit it . . .?

Then she suspected some kind of pack instinct would take over. They'd be upon her in the blink of an eye.

Let it touch. Let it make contact.

She swallowed nervously as the tips of its fingers eagerly stretched out and brushed lightly against her hair.

'Hair,' she said.

The fingers curled through the strands, flicked at them, played with them.

'It's hair,' she said again, softening her voice, trying to steal the fear from it.

The thing's mouth seemed to widen, stretch, exposing a few snaggled teeth emerging from bloody gums.

My God . . . is that a smile?

A soft *sing-song* humming vibrated up from the creature's narrow bony chest into its throat. It became an almost childlike cooing. Like the contented noise of a baby suckling a bottle.

Sal found her hand stretching out towards it. Copying the gesture, showing the same curiosity seemed like the right thing to do. Her hand brushed against the thing's forearm. She expected it to be cold and clammy . . . but it was warm and dry. Just like any human's skin should be.

And she returned the smile.

'Pleased . . . pleased to meet you,' she said.

'Eeeeee . . . eeeee-ooo-eeeee-oooo.'

It was then she heard the clatter of rubble disturbed behind her.

'You should keep very still!'

It was Maddy's voice. Not a shout, but a coarse whisper echoing across the stillness.

'No sudden moves. OK?' That was Foster's voice. 'Keep your eyes on that thing, Sal. Do *not* look away. Do you understand?'

She nodded.

'All right, Sal, you should take a slow step back now.'

She wanted to look back over her shoulder. To see where her friends were, how far away they were.

'Don't!' hissed Foster. 'Keep your eyes on it as you back off.'

'W-why?' she managed to whisper.

'Just do it!'

She did as instructed, taking one careful step at a time, feeling her way across the uneven ground with her feet, keeping her eyes locked on the thing in front of her.

The Gollum frowned. The humming quickly became a frustrated growl as it shuffled forward, reaching again for her hair.

'It's – it's not going to let me g-go,' uttered Sal. 'Ouch! It's got hold of my hair again!'

'Just keep coming, Sal . . . Don't stop,' said Maddy. She sounded a little bit closer.

The creature was holding tight to a lock of her hair, winding its claw-like fingers through it to get a better hold. And then she saw something in its face, innocent curiosity vanishing, replaced by some dark instinct. It opened its mouth and let out a cry that almost sounded human, but certainly didn't resemble anything like a language.

The other creatures suddenly surged forward.

'Oh no!' cried Maddy.

There was the deafening blast of a gunshot. The creature holding her hair was suddenly hurled on its back, spattering dark blood across the rubble.

'Sal, quick!'

She turned and saw Maddy and Foster ten yards beyond, a blue veil of gunsmoke clearing as Foster pumped another round into the gun. She scrambled on all fours towards them, clattering noisily over a mound of loose bricks and masonry, expecting at any moment to feel claws in her hair again, yanking her off her feet from behind. Instead, a moment later, she was stumbling into Maddy's open arms.

'Oh God! Sal! Are you all right?'

She was too frightened to answer.

'Run!' she whispered. 'We – w-we should run!'

Maddy stood her ground, held her tight. 'It's OK, Sal . . . it's OK. Look.'

Sal turned to look over her shoulder to find the creatures had gone. Every last one of them except for the twitching corpse in front of her had . . . simply vanished within the space of a few heartbeats, as if they'd never been anything more than mere wisps of smoke, carried off by a gusting wind.

'The noise of the gun scared them off,' said Foster.

Maddy looked anxiously around at the dark husks of ruined buildings on either side of them. 'They're hiding in there. We should head back while they're still spooked.'

Foster nodded and waved them past. 'Come on.'

The girls stepped around him quickly and backed away. Foster followed, his shotgun still shouldered and ready to fire.

CHAPTER 52

1956, New Jersey

Feldwebel Johan Kernst rubbed his hands to warm them as he watched the distant truck approaching the east entrance to the prison camp, Gefangenenlager 63. From this distance it seemed to be approaching them far too quickly.

'Wake up, lads,' he barked at the men manning the barricade.

He shielded his eyes from the glare of the sun on the snow-covered fields either side of the rutted gravel track. He sensed something wasn't quite right.

'Ready the M96,' he snapped.

Two of the guards shouldered their carbines and manned the heavy-calibre sentry gun – four high-velocity barrels that could chew up an un-armoured vehicle in a matter of seconds, mounted on a sturdy tripod and sandbagged for stability.

The truck was still showing no sign of reducing speed as it rolled down twin ruts in the road, splashing fans of slushy mud up on to the banks of snow on either side.

Kernst took several steps forward in front of the vehicle barrier and waved his arms, indicating to the driver that he should slow down, stop and have some papers ready to show. That, or risk being fired upon.

He cursed under his breath as he heard the rumble of the truck's engine increasing in pitch.

He's speeding up.

The German sergeant stepped out of the muddy ruts in the middle of the road to one side and nodded at his men to fire a short warning burst. The M96 buzzed for a second, spewing a small cascade of steaming shell casings on to the ground. Divots of slush and mud danced into the air several dozen yards in front of the closing vehicle.

But it showed no sign of slowing down.

Kernst shook his head. The stupid fool driving that vehicle was no doubt some hot-headed American kid trying to break in and rescue a relative, a loved one. Well, the fool was about to die.

As the truck closed the remaining distance, only fifty yards away now and picking up further speed, Kernst nodded to his men once more. They levelled the M96's thick barrels at the truck itself, aiming at the windscreen.

And fired.

The windscreen exploded. The metal grating at the front of the truck began disintegrating amid showers of sparks. But momentum was still carrying the heavy four-ton vehicle relentlessly forward.

Kernst found himself diving out of the way at the very last moment into a deep bank of snow as it cannoned past him, careering into the M96 gun emplacement and through the barrier beyond. The vehicle flipped over on to its side and slewed on another ten yards, pulling down a good fifty-yard stretch of chain-link perimeter fencing as it ground to a halt on the snow-covered courtyard in front of the first row of the prison camp's huts.

Kernst pulled himself out of the waist-high snow bank and unslung his carbine. He cautiously approached the vehicle, now utterly still . . . except for a solitary wheel still spinning and a plume of smoke and steam issuing from the jagged and twisted remains of the truck's front grille.

The driver's-side door suddenly burst open and a man emerged, pulling himself out and dropping off the side of the cab on to the ground with surprising speed and agility.

Kernst fired a dozen rounds at the man. Most of them missed, but (he'd swear later on in the afternoon when asked to recall what he claimed to have witnessed) at least a couple of his shots hit the target square in the chest.

The man was large, muscular and apparently utterly fearless. He didn't go down screaming and clutching at his wounds. Instead, his head calmly swivelled round and spotted Kernst. He brought up both his arms, each hand holding a heavy pulse carbine, and fired.

The German found himself head first in the snow bank again as a hail of bullets zipped over, mere inches above him. Kernst decided he was probably best staying right where he was for now.

The muscular man strode across the open space, eyes scanning the long squat wooden huts in front of him. A moment later doors began creaking open. From within the dark interiors, faces peered out. Dozens of them.

[Scanning]

His eyes locked on each face one after another for a micro-second.

Nothing.

No Liam O'Connor.

Bob strode towards the nearest hut just as an alarm went off across the camp. The shrill sound of orders being barked in German echoed in the air.

He kicked in the nearest door and pushed his way into the dark interior, his eyes adjusting instantly to the gloom inside.

[Scanning]

None of the pale and frightened faces within were that of his mission operative.

'Have . . . h-have you come to f-free us?' a frail voice cried out from among the shivering cluster of prisoners.

Bob cocked his head thoughtfully. 'Negative.'

'P-please . . . h-help us. Help us.'

[Tactical assessment]

Bob could see that the confusion of escaping prisoners would help him rather than hinder him. Standing out there alone, if he attracted too much fire, took too many hits, his genetically enhanced body would struggle to repair the damage done. Even though he was an *artificial* human, he was still just blood, bones and organs. It was a body that could be killed.

With hundreds of people fleeing in all directions, the guards would be confused; their fire would be divided, turned on the fleeing prisoners as well as him.

Bob looked down at them. 'You are free to leave,' he uttered in a monotone voice.

Fifty-four huts. Bob proceeded to each one in turn, ushering out those brave enough to make a run for the flattened section of perimeter fencing. His eyes quickly and systematically scanned the faces of the prisoners huddled inside.

Outside, the camp courtyard was thick with chaos. People scrambling towards the downed fence, the snow scuffed and flattened with footprints and stained pink with blood. The air was full of screams and crying, the percussive rattle of shots gunning prisoners down, barked orders, vengeful shouts.

He observed half a dozen guards, taken by surprise, overrun, beaten and then shot as they pleaded for mercy. Bob, himself, had casually tallied thirty-six kills by his own hand, a number that would be taken into account when his silicon mind later evaluated his mission performance.

As he followed the fleeing crowd of people out of the camp, his eyes momentarily logging each face and coming up with a negative, a small, lean man jogged across the snow to join him.

'Hey, you!'

Bob turned to look at him.

'Yeah, you, big guy!'

A gun rattled in the distance and several rounds zipped by his head. Bob swung his carbine round, levelled the weapon and fired a short burst in one swift reactive movement. Fifty yards away, a guard doubled over amid several puffs of crimson.

The small man's jaw dropped open, revealing a mouthful of tobacco-yellow teeth.

'Jeeeez, man . . . now that . . . that was some shot!'

Bob continued quickly striding towards the downed fence. 'Information: the standard accuracy of this firearm is effective at up to one hundred yards,' he explained crisply.

The man shrugged. 'Yeah, well, sure . . . but you just kinda swung that thing up an' just fired without even aiming –'

'This tactical situation is hazardous. Reinforcements will be deployed here soon,' Bob announced, stepping across the twisted and crumpled remains of the chain-link fence. 'You must leave the vicinity immediately.'

'No kidding,' replied the man. 'Those guys are going to be mighty annoyed when they arrive. I sure ain't stickin' around for that!'

Bob was already over the fence and jogging across the snowy field beyond. The small man caught up with him again, panting already as he struggled to keep pace with him.

'Hey! My name's Panelli. Raymond Panelli,' he gasped. 'But I let my friends call me Ray, 'cause it's . . . Ow!' He stumbled on a rock buried beneath the snow, cursing as he hopped and cradled his foot for a moment before struggling to catch up again with Bob.

'So . . . so, what about you?' he wheezed. 'What's your name?'

'My name is Bob.'

'Bob? . . . Bob? That it?'

They jogged in silence across the field for a while, heading towards the cover of a treeline. Panelli was rasping like an asthmatic old man beside him.

'So, Bob?'

Bob continued in silence. Eyes scanning the faces of other prisoners streaming across the snowy field. Inside his skull, the computer was busy assessing his mission's performance score, evaluating the tactical situation. Meanwhile his body was already hard at work dealing with five gunshot wounds sustained during the raid, congealing the blood around the wounds, white blood cells already coalescing to combat any infection.

'Hey, Bob!'

The small man running beside him was becoming a useless distraction. Bob turned to look down at him. 'What do you want?'

'Uh . . . mind if I sort of . . . team up with you for now? You kicked some butt back there, I mean *really* stuck it to them guys. It was just amazing.' Panelli shrugged. 'So, I figure you're a good guy to have as a friend.'

Bob evaluated the small man. He could provide assistance in some way.

'As you wish,' he replied flatly.

CHAPTER 53

2001, New York

Thursday/Friday? (I don't know)
Three days now. I think it's three – it's hard to tell. The tins of food in the cupboard are running out and we'll be going hungry soon.

Foster and Maddy went out there a few times looking for supplies. They've not found anything so far, just ruins and bones.

And those creatures outside. We now know they're cannibals.

Foster found the leftovers of one of their own kind, half eaten . . . and nearby the bones of loads of others. Those things seem to exist in small tribes, feeding off each other. When I think now how close I came to being taken . . . That creature running its hand through my hair must've been sizing me up! Working out if I could be eaten.

I don't want to die like that. I'd rather anything else. I keep expecting to hear them at any moment outside the garage door, scratching at it, trying to find a way in.

I've never been so jahully-chuddah scared in my life.

'I . . . I don't want to go out there again,' whispered Sal. 'Never. Never again.'

Foster could see the terror in the poor girl's eyes by the

guttering glow of the candle on the table between them. The rest of the arch was lost in the darkness.

'We have to,' he said firmly.

'But . . . but, those things . . .'

Those things had once been human beings. But something had happened. He suspected some sort of a nuclear war. There was plenty of blast damage, scorched walls and debris suggesting a moment of intense heat. Decades of radiation sickness would account for their pitiful condition, anaemic complexion, the running sores, toothless mouths.

'Foster's right,' said Maddy. 'We can't hide in here forever.'

'But . . . they . . . those things are . . . *cannibals*.'

'Yes, we know exactly what they are,' Maddy snapped.

'Perhaps we might be able to communicate with them,' said Foster. 'If some sort of nuclear war happened in 1956 and we're in 2001, then those creatures will be the *grandchildren* of the few that survived. Post-apocalypse children who've only ever known ruins and rubble. It's possible the eldest of them might just remember some language.'

'You're kidding, right?' said Maddy. 'They dribble, they don't talk. They see us as a free-range meal.'

Perhaps she's right. Those things would probably kill them before he could find a way to communicate with them.

He sighed. 'All right, well . . . we've wasted enough time. I was hoping another time ripple would arrive, perhaps one that would improve our situation. But it looks like this is what we're stuck with. So we've no choice. We need to find some way to generate power. Enough to reboot our computer system . . . and enough, if we can, to open a window and pull back Liam and Bob.'

Maddy frowned. 'Sounds like we're gonna need a lot of power.'

'Even if we only have enough to pull *one* of them back, we might learn exactly where and when the timeline was changed.'

She pulled her glasses off her face, and wiped the scuffed lenses. 'But then we'd also need enough power to send them back to that point in time to fix it, right?'

'Yes.' Foster managed a grim smile. 'But, look, we'll worry about that when we get to it. One thing at a time.'

'Oh jahulla, we're so-o-o-o doomed,' whispered Sal.

'No, we're not,' he replied sternly. 'If there's one thing I've learned over the long years I've been here working for the agency, it's that everything is *fluid* . . . nothing is *fixed*. We can, we *will* . . . *we must* . . . change it all back. Do you understand? Failure is not an option.'

Both girls stared at him silently.

'Nobody's going to do that for us. It's down to us. If we just sit safely in here until we starve to death, well then . . . that's it. That world outside our shutter doors is what will remain forever more.'

He let those words hang above the table, their three faces caught in the flickering glow of the candle, still and impassive.

'So . . . we have a generator in the back room where the clone tubes are. We need to find some diesel fuel for it.'

'Why don't we have stores of diesel?' asked Maddy. 'What's the point of having a back-up generator if there's no fuel to run it?'

Foster shook his head. 'We used to maintain a store of diesel fuel . . . but there's something about the energy of our field office's time bubble that corrupts it at a chemical level.'

'Meaning?'

'Meaning the diesel degrades. The fuel we have in the back room is useless. We need to get out there and find some more.'

He was silent for a moment, listening to the haunting wind outside their shutter door moaning softly.

It was Sal who broke the silence. 'Then I . . . I guess we'd better get off our butts and start looking.'

Maddy nodded. 'Yeah. We've got your gun. Those creatures will keep their distance.'

'Out there in New York somewhere – maybe in someone's basement, in a storeroom – there's got to be some diesel fuel.'

Maddy nodded. 'Right.'

Sal pursed her lips pensively then eventually nodded too. 'Let's do it.'

Foster reached out for their hands. Grasping them tightly, he smiled proudly at them. 'You know, I've got a feeling you two, and Liam, are one day going to turn out to be a formidable team. The agency's best yet.'

The girls both managed a brave grin.

CHAPTER 54

1957, Prison Camp 79, New Jersey

Liam tugged the coarse grey blanket tightly around himself, trying to seal in what little warmth his body had managed to generate. He was beginning to lose track of how many weeks he'd been there. He wasn't sure whether it was four or five months now.

Had to be about that.

His eyes drifted across hundreds – no, thousands – of other people wrapped in similar grey blankets and gazing out listlessly through the chain-link fences at the barren winter countryside around the prison camp.

'Look, it's just hard to accept . . . to believe,' said Wallace, standing next to him. He'd been quiet for a while. Cupping his hands and blowing on them as he thought things through. 'I mean . . . yeah, I saw your friend, *Bob*, take Lord knows how many bullet wounds back there at the White House, and he just kind of shrugged it all off. I can't say I *ever* saw anything like that.'

'So then you *do* believe me?'

Wallace's jaw was dark with a thatch of unshaven bristles. He scratched his chin irritably. 'You're really asking me to believe you're from the future?'

'Yes.' Liam shrugged. 'Well, actually I'm from 1912. But –' he offered a tired smile – 'yes . . . I came *here* from the future.'

'And you say you came back to today . . . to 1956, to fix history so that the Germans actually *lost* the Second World War?'

'Yes. To *correct* history.'

Wallace shook his head and laughed. A plume of his breath billowed out and quickly dissipated amid the cool morning air.

'That's completely insane. Listen, I'm tellin' you, them Nazis never even came close to losing that war. They took Poland, Belgium, France, Britain . . . the rest of mainland Europe in the space of just two years. There's no way on earth they could have lost the war. No way.'

Liam shrugged. 'Well, where I came from they did. That's what I was told. And they lost *badly*. Their leader, the Hitler fella, is supposed to have made some pretty big mistakes, like starting a fight with Russia at the same time as he was fighting the –'

Wallace scratched at his chin again. 'Well . . . the old guy, Adolf, was pretty nuts. That much is true. That's why there was a change at the top in '44. That's when Kramer took command of Germany.'

Liam turned to Wallace. 'Tell me more about Hitler and this other fella, Kramer. I need to know more. See, all of these things happened forty years *after* I died and I'm doing my best to catch up and make sense of it all.'

'Died? Oh yeah, you say you were on the *Titanic*, right?' added Wallace sceptically.

'Yes, on that bleedin' – supposedly *unsinkable* – hunk of metal.'

Wallace snorted. 'You're serious, aren't you?'

Liam sighed. 'Just tell me about them, would you? Hitler and Kramer?'

The man sucked in a deep breath.

'Adolf Hitler was the leader of the Nazi Party. They came to power in Germany in 1932 because the country was bankrupt and broken and Hitler promised the people he could fix things for them. And, for a while, he did too. He got that country going again and his people loved him for it. But then . . . he started going a little crazy in the head, mad with the power, I suppose. He had his country build up their armed forces, and then it was inevitable. In 1939, they invaded Poland. That started the Second World War.'

'*Second* World War? So there really was a *first* one?'

'The First World War? Yeah, of course. You want me to wind back and tell you all about that too? It happened not long after you say you . . . uh . . . *died*.'

Liam shook his head. 'No . . . this is confusing enough for me already. Just carry on with Hitler and Kramer.'

'OK. So the Second World War started. The Germans took Poland, Belgium, France. They kicked the British army out of France at a place called Dunkirk. And then they spent a year just digging their heels in and building up their defences. Over here in America, although President Roosevelt wanted to enter the war, Congress and the Senate stopped him and kept us out if it. Which, back then, I think most Americans thought was a pretty smart idea. We figured it was a European problem. Not ours.

'So,' Wallace continued, 'there were rumours that Hitler had plans to invade Russia next. He was certainly preparing something. I saw intelligence reports coming in for the president that the Germans were massing tanks and infantry in the east. Then, all of a sudden, it's like Hitler had a complete change of heart.'

'What do you mean?'

'I mean, he decided *not* to invade Russia. In the early summer of 1941 the Germans and Russians, out of the blue, signed a peace treaty. And that was the very same year that Paul Kramer came to public attention as Hitler's deputy. That was an incredible and very sudden change of heart. Because it was well known that Hitler despised the Russians, Stalin, communists. We all thought they were the next on his hit list.'

'Do you think it was Kramer who changed his mind?'

Wallace nodded. 'Yes . . . yes, absolutely. I think Kramer had Hitler's complete attention from the very first moment they met; he became his closest adviser, his deputy. And then three years later that sly dog Kramer kicked that crazy old lunatic Hitler out of power.'

Liam looked at Wallace. 'See, where I've come from – the future, the story I was told is different. This Hitler fella stayed in power and he went and *lost* that world war. Died in a bunker, if I recall correctly. Took his own life, I think. No mention of a *Kramer*.'

Wallace looked at him incredulously. 'And you're saying in your history books there's no Paul Kramer?'

Liam nodded. 'As far as I know.'

Wallace stared at him, struggling to believe such craziness. 'Good God, if only that were so,' he replied, shaking his head. 'The world has watched that man with bated breath. He's never put a foot wrong. He's a genius and a madman. We've watched his empire grow stronger and stronger, his military technology become so much better than ours. An ever-increasing threat to America over the last fifteen years.'

Wallace puffed air into his cold hands. 'But we thought – we *hoped* – he'd leave us alone over here. There was a hope that Kramer was finally ready to sign a truce between the Greater Reich and America. That the cold war between us was over.' Wallace sighed. 'Turns out we were fooled.'

Liam watched a couple of armed guards patrol the outside of the perimeter fence nearby, their black uniforms and death's-head insignia covered by thick winter capes.

Kramer? Is it him? Is he from the future?

Liam shivered inside his blanket. 'Listen, it's just possible this Kramer is someone like me . . . another time traveller.'

Wallace laughed. 'Look, your story is getting too far-fetched, kid. Even for me.'

'Oh, I'm quite serious.'

Wallace made a face. 'Back there in the White House, I thought you and your buddy were maybe Secret Service guys. That maybe there was something special or secret about you two. Now –' he shook his head – 'now . . . I'm sorry, I'm just thinking you're some crazy kid with a little too much imagination.'

'I'm telling you, time travel *is* possible.'

'Then, you know what? Why don't you go make a time machine and kill Kramer all by yourself?' Wallace scoffed. He looked like he'd finally had enough of Liam's crazy story.

Liam sighed. 'I'm just a dumb ship's steward. Or at least I was. Anyway, even if I had the brains to actually make a time machine, I'd need to know where and when to go . . . to the very first moment Kramer entered your history.'

Wallace shook his head. 'Well, everyone knows that – except you, I suppose.'

'Uh? What do you mean?'

'There's an account of Hitler's very first encounter with him. It's in Hitler's second autobiography, *Mein Sieg . . . My Victory*, the one he published in 1944, just before Kramer ousted him.'

'Go on.'

'It was April 1941. It's a well-known encounter. He describes Kramer as a messenger from God, an angel. Divine intervention, he called it. In his book he tells how Kramer arrived in the dark of a wintry night at the notorious Eagle's Nest. The night of the fifteenth of April, if my memory serves me well.'

Liam felt his heart pounding.

Oh my . . . that could be it. The time and place we should have gone to.

Wallace turned to go, then stopped. His gaunt face smiled, teeth showing through his dark beard. 'I guess I'd like to believe in your story, kid, that there's a better history out there somewhere.'

'There is!'

He laughed, puffing a cloud of breath before him. 'Well, let me know when you find it, eh?'

Liam watched the man turn and go, feet crunching across the snow, huddled in his own grey blanket. A bleak figure. As Wallace merged with the other prisoners, huddling for warmth, Liam's mind turned to a possibility, a ray of hope. If he could only get that information to Foster and Maddy . . . that particular place and date.

Perhaps they'd also stumbled across this information somehow – this supposed inspirational meeting of Kramer and Hitler. Perhaps Bob had made it back through the scheduled portal and right now he and Foster were on their way back to put things right. Back to 1941 to find this Kramer.

And to kill him.

It was a hope, wasn't it? Something for him to hang on to.

CHAPTER 55

1956, command ship above Washington DC

Karl Haas smartly saluted the two SS Leibstandarte standing guard either side of the doors to the Führer's observation deck. They snapped crisply to attention, and then swung open the double doors for him.

He proceeded down the oak-panelled passageway towards the second, inner, doors leading on to Kramer's extravagantly decorated quarters, the heels of his black leather jackboots no longer clacking noisily on metal plating, but softly thudding against the luxuriously thick carpet.

What is wrong with Paul?

Karl was becoming concerned with his leader. In the last couple of months, since their final assault on Washington and the taking of the White House, Kramer had become very distracted. It was becoming increasingly difficult to convince him to attend the weekly situation briefings with the regional Gauleiters and invasion fleet's senior commanders. And when he did turn up he appeared not to be listening.

It was even getting harder for Karl to see his old friend alone. With increasing regularity it seemed, Kramer insisted he was far too busy to see anyone.

What is wrong with him? Surely not that body?

The worst it could possibly mean is that some future agent

had tried and failed to get to Kramer. A failed assassination attempt, nothing more.

And the rest of the news was all good. Back home in Europe the people of Greater Germany were ecstatic with the newsreels they were watching in their cinemas. Footage of their invasion forces marching proudly through the streets of New York, Washington, Boston. Some of that good cheer was evident even among the provinces of Britain and France . . . who, despite being conquered over a decade ago, had come to realize the Führer was a good man, intent on uniting all people, not enslaving them.

The announcement of Unity Day, a day to celebrate the end of war and a uniting of the western nations, had been met with rapturous approval by the citizens of the Greater Reich. Karl was certain future Unity Days would be celebrated with street parties everywhere, people in every city in every country of Kramer's empire happy to draw a line under two thousand years of bloody history. Wars, crusades, religious intolerance, inquisitions, torture, ethnic cleansing, holocausts – all of those dark things in the past now.

He rapped his knuckles against the thick wooden doors, waiting until he heard Kramer beckon him in. He pushed them open, stepped inside and saluted his leader.

Kramer was sitting in the window alcove, looking down at a misty morning. He could just make out the dome at the top of the White House poking through the pale blanket covering Washington, the orange glow of street lamps along Pennsylvania Avenue and the pinprick headlights of slow-moving cars making their way sluggishly to work.

Presently, he turned to look at Karl and offered him a warm smile. 'Good morning, Karl. How are you?'

Karl relaxed his posture, dropping his stiff salute and stepping towards his leader, his friend. 'I'm well.'

Kramer shook his head. 'It's amazing how quickly normality returns, isn't it? Out there . . . people go to work, go to school, visit their friends, their loved ones, just as they always have. They have a new leader, a new flag . . . but life simply goes on for them.'

'Yes . . . Paul.'

'The American people, it seems,' continued Kramer, 'have already accepted the way of things.'

Karl stirred uncomfortably. *Except, of course, those troublesome people attacking the prison camps.*

'So,' said Kramer, 'shall we get on with this morning's briefing? I have other matters to attend to.'

'Of course. I have the usual stack of papers for you to sign; most of them are approvals for regional state governors – sympathetic politicians mostly.' Karl leaned over and placed the papers on the desk. Kramer got up from the window seat and sat down at the desk, flicking wearily through the forms and signing them absent-mindedly.

'So much paperwork these days,' he sighed.

'The remaining US military forces regrouped in Texas have agreed informal terms for surrender. I believe it's General MacArthur who's in charge there.'

'Good . . . good. Silly their fighting on needlessly.'

'He's hoping that we'll grant clemency for the senior officers, allow them to return to their families.'

Kramer continued scribbling his name as he talked. 'To be honest, it's the senior officers I don't trust. Tell MacArthur his troops will be disarmed and allowed to disband, to go home. But I'm afraid he and his high command will be interned along with all our other political prisoners,' uttered Kramer, leafing impatiently through the papers. 'Until, that is, I'm satisfied they won't be tempted to lead any troublesome uprisings.'

Karl shuffled uncomfortably. 'On that subject . . . we are having a few problems in the Washington area.'

'Hmm?'

'Raids. Some insurgents attacking our prison camps.'

Kramer looked up at him, his pen poised.

'Five camps have been raided so far,' Karl continued. 'The garrisons were over-powered and quite a few detainees managed to escape on each occasion.'

'I presume these insurgents are some rogue US army unit? How many of them are we talking about?'

'Well, there's some confusion there, sir,' said Karl awkwardly. 'Eyewitness reports on the earlier raids indicated a very small raiding party.'

'How small?'

'Well, actually, just one man.'

'What?'

'Clearly it *can't* be just one man. That would be madness. But among some of the prisoners that we've managed to recapture there's a spreading rumour that some sort of . . . of a *superman* . . . has come to their aid. They describe a large figure off which bullets bounce –'

'A *superman*?'

Karl smiled. 'Clearly it's wishful thinking, a fantasy. The Americans have always liked their comic-books, their heroic figures in silly costumes. It's not unreasonable that their hopes and prayers have taken the form of this kind of mythical figure.'

Karl was unsettled by the sudden look of distraction on his Führer's face, as if half his attention was elsewhere, listening to a faintly heard tune, or a conversation coming from the room next door.

'In all likelihood, sir, the insurgents may well be a small group of well-trained soldiers, US marines . . . US airborne, highly motivated and well equipped and so far they've just managed to be very lucky.'

Kramer nodded. 'Yes . . . yes. Perhaps you're right.'

'Nonetheless, sir, I suggest it would be wise to double the garrison strengths on the other camps in the region. Too many successful raids like these might just encourage other insurgents to join in.'

Kramer was silent, his face clouded, his brows locked in a frown of concentration as if he was trying to listen to someone else. Karl noticed he'd not shaved this morning, a faint blur of silver-grey bristles on his chin, and he spotted the slightest sporadic tremble in the man's jaw. Small things that only a close friend would notice.

Small things that worried him.

He's having some kind of a breakdown?

'Paul? Are you all right?'

'Yes . . . yes, of course,' said Kramer absently. His gaze returned from where it had been and focused back on to Karl. 'Take what action you think is necessary with these raids.'

Kramer hastily scribbled his signature on the last few sheets of paper, handed them back and offered him a flickering smile. 'Thank you, Karl. You may leave now.'

'Yes, sir.'

He offered a clipped salute, turned on his heel and departed the observation lounge.

Kramer waited until he heard the footsteps recede down the hallway outside.

To work.

'To work,' he agreed, stepping quickly across the polished floor towards his study door. He turned the brass handle and stepped through into his *sanctum sanctorum*: book-lined walls, several leather armchairs and a work table littered with drafting materials. It was very much a replica of his private study back in the Reich Chancellery in Berlin, a place to think, to tinker with his weapons designs, to ruminate on empire-wide policy.

From his desk drawer he pulled out a little black notebook, the corners curled and scuffed, the pages of handwritten notes beginning to yellow with the years now. A precious book of thoughts and ideas, theories and secrets. His younger handwriting so scribbled and impatient.

In the year 2056, he'd been barely twenty years of age and such a devout fan of the mysterious inventor Roald Waldstein. His reputation as an elusive genius, the one and only man to mathematically formulate a displacement field that could fold a gap through space-time. The *only* man to have actually tested the theory with a working prototype. An honorary director of the International Institute of Quantum Research, and the American Museum of Natural History, a wealthy entrepreneur, a scientific adviser to presidents . . . a complete enigma.

Kramer's hard work and promising talent had earned him an internship at Waldstein's prestigious New Jersey research centre, several months in the company of the great old man himself. Waldstein liked to be in the company of keen young minds. He'd taken warmly to Kramer. The other keen young minds, jealous fellow interns, suggested that Paul Kramer reminded the sentimental old man of the son he'd lost many years before.

Kramer smiled at the pleasant memories, those weeks with that great mind, earning his confidence, listening to his theories about how the unseen dimensions of the metaverse held everything together in a way beyond the comprehension of most human minds. Struggling to keep up with him, yet understanding *just enough*, parts of it fitted together in his young head.

The old man's over-riding passion, though, what kept him

awake late at nights and fired him up with a preacher's zeal, was to bury the technology he alone had pioneered – the potential for time travel. To ensure absolutely *no one* followed in his footsteps. For Kramer, it had been frustrating to be discussing with this great man his most advanced theoretical work and then for Waldstein to suddenly grow cautious on the subject of displacement theory.

An old man. He must have been about sixty then, but he seemed so much older and frailer than that, with hands that shook and trembled constantly, and watery eyes that always seemed to dart towards dark corners. And his bizarre rituals – every morning after breakfast, Kramer watched him shuffle towards a curious sheet of yellowing newsprint, framed behind glass and hung on his wall. Waldstein stared at it for several minutes every day with eyes that leaked tears down his sunken cheeks.

Kramer had glanced at it once, nothing more than a page of personal ads from some old newspaper, lonely men seeking lonely women.

Waldstein was losing his mind . . . and in the quiet moments, sitting with young Kramer beside the warming fire, he let slip perhaps a little too much. Old enough and perhaps trusting enough of Kramer to let him know a little more than he should have.

Kramer fingered his tatty old notebook now. Pages of mathematical characters and equations, the parts of the old man's puzzle that he'd carelessly let go, interspersed with pages and pages of angrily crossed-out formulae that Kramer himself had worked on over the years. Pieces of equation that he'd tried to squeeze into the spaces, to *make right* with Waldstein's elegant work . . . and that always seemed to not quite fit.

He smiled at the notes scrawled across the draftsman's sheet on the desk.

It fits together now, though, Paul. Doesn't it?

Some of it did – the 'Waldstein displacement field'. It had taken

Kramer fifteen years on and off, thinking the problem over in his private moments. A personal hobby, an affliction, perhaps.

The field – the Waldstein field – in theory, on paper, was merely a method to crack open the tiniest gap in space-time. That alone didn't make a time machine, just a way to open a peek-hole into the very fabric of space-time. Kramer needed computing power at his fingertips to make a time machine. Computing power to precisely navigate through the swirling chaos of a dimension that mankind had no business entering. There were no Apple Macs here in 1956, no PCs, no palmtops or organizers that could be cannibalized, adapted.

The schematic sketched out on the sheet of paper in front of him was for a device he could construct merely allowing him to open a tiny window and tap infinite energy from the swirling chaos beyond.

There'd been something Waldstein had once said to him: 'To open time-space is to open a door into Hell itself.'

You've been through that door before.

'Yes,' he uttered softly, 'stepped into Hell.' His voice trembled with a mixture of fear and excitement. Waldstein had also once said something to a much younger Kramer, something that had unsettled him back then, and did so now.

'*Consider this, Paul . . . If a man can place a foot in Hell, then whatever exists there might just as easily use the same door and place a foot in our world.*'

Those words tormented him now because he realized it was something far worse than some agent from the future after him. Something far more frightening.

You must hurry, Paul . . . before it seeks you out.

'To work,' said Kramer, pushing a forgotten plate of food aside on his desk.

CHAPTER 56

1957, New Jersey

Bob studied the map in front of him. A dozen crosses scrawled on the map indicated the locations of other prison camps between Washington DC and New York. Simple logic dictated that Liam O'Connor had to have been taken to one of these. So far nine of these scrawled crosses had been paid a visit: nine prison camps broken into, searched and left behind in a state of chaos, prisoners surging out the way he'd smashed in, buildings on fire, the bodies of guards and unfortunate civilians littering the ground.

And so far he'd been unlucky. Nine camps . . . no sign of Liam.

[Mission evaluation: success probability reduced to 31%]

The camps were becoming harder to break into. There seemed to be more guards stationed at each now and they were more alert – ready and waiting to be attacked. After the last raid Bob had walked away with at least a dozen bullet wounds across his body. It had taken five days for the wounds to heal. Five days of lying still, devoting all of his body's energy towards the process of recovering.

The small man who had decided to tag along with him, Raymond Panelli, had watched over him, taken care of him as he lay motionless in a state akin to suspended animation, healing. Bob wondered why Raymond Panelli would care to do that. For that matter, he wondered why a growing band of humans was following him around from camp to camp. With each of his raids, he seemed to be picking up more and more of them. Tactically speaking they were, of course, *useful*; they drew some of the enemy fire from him.

His stomach rumbled noisily and Bob's computer brain reminded him that it was time to refuel his body with some protein. The food being served up by his growing band of camp followers – a variety of stews, broths and soups – wasn't as nutrient-rich as the highly efficient protein solution he was used to consuming back in the field office's birthing tubes, but it would do as a stopgap.

He folded the map carefully and emerged from his tent, stepping through the briar and undergrowth, stooping beneath the low-hanging branches as he made his way towards the campfire.

As he approached, one of his followers hurried over to him with a steaming bowl of soup.

'For you, *Captain Bob*, sir.'

Bob took the bowl and stepped towards the fire, finding a space on the ground amid the silent crowd of men. They followed his every movement with wide eyes. He sat down heavily, cross-legged, stared at the flickering fire and began mechanically spooning soup into his mouth.

The human called Raymond Panelli leaned forward. 'Captain Bob, we've got ourselves another bunch of fighters for the cause. Joined us just this evening.'

Bob stopped mid-spoon and looked up from the fire at him.

'These guys right here,' said Panelli, pointing out some men clustered near the fire. They stared in awed silence, clearly wondering what to make of the large muscular superhero in front of them.

Bob's eyes panned across them, one to another. He identified tattered US army uniforms on seven of them. They looked physically fit and by and large of optimum combat age. More bodies for the enemy guards' fire to be distracted by, more bodies for them to aim at and fewer shots directed specifically at him.

[Mission evaluation: success probability increase +1%]

Bob nodded. 'That is good. With more men, probability of mission success increases.'

A softly taken gasp rippled around the campfire at the timbre of his deep rumbling voice, a commanding sound.

One of the men, a young corporal, turned to Panelli. 'Can . . . can I ask him, ask Captain Bob a question?'

Panelli gave it some thought, then nodded reluctantly. 'Just one, OK? The hero needs his rest, needs to be thinking about our raid tomorrow.'

The young man swallowed nervously. 'Excuse me, s-sir?'

Bob's steel-grey eyes slowly swivelled towards him.

'Word's been spreadin' across the state . . . you're some kinda superman, can be shot over and over, an' never die.'

Bob stared at him silently, his face devoid of any emotion or reaction.

The young man's lips twitched anxiously. 'I'm . . . I'm a . . . I believe in the Good Lord, and –'

'Well, that's great, son,' said Panelli, 'but the captain's got better things to do than listen to your Bible-thumping.'

'I gotta ask you, Captain Bob,' the young corporal interrupted, 'did God send you to save us, sir?'

Bob's silicon mind momentarily suspended work on an array of mission assessment calculations to deal with the curious question posed by the young man. His computer offered a list of the most appropriate replies to the question.

The fire crackled noisily in the silence. Far away through the trees an owl hooted, as if urging Bob to hurry up and say something appropriate.

He picked a biblical quotation from his database that seemed to have the most relevance at this moment.

'When trouble comes, the Lord is a strong refuge. He will sweep away His enemies in an overwhelming flood,' he replied, his deep voice like a roll of thunder. Bob wasn't entirely sure what the words meant, but it seemed to have a suitable effect on the men gathered around the campfire.

'Amen,' someone muttered after a while.

CHAPTER 57

2001, New York subway

Foster's torch probed the darkness of the subway station. The beam picked out the glint of twin metal rail tracks to their left over the edge of the platform and the glimmer of pools of stagnant water between them.

Further along the tracks Sal could see an old pram lying on its side, half in, half out of the water.

They could hear skittering sounds along the rails, in, around and under the rotting wooden sleepers; the pattering of little vermin feet and the steady metronome-like *drip*, *drip*, *drip* of moisture from the curved tunnel roof above them echoed through the station.

Along the tiled walls of the station's platform Sal was fascinated by long-faded advertisement billboards. She passed by the faded image of a happy family gathered around a traditional oak kitchen table, all smiling, with well-scrubbed rosy cheeks, enjoying all the pleasures a tin of *Colonel Johnston's Oatmeal Cookies* could offer.

'What're you expecting to find down here?' asked Maddy.

Even though she spoke in little more than a tremulous whisper, her voice seemed to echo endlessly down the station's walls and curved ceiling and off into the dark tunnel beyond.

'An emergency storeroom of some sort,' whispered Foster. 'I remember reading that most of New York's subway stations had back-up generators installed during the Second World War. Hopefully we'll find one and, along with it, some containers of fuel.' Foster looked back at them. 'I know. It's a long shot.'

'I never knew they had an underground system back then,' said Sal.

'Yeah, of course they did,' said Maddy. 'I did a school project on the New York subway once. They started digging out the tunnels as early as 1904, I think.'

Foster nodded. 'That's right. Brought in Irish workers by the tens of thousands to work on it . . .' Foster was about to say more, but stopped himself.

So far, mercifully, they'd yet to encounter a single one of those creatures. They'd come across signs of them on the streets above: clusters of small bones, rat carcasses, remains of cats and even dog carcasses. And of course, more ominously, here and there discarded piles of larger bones, sometimes carefully stacked or arranged by size. Sal found that even more unsettling – the thought of several of those creatures sitting down and carefully sorting through the bones of someone they'd eaten.

She shuddered.

On 5th Avenue she thought she'd seen a pale face peeking out at her before it dipped back into the dark shadows beyond a department-store window frame. And on Broadway, the faintest slither of movement among some storefront mannequins, their plastic scorched black in places, fingers and thumbs little more than melted stubs. But she was prepared to believe she was mistaken. Preferred to believe that, in fact.

Mind you, if those things were really there, watching from the darkness, then at least they were keeping their distance, still very much wary of Foster's gun. She wondered, though, how long that would last. How long before insatiable hunger for their comparatively plump, well-fed bodies would overcome their caution.

'Up ahead,' whispered Foster. 'Look!' He swung his torch along to the end of the platform, to a small door with a faded STAFFROOM sign on it. Beneath that another sign warned of an electrical hazard.

He picked up the pace, his shoes *clacking* along the platform surface, kicking aside several fallen tiles that clattered noisily across the platform, over the edge and sploshed into the puddles of water below. Sal cringed as the noise echoed interminably down the tunnel.

Foster reached for the handle and tried it, rattling it hard. It came off in his hand amid a shower of rust flakes.

'Oh, that's just great,' he snapped.

'Let me have a go,' said Maddy.

She lifted a booted leg and kicked the door by the rusted stub of the handle. With a sharp crack, the door rattled inwards on its hinges, shards of rusted lock and splinters of wood cascading to the floor.

Foster waved a cloud of dust away from his face. 'Shall we?'

'Age before beauty,' said Maddy.

He replied with a thin smile and the flicker of a wiry eyebrow, then stepped into the room beyond, swinging his torch quickly from side to side, the light picking out surfaces covered in half a century of dust.

Maddy stepped in behind him while Sal cast one last glance over her shoulder at the empty platform behind, now robbed of the light from Foster's torch as he made his way further inside.

She hurried in after them.

Foster panned the flashlight around slowly. She could see a table and chairs in the middle of a small room. Several enamel mugs were on the table, along with a yellow tattered and faded copy of *The New York Times* opened on the funnies page and dotted with rat droppings. On the walls were coat hooks, lockers and pin-ups of beautiful movie stars, forgotten faces her mum and dad might have once been able to put a name to.

'It looks untouched since ... well . . . since whatever happened, happened,' said Maddy.

Foster nodded. 'Doomsday.'

He stepped over to the table and shone his torch down on the newspaper. 'Wednesday, thirteenth of March 1957.' He looked up at them. 'I was never that keen on Wednesdays.'

Maddy snorted. Sal smiled, comforted by his lame attempt to lighten the mood. She leaned over the paper, scanning the headlines.

Terrorists Continue Attacks On Resettlement Camps

Teacher Arrested For Teaching Pre-unity History

Führer Absent at Unity Day Parade – Rumours Of Ill Health

'Superman' Just A Myth Spread By Troublemakers

At the far end of the room was a door with another electrical hazard warning screwed on to it. Below that, another sign read AUTHORIZED ACCESS ONLY.

'Maybe we'll find something useful in there,' said Foster. He stepped around the table and tried the door handle. This time it opened without putting up a fight, although the hinges creaked drily. He pushed it open and flicked his torch from side to side in the dark void beyond.

'See anything?' asked Maddy.

'I see shelves both sides . . . I see coils of cable . . . some tools . . . oh.'

Silence.

'What is it?' asked Sal.

'Yeah,' Maddy chorused more loudly. 'What have you got?'

'Just a second,' said Foster, stepping further inside. He let the door go behind him. Maddy grabbed it before it could slam with a loud bang.

'Foster?'

Over Maddy's shoulder Sal could see his silhouette inside, dancing shadows, the flicker of reflected light off dust-covered pipe conduits suspended from a claustrophobic low ceiling. He paced down a narrow walkway flanked on either side by racks of floor-to-ceiling shelves.

'Useful supplies in here. Just taking a look. You stay there,' he called back. He made his way down to the end of the racks of shelves then turned right, slipping out of view.

Sal wanted to call to him to come back, to say that they should all remain close together. But she didn't. Maddy was right there next to her.

Light flickered over the tops of the shelves and shadows danced across the low ceiling as he moved around the end of the shelves and out of sight. They could hear his feet tapping and scraping across the cold concrete floor.

'Come on, Foster. Is there anything we can use in there, or not?' Maddy called out.

The sound of movement stopped and the torchlight hovered where it was for a while. 'Just a sec,' he replied.

Foster was taking his time. 'What's he doing?' Sal whispered.

'Checking something out, I guess.'

Sal bit her lip, trying to keep her cool.

That's right. He's just round the corner, not far. No need to panic, Saleena Vikram.

However, right then it occurred to her that the *only* gun they had was round the corner with him. What if those things were back in that tunnel leading out of the station, watching patiently from the shadows? Perhaps waiting, perhaps growing bolder with each passing second. They might be on the platform, approaching the door to the staffroom right now, standing just outside and curious to see what was going on inside. Curious to see how close they could get without being spotted.

She glanced back anxiously over her shoulder at the small room. It was almost pitch black now. She could just about make out the square edge of the table from what little light was reaching them from Foster's bobbing torch, a faint glint from one of the mugs. One or two of the chairs were visible. But nothing else. She turned back to see how the old man was doing.

'Foster?' called Maddy, quieter now. 'You gonna tell us what you got there?'

The shards of light on the ceiling shifted slightly in response. Then they heard movement, footsteps across the floor and the shadows danced once more. He was on his way back to join them.

'You find anything?' called out Maddy.

A beam of light emerged around the end of the long racks of shelves, flashing into their faces as it approached them.

'Foster?'

'We're in luck,' his gruff voice replied. 'There's a generator in the back . . . hopefully we'll find some fuel somewhere on these shelves –'

His voice cut off suddenly.

He's seen something.

Sal felt her blood run cold.

Something behind me?

Quickly she turned round to look back over her shoulder again and saw two pale eyes. Milky boiled-fish eyes in a ghostly face, just a few feet away, rounding the end of the table and gliding rapidly towards her.

'GET DOWN!' shouted Foster.

Maddy reacted instinctively, stepping to one side and pulling Sal with her.

The small room was filled with the deafening boom of Foster's shotgun. In the flickering instant of muzzle-flash she saw a freeze-frame image of one of the mutants as it rose up from a low stealthy crouch, one long thin arm reaching out towards her, only inches from where she'd been standing. Behind it were a dozen more of them, caught in the flash as they were filing in through the open door to the staffroom, rounding the table and closing in on them.

Darkness.

She heard something tumble on to the table and thrash noisily for a moment. Then the skittering of a host of panicked feet, the heavy clatter of a mug as it dropped and bounced, squeals of terror and snarls of frustration.

BANG!

Another blinding moment of muzzle-flash, a glimpse of a creature sprawled across the table, still twitching, a dark almost black jagged hole in its chest and a slick of liquid pooling beneath it. By the door a tangled nest of pale limbs and skeletal torsos pressing through the narrow doorframe. All of them trying to escape through the doorway at once.

And then dark again.

She heard the slap of bare feet fading as the creatures fled down the platform, mewling, crying with both anger and fear as they retreated.

Then silence except for the rasping sound of her and Maddy's breath, the distant repetitive drip of moisture from somewhere above and the sound of an enamel mug rolling back and forth across the floor.

'Oh my God,' exhaled Maddy.

'That was close,' said Foster. The torch was on the floor at his feet. He'd dropped it in the panic. He bent down and picked it up, panning it quickly across them.

'You – you two all right?' he puffed.

'Yes,' said Sal, her voice robbed of everything but a whisper.

Maddy's eyes met hers. 'They were right behind us! I mean,' she gasped for air, 'I mean they were *right behind us*!'

'We best get a move on,' said Foster quickly. 'They may well come back.'

CHAPTER 58

2001, New York subway

They found what they were looking for in a locked storage cupboard towards the back of the storeroom: three large metal drums of diesel fuel that sloshed encouragingly as Maddy struggled to ease them out on to the floor.

'They're way too heavy. I can barely move them, let alone carry one all the way back to our archway,' she said.

Foster pulled a face. 'You're right.' He considered the problem, his eyes darting along the storage shelves for inspiration. 'All right then, we can pour the fuel into a load of smaller containers that we could carry between us.'

'But how much will we need?'

The truth was he didn't know. He'd never used the generator, never needed to so far. Last time it had been checked out it had chugged away quite happily for a few minutes. If he knew something about diesel generators, if he was a mechanic, he could have probably made an educated guess as to how much fuel they were going to need.

Thing was . . . what he did know was that the time-displacement machinery was going to need to charge itself up before they could use it. Since the power had been cut for quite a few hours now the charge would be flat. It was probably going to need the generator running a dozen, maybe twenty-four hours before they'd be able to do anything. He had no idea at all how much fuel they needed for that. Probably quite a lot.

The girls were looking at him, hoping he had an answer.

Come on . . . think. How much will we need?

That depended on what the plan of action was. As it stood, they needed to transmit a message through time to Bob to arrange a new return window. *Where* and *when* they opened the window were factors that would decide just how much of a charge the displacement machinery needed.

And even if they did manage to get Liam and Bob back they'd need enough energy to send them back to the correct time and place to try to fix history.

There were too many variables for Foster to work out precisely how much fuel they needed.

'Foster? How much do we need?' asked Maddy again.

'As much as we can carry,' he replied. And if that wasn't enough, they would have to come back down here and get some more. A prospect he wasn't too happy about, and the girls most certainly wouldn't be.

He looked around. There were half a dozen jerry cans further along the bottom shelf. If they emptied those out and filled them up with diesel, then between them they'd be carrying twelve gallons of fuel.

Enough?

It would have to be.

'See those jerry cans?' he said, pointing towards them. 'We're going to fill them all up. That'll give us twelve gallons.'

'That going to be enough?'

Maybe. I hope so.

'Foster?'

'Sure,' he replied. 'That'll do us fine.'

Maddy nodded, satisfied for the moment with his answer.

'The next thing we're going to have to figure out, though,' he added, 'is how we're going to carry those jerry cans back home. Filled, they're going to be very heavy. We'll have to take them between us, one at a time. That's six journeys.'

Sal turned to them both. 'Hang on, I've got an idea.'

They emerged up the stairs from the subway station. Between them they lifted the pram laden with sloshing cans of fuel up off the last few steps and on to the rubble-strewn pavement. The pram's large old-fashioned spoked wheels coped far better with the rubble and debris than some shopping trolley with tiny little castor wheels would have.

It was getting dark. Foster had intended for them to be back at base safe and sound before too much of the pallid grey daylight had gone from the sky. But things had taken them longer than expected.

Never mind. They were above ground now, and even though dusk was settling across the lifeless city, the three of them felt happier out in the open than they had down below. They eased the pram through the cluttered street, feeling those eyes upon their backs . . . watching and waiting.

'We'll be back home soon,' said Foster quietly.

Sal nodded. It wasn't too far now. Just down East 14th Street, a right on to 4th Avenue all the way down to Delancey Street, then left over the bridge and home.

Maddy grinned anxiously.

'Just takin' the little ol' baby out for a stroll down the avenue,' she muttered with a shaky sing-song tone. 'Uh-huh . . . Just minding our business and heading home. *Oh yes indeedy*.' Her eyes darted from one dark window to another.

'How about we do those things quietly?' said Foster.

Maddy giggled, then shut up.

Nerves.

The wheels rattled noisily over a scattering of rubble.

'I reckon we're being watched anyway, Foster,' she replied quietly. 'Might as well make 'em think we're not scared.'

Foster nodded. *Maybe she's got a point.*

'Well, a good day's work, I think,' he announced loudly. 'I got a feeling that the worst of this is over.'

Sal looked up at him. 'Do you think so?'

'Sure. We'll get this lot back. I'll crank up the generator, get things charging up. We'll have a nice hot cup of coffee whilst we wait. How does that sound?'

'Wonderful,' she replied.

'How long will it take until we can try bringing them back?' asked Maddy.

Foster made a show of shrugging casually. His eyes, though, were on the lengthening evening shadows on either side of the street. 'I'd say about twenty-four hours until we can actually try opening up a portal.'

'Twenty-four hours!' Maddy's voice bounced off the nearest walls and rippled off down the deserted ruins of East 14th Street.

'But –' he smiled – 'the good news is that we should be able to transmit a message through to the support unit and Liam much sooner.'

'Bob,' said Sal. 'That's what we agreed to call him.'

'Yes, I'm sorry . . . Bob.'

'So, how does that transmitting-messages-through-time thing work exactly?'

'I'm no physicist, Madelaine, so don't start throwing questions at me. But the explanation I was given is that it's all to do with tachyon particles. They're particles of matter that can travel faster than light and thus are able to travel through time. If we aim them at roughly where we expect Liam and Bob to be, then

Bob's on-board hardware will detect them and decode the message.'

'But they can't send a message back to us?'

Foster shook his head. 'No. The particles can only travel back through time, not forward.' He snapped his torch on, throwing a cone of light down the darkening street. 'We know they're somewhere around Washington, so we'll aim the tachyon array in that general direction.'

'It doesn't need to be that precise, then,' said Sal, 'you know, aiming the signal?'

'Well, the more precisely you can aim the particles, the fewer particles you need to send, which means you need less energy. If we knew *exactly* where they were standing, it would take a lot less energy. So, if we keep the message nice and short and spread the beam wide . . . it amounts to just about the same power burn.'

Maddy nodded. 'I think I get it. It'd cost the same energy if we had a longer message but used a narrower beam.'

'You got it.'

They walked in silence for a little while, accompanied only by the sloshing of the jerry cans in the pram and the clatter of its wheels over the rubble-strewn pavement.

'I hope Liam's all right,' said Sal. 'I know it's been only a few days since he went back, but it feels like he's been gone for ages.'

'He has . . . from his point of view nearly six months has passed.'

She frowned. 'That's just so weird.'

They walked in silence for a while as she struggled with the idea that Liam's experience of this crisis had stretched over nearly half a year. 'So . . . so how long have *you* been a TimeRider?' asked Sal. 'You're pretty old, so I guess you must have been doing it for a while?'

'Long enough, Sal,' he replied, 'long enough.'

'Does it all make sense to you, yet?'

Foster shook his head and snorted dismissively. 'Does it heck. It still messes with my mind.'

CHAPTER 59

1957, Prison Camp 79, New Jersey

Liam was exhausted. Barely an hour into the morning shift digging the ditch alongside the camp's wire perimeter and he felt drained, barely able to lift his spade. Nearly six months of poor food, little more than a starvation diet, had left him feeling weak and unable to sustain any sort of physical exertion for long.

He leaned on the spade, trying to catch his breath, giving his aching muscles a moment to recover. Sweat rolled down the small of his back, soaking his shirt. Clouds of his hot breath puffed out into the crisp winter air in front of him.

'You better not let Kohl see you,' whispered Wallace in the ditch beside him.

Kohl was one of the more ruthless guards. Last week he'd pulled a man from the defensive ditches being dug around the camp and beaten him repeatedly with the butt of his pulse carbine for stopping and taking a rest. News was the man had died later on from his injuries.

It was from one of the guards that Liam had learned *why* they were digging these defensive ditches around the wire-fence perimeter. There'd been some raids, successful raids, by a small band of resistance fighters. Several camps had been overrun, the prisoners freed and most of the soldiers who'd been guarding them killed. There was a rumour spreading among the guards that these fighters were being led by some demonic entity. There were varying descriptions of this thing; some of the guards who'd survived described a giant, eight or nine feet tall, with the horns of a devil protruding from its head. Another eye-witness described this demon as being made of iron, yet able to move at a terrifying speed with the agility of a tiger.

They even had a nickname for this thing.

Der Eisenmann. The Iron Man.

One of the guards further down the line spotted Liam resting on his spade and barked a shrill order at him.

'*Weiterarbeiten, Du Amerikanischer Haufen Scheiße!*'

He started digging again, relieved that it hadn't been Kohl.

'O'Connor, you're going to get yourself killed if they see you slacking like that again,' hissed Wallace.

He's right.

The rumours of *Der Eisenmann* had put these soldiers on edge. Liam could see fear in their eyes as they scanned the distant treeline, unhappy with being outside the wire fence of the camp.

The Iron Man.

So much time had passed in here that Liam had *almost* begun to believe his short time as a TimeRider had just been a figment of his imagination. That time travel was just a fairytale . . . perhaps his life even, his childhood in Ireland, his working a passage on the *Titanic*; all those things had been some dream. And in fact this dreary camp, his fellow starving prisoners in their grey rags, the long low wooden huts – that was his real world. His real life.

But then he'd heard those rumours about *Der Eisenmann*. A desperate hope had surfaced, a long-discarded possibility, that Bob was behind this Iron Man story somehow. He hated himself for allowing that hope to momentarily flicker to life. Common sense tried telling him that this Iron Man nonsense was nothing more than the superstitious prattle of spooked soldiers completely unused to being on the losing side of any kind of a fight.

You're here for good, Liam. Now, just you bloody well get used to it.

It was hard, though. Hard not to hope that one day, totally without warning, a shimmering sphere might suddenly pop up beside him, and Foster and Bob and the girls would appear and take him back.

Stop it! No one's coming for you now. It's been nearly six months. No one is coming.

Five months and three weeks. A hundred and seventy-five days. He knew exactly how long now . . . One of the prisoners worked as a cleaner in the kommandant's office and had spotted a calendar on his desk. The prisoners kept track of time – marked the endless, identical days passed inside here – through him.

'You all right there?' whispered Wallace. 'You mustn't give up hope, kid. You give up . . . you die.'

He was right. It was the thin sliver of hope that came in the form of whispered rumours, overheard conversations between guards, that was keeping them going. Keeping them alive.

Liam turned to Wallace and gave him a thin, weary smile. 'I'm all right.'

'You know, lad . . . things *will* get better,' he replied quietly. His thick, dark beard parted with a smile. 'The American people won't stand for this. They'll fight back. I know they will.'

Liam wondered about that. From what he'd heard, the camps were filled with those people who might have organized or led some sort of a resistance movement: army officers, civic leaders, congressmen, lawyers, teachers, college professors, newspaper editors. The rest . . . those who'd been spared imprisonment and left to continue their lives so long as they posed no threat to their new masters, were never going to risk their lives, their family's lives, as long as some semblance of normal life remained for them.

Liam could see this Führer's plan with stark clarity – lock up all the potential trouble-makers and either starve them or work them to death. Either way they were never going to see the outside world again. Meanwhile, the rest of the population would get used to the new regime, get used to obeying their new masters, until finally they'd forgotten what it was like to be free. Just as long as their new ruler – their Führer – continued to ensure there was food and water and electricity. What was it he heard someone muttering last night in their dormitory hut?

'*. . . Long as them Krauties keep the trams runnin', the shops well stocked, the cinemas playing those cowboy movies, the Major League baseball play-offs on schedule and you can still get yer long-boy hot dog covered in mustard an' ketchup from the vendors 'tween innings, people'll be content enough to let things go on as they are. They'll forget all about us in here . . .*'

Those on the outside might resent being lorded-over, but as long as things were kept ticking over, kept comfortable enough, they were never going to rise up.

We're stuck in here . . . forever.

WHUMP!

A geyser of muddy soil erupted from the ground a couple of yards away and sprayed down on him.

'Uh?'

CHAPTER 60

1957, Prison Camp 79, New Jersey

Liam felt it rather than heard it.

Another *whump* nearby that punched his chest softly.

A geyser of snow and soil was tossed into the air a dozen yards from him. Then another one further away. And another.

'Mortar shells coming in!' shouted somebody in the trench.

From the treeline across the field he saw flashes of light amid the undergrowth and moments later heard the distant percussive rattle of gunfire.

The guards reacted swiftly, dropping down into the ditch alongside the prisoners and returning fire on the treeline. An officer quickly issued orders to several of his men to escort the prisoners back inside on the double.

They barked hasty orders at the prisoners, shooing them along with their carbines. 'Prisoners must go inside, now!' one of them shouted. 'Move . . . MOVE! *Schnell!*'

Liam did as he was told, keeping his head low as he ran along the ditch towards the open gates at the front of the camp. Divots of soil spat into the air just above his head as shots landed home from across the field.

Another half a dozen *whumps* landed either side of the ditch, showering them with clumps of wet soil. A prisoner in a tattered olive-green marine uniform just in front of Wallace shouted out: 'Those are US army mortar shells!'

The guards bellowed shrilly at them to move faster and Liam soon found himself climbing up out of the ditch and running into the compound through the open gates, herded in by half a dozen more soldiers.

Wallace, behind him, slapped his shoulder, grinning and gasping at the same time. 'What did I tell you, kid?'

The guards standing nearby had their eyes on the increasingly intensive exchange of gunfire going on in the field and warily on the jubilant prisoners. Liam could see they were nervous – as much worried about the growing jubilation among the prisoners inside the camp as they were about the attackers in the treeline.

'Yeah!' yelled Wallace triumphantly at them. 'They're coming for you, you scumbags!'

Several of them turned towards him, eyes darting from Wallace to the growing crowd of prisoners emerging from their huts into the courtyard to see what was going on.

'Come on!' Wallace cheered on the distant attackers. 'Come get these Krauties!'

Liam grabbed his arm. 'Wallace, hey, keep it down!'

A mortar shell landed amid several of the guards in the ditch outside, blowing them to bloody shreds. Wallace and several other prisoners cheered noisily, punching the air with glee.

The camp kommandant emerged from his hut at a trot, flanked by a dozen more guards. There was a brief, harried conversation barked over the increasing noise of battle. He gestured towards the growing crowd of jeering prisoners. The guards standing around them nodded at his orders and slowly raised their guns.

Liam realized by the calm, ruthless expression on the kommandant's face that he'd just given the order for them all to be executed on the spot. None of the other prisoners seemed to have noticed, their eyes on the gunfight across the field outside.

I have to run . . . run now!

Liam began to shoulder his way back through the jeering, defiant prisoners, as the guards silently raised their pulse carbines.

Jay-zus Christ.

The rattle of guns being cocked to fire alerted the rest of the prisoners, their eyes darting back to the line of guards. Before they could react, the kommandant barked a single word. '*Feuer!*'

The guards opened fire.

Suddenly the air about Liam was alive with the hum of passing bullets, the hard thud of rounds impacting bodies, the muffled gasps of those falling and dying, the screams of the wounded and terrified.

He stumbled back through the panicking crowd, expecting at any second to feel a hard, sharp blow between his shoulders, punching the air from his lungs and throwing him down on to the compacted snow and muddy slush.

The opening volley of shots came to a rattling conclusion as ammo clips emptied and the guards began to reload. In the pause the air was filled with moaning and crying and wailing, and the nearing sounds of fighting across the field.

Liam realized he wasn't running. He was on his knees in the mud surrounded by bodies twitching and flailing.

Run!

He scrambled to his feet, stepping over and on the bodies around him. He glanced back to see the guards finish loading their carbines and begin to level their barrels at the remaining prisoners still on their feet. Many of those still standing were rooted to the spot in shock. Others who'd been towards the back of the crowd were now on the run, scrambling away from the guards towards the open doors of their huts.

The guards began firing again at will, now picking out

individual targets with short aimed bursts, mechanically aiming and firing . . . aiming and firing . . . like automatons, obeying their orders mindlessly.

Liam rose from a crouch to run for the nearest hut. The lurch of movement caught a guard's eyes and he swung the barrel of his gun in Liam's direction. Several shots whistled past him – close, very close – and over his head as he dived, staggered and fell across a writhing carpet of dead and dying towards the open door of the nearest hut.

He fell into the dark interior and scrambled on hands and knees across the rough wooden floor to hide beneath the nearest of the wooden bunks.

Outside the firing continued. Sporadic clusters of shots, short bursts, long bursts and single taps to finish off the wounded as the soldiers stepped forward among the bodies. Meanwhile, the rattle of gunfire in the field outside was coming closer. He heard the muffled thud of more mortar shells landing, this time inside the perimeter of the camp.

He heard the shrill sound of panic in the guards' voices.

Liam prayed. It wasn't something he often did. Rarely, in fact. Catholic faith, drummed into his head since birth by his mother, father and every schoolteacher he'd ever had, had never managed to take hold of him. But he certainly was praying now, begging the Virgin Mother of Jesus to make sure that none of those soldiers outside had decided to stick his head in through the open door and finish him off.

He heard heavy jackboots slapping through the mud outside, running past the open door, the guards' attention now on the approaching attackers. They began taking up defensive positions as the noise of exchanged gunfire seemed to be reaching a new intensity.

It sounded like the fight was now within the camp itself.

A row of jagged holes suddenly stitched its way across the thin plywood walls of his hut, sending a shower of wood splinters on to the floor and leaving a line of pale sunbeams lancing through the air.

Another explosion, deafening this time, amid the mud and bodies right outside the hut, hurled a wet spray of soil inside through the open door.

The guards were screaming in German. Not the barked orders of professional soldiers, but cries of sheer terror.

'*Der Eisenmann! Das ist der Eisenmann!*'

'*Töten Sie ihn! Töten Sie ihn!*'

Liam heard the appalling sound of a protracted scream, suddenly ending with a fleshy ripping sound. Other cries. Across the compound, faintly, the sound of American voices could be heard.

'Kill the guards! You kill them all!'

Then the rattle of gunfire and feet splashing the bloodied ground outside. 'You men! Get those guards . . . They're running! Take them down! We're not taking any of these *scum* prisoner, understand? Not a single one of them!'

Liam wanted to climb out from beneath the bunk, but fear kept him cowering in the dark. There were plenty of shots still echoing around the camp, snarling angry voices of men appalled at the carnage in the compound.

'Ahh man . . . ohh Jesus,' he heard a man outside crying. 'They massacred them. Before we could rescue 'em, those scum shot 'em dead . . . ain't never . . . seen . . . Oh Jeeez.'

The distant pleading of a German voice . . . '*Nein! Nein! Ich . . . ich habe niemanden erschossen –*' . . . ended with the single crack of a gunshot echoing among the rows of huts. He heard another pleading German voice silenced by a single bullet further away across the compound. And the distant rattle of gunfire as the fight continued somewhere on the far side of the camp.

'Is Liam O'Connor here?'

A deep and monotone voice without any sense of expression.

'Is Liam O'Connor here?'

Louder, closer, like a foghorn – without any variation.

'Is Liam O'Connor here?'

He heard the heavy splatter of boots in mud just outside the door and then the hut was thrown into darkness as a large body stepped into the doorway, blocking out all but the thinnest glimmer of light.

'Is Liam O'Connor here?' the voice bellowed deafeningly into the hut.

It was almost too much for him to react. Almost too much. He'd convinced himself that he'd never see that big robotic ape again. The truth took a moment to sink in.

Bob hovered a second longer then stepped out of the doorway.

'Bob!' Liam cried out weakly, scrambling on all fours to pull himself out from under the bunk. 'Bob! Wait! I'm here!'

A pair of broad shoulders and a small head crowned with a tuft of nut-brown hair leaned back into the hut. 'Liam O'Connor?'

Liam looked up. 'Oh sweet Jay-zus-'n'-Mary-mother-of-mercy! It's good to see you again, Bob, so it is.'

The support unit stepped inside and then squatted down on his haunches, studying the frail form of Liam on the floor, his calm grey eyes quickly adapting to the darkness inside.

Liam could have sworn that in that moment of recognition, as Bob's computer mind confirmed Liam's visual identity and verified the signature tone of his voice, he saw a tear in those dull, expressionless grey eyes of his.

Then, of course, he went and ruined that sentimental moment

of reunion by grunting emotionlessly: 'Target successfully acquired.'

'Good to see you too, Bob,' replied Liam weakly, choking back his own tears and grinning as best he could.

CHAPTER 61

2001, New York

'It really smells bad back here,' complained Sal. 'Phew. Smells like something's gone off.'

Foster panned his torch around. They'd not been in the back room of the archway since the power had failed them several days ago. His torch flickered across the row of large plastic birthing tubes along the back wall.

'It's them,' he said, 'the embryos inside have died.'

Sal stepped across the floor towards them. She stared in through the murky plastic at the dark forms inside – the foetus, the baby, the small boy, the teenage boy.

'They're all dead?'

Foster nodded. 'Filtration system stopped running. Their own effluence must have backed up and poisoned the nourishment solution.'

'What does that mean?'

'They choked on their own poop,' said Maddy helpfully as she poured a jerry can of diesel into the generator. 'Hey, Foster, you sure this is the right kind of fuel I'm pouring into this thing? How do we know it runs on diesel and not, like, gasolene?'

He stepped over towards her. 'It's diesel. Although whether this is the right kind we'll know soon enough.'

'My grandad used to have a generator in his basement,' said

Maddy, 'and he was very particular about the kind of fuel you poured into it . . . two-stroke or whatever. He said you pour the wrong kind of fuel in and it eventually clogs up the carburettor or something. Costs a bunch of money to fix.'

Foster shook his head. 'Just as long as this generator keeps working long enough to get us out of this fix, then I'll be happy. If it clogs it up and we need to replace it, then we'll worry about that later, OK?'

Maddy shrugged. 'OK.'

Foster finished emptying the last can and screwed the cap back on the generator's tank. 'Right,' he said, licking his lips, 'right then . . . Fingers crossed.'

He worked a manual lever on the side of the generator several times, grunting with the effort of pulling it down. With one last look at Maddy, he punched a red button on the front. The generator coughed to life and turned reluctantly over several times before spluttering and dying.

'Well, that didn't sound too good,' uttered Maddy.

'She's just clearing her throat, that's all,' he said with a less than convincing nod. He pumped the lever several times, his breath catching from the effort, before hitting the button once more. The generator thudded to life again, this time with far more enthusiasm. After a few perilous seconds, it found a slow chugging rhythm, then began to pick up the pace. The slow thudding, at first like a giant heartbeat, became a rapid stabbing, then a clattering purr that filled the back room with its deafening volume.

Foster stepped to the side of the vibrating machine and flipped some circuit breakers on a fuse board. A cobweb-covered light bulb in the ceiling glowed to life, bathing the room with a flickering red light.

'Yeah!' yelped Maddy. 'We did it!'

Foster nodded and grinned, clearly relieved. 'So now we've

got power again,' he barked loudly, struggling to compete with the generator's noisy chug.

He turned to Sal, still staring at the dead bodies in the tubes. 'Hey, Sal, cheer up! We're well on the way to getting the others back!'

She turned round to look at him, eyes red-rimmed and wet. 'But too late for *them*, though.'

He shook his head firmly. 'Although they *look* human, you must try not to think of them as such. They're nothing more than meat robots, Sal, nothing more. Come on,' he said, gesturing towards the sliding metal door leading back into the archway, 'let's get the displacement machine charging up.'

He ushered them out, Sal craning her neck one last time to look at the tubes as they stepped out.

'What will you do with them?' she asked.

'I'll deal with them, don't you worry about that.'

'But what will you do with them?'

Foster shook his head. 'We've got far more important matters to be thinking about right now.'

He closed the door on the smell and the noisy rattle of the generator and made a mental note to dispose of the clone bodies when Sal was fast asleep. The last thing she needed to see right now was him carrying their bodies out.

He stepped over towards the machine beside the large perspex cylinder, and flipped a switch. A long row of small red LED lights winked on. The first of them almost immediately flickered and turned from red to green.

'OK, it's charging,' he said.

He joined the girls slumped in chairs around their mess table. 'We've been through a lot. And there's still a lot more we're going to have to do. When the machinery is charged up enough, we'll need to get that message through to Bob. And, of course, we'll need to decide exactly *where* and *when* we're opening the return window. But for now,' he said, sighing, 'right now . . . I could murder a cup of coffee.'

The girls, both grimy and tired, looked up at him. 'Just what the doctor ordered,' said Maddy.

Foster settled back in his chair, suddenly feeling as old as the hills. 'Come on, then, whose turn is it to brew up?'

CHAPTER 62

2001, New York

'The shorter the message we try to send, the less energy we'll use,' said Foster. 'We need to keep it precise and to the point. That way we can spend more of the energy of the tachyon burst on creating a wider spread of particles.'

Sal pulled a face. 'I still don't get it.'

Foster scratched a chin thick with several days of white and grey bristles. The first thing he planned to do once things had returned to normal was to get a nice clean wet shave.

The idea of beams of sub-atomic particles that could be fired backwards through time had been a hard concept for him to get his head round back when he'd first been recruited as a TimeRider. In fact, a lot of the concepts, the technology, the gadgets had been alien to him. His young mind had struggled hard to absorb it all. But he'd managed.

'Look,' he said, 'it's like this. What we're doing, in effect, is spraying an area of America in the past, fifty years ago, with a shower of tiny particles – these *tachyons*. Now, if we knew *precisely* where Bob was standing at a certain time, then we could aim our transmitter right at that point and fire off a message using very little energy, needing to send only a small number of these tachyon particles. However, we don't know where Bob is right now. We just have a general direction.'

'But why don't we aim the beam to the location and the point in time that we sent them back to? You know . . . the White House front lawn, say . . . thirty seconds *after* they'd arrived there. They won't have been able to wander too far in, like, half a minute,' said Maddy.

'True,' said Foster, 'but then they won't have had time to gather any useful intelligence in just thirty seconds. We'd be right back where we started, none the wiser and with no information to work from.'

He looked across at the machine beside the perspex tube. The winking row of red lights showed the displacement machinery was still a long way off from being charged up enough to use.

'Look, I'll be honest. I really don't know yet whether we're even going to be able to get *one* of them back, let alone *both* of them. The point is – and this is really important – we have to hope they've found out enough in the past to be able to tell us *exactly* when and where this wrong history diverged from our own. Because,' he said, looking up at both of them with a stern expression, 'we may only have enough power left to get *one* shot at sending someone back. One last shot.'

He sipped from his mug.

'Just one shot to put things right.'

'Right,' said Maddy quietly.

'So, we know they missed the return window, and the back-up window an hour later . . . and the last back-up twenty-four hours later. Which means they must have run into trouble. But that's not necessarily such a bad thing.'

Sal made a face. 'It's not?'

'No. From my many years' experience as an operative, running into trouble is inevitably how you end up learning things.' Foster smiled. 'The more trouble they've been in, the more they've probably learned about the world in 1956.'

'If they're still alive, that is,' added Maddy.

'Liam is a very resourceful young lad. He's a quick learner. And the support unit with him, well . . . they're very tough things. Takes quite a lot of effort to kill one of those. Between them, I'm sure they will have managed a way to lie low, to gather information and await a message from us.'

'So then . . . what message *are* we going to send them?' asked Sal.

Foster looked at her. 'We send them a time-stamp: a location and moment in time for them to make their way to.'

'Right.'

'We can assume they have remained in the area of Washington.'

'You sure?' cut in Maddy. 'Can we assume that?'

'Yes, because it makes sense. Bob will assume we'll pick them up from roughly the same area. So he'll have kept as close to the White House as is safe to do.'

'We're doing a lot of guessing here,' said Maddy, a note of scepticism in her voice.

'Guessing is all we've got, I'm afraid.'

Neither girl looked too happy with that.

'Look, here's the plan,' he said. 'We're going to turn on the computer system, pull up a street map for Washington and try to find some quiet backstreet not too far from the White House . . . say within a mile or two. That'll be *where* we'll open the return window. We'll write down the co-ordinates, turn the computers back off since they're drawing power from the generator and we'll have what we want.'

'OK.'

'So the other part of the message is the *when*. That's the part of this we've got to guess right.'

'How about the day *after* the twenty-four-hour back-up?' suggested Sal.

'Could do . . . but if they failed that, then something must have prevented them getting there. I'd say we need to give them more time.'

'Something prevented them?'

Foster shrugged. 'Many things. Bob or Liam might have been wounded, incapacitated somehow . . . unable to move. They might have been arrested. The area might have been sealed off or hazardous.'

'So, how long after that, then?' asked Sal. 'Two days? Three days?'

His lips tightened. 'As long as we possibly can. We don't know what their situation is, how much planning or recovering they might need to get to this location.'

'How much time are we talking about?' asked Maddy. 'A week?'

'The maximum mission time possible. Six months,' he replied.

Maddy pulled off her glasses and absent-mindedly wiped the lenses. She narrowed her eyes. 'Maximum mission time? You mentioned that once before.'

'Maximum mission time,' repeated Foster. 'Twenty-six weeks. Six months. That's the support unit's *expiry point*.'

'Expiry point?' said Maddy. 'I don't like the sound of that.'

'The support unit, Bob, is programmed to destroy himself if he's not been returned to the present after a period of six months.'

'Why?' asked Sal.

'To prevent him falling into the wrong hands . . . to prevent him becoming a dangerous weapon.'

'Dangerous?'

'His mind is adaptive AI. It's software that learns. Imagine if Bob fell into the wrong hands. Imagine if Bob's software began to learn about the world from someone evil, or mad. Imagine if Bob learned about the world from someone utterly insane like the Roman Emperor Caligula. Or was used as a weapon by Napoleon, or Genghis Khan.'

The girls considered that prospect in silence.

'Worse still,' Foster continued, 'since his organic body doesn't age, and provided he's able to eat, he could live indefinitely. A strong man, almost impossible to kill, who never ages. Think about it. Something like that could end up – particularly back in a superstitious time – being worshipped as a . . . well, as a *god*.'

'Sheesh,' whispered Maddy, 'I bet ol' dumb-nuts would love that.'

'Point is that it's a particularly bad idea leaving a support unit behind in history. So they're programmed to self-terminate after six months.'

Sal frowned. 'So what will Bob do? Blow up?'

'Nothing quite so dramatic. The computer brain short-circuits and burns itself out. You're left with nothing but a nugget of metal that's useful to no one.'

'And the computer burning itself,' said Maddy, finishing off her coffee, 'that, like, that'll kill Bob?'

'Not exactly. With no computer in his head, the support unit will be nothing more than a large, able-bodied adult male with the undeveloped mind of a newborn baby.'

'He's left a gibbering idiot for the rest of time,' said Maddy. 'Nice.'

'No. He'd most probably die eventually. Being unable to actually *think*, he'd be unable to care for himself, feed himself. The body would die of starvation after a few weeks, just like any other human body. In fact, unable to figure out he needs a drink, he'd die within just a few days.'

'Poor Bob,' said Sal.

Foster leaned forward and rested a hand on her shoulder. 'Meat robot . . . OK? That's all he is. Just a meat robot.'

She nodded slowly. 'Meat robot,' she repeated to herself, 'meat robot.'

'So,' said Maddy, putting her glasses back on, 'that's the time-stamp we're gonna send back to them? That they gotta shift their butts to somewhere in the neighbourhood of the White House for a portal that opens six months after they first arrived there?'

'Maybe a couple or more days before the termination date. Just so we're not cutting it too fine. But yes,' he replied. 'I think that's our best shot.'

'Right.' Maddy nodded towards the computer monitors. 'I guess I better boot up the computer, see if the thing still works an' rustle up a map of Washington.'

'Good girl.'

CHAPTER 63

1957, woods outside Baltimore

'So, er . . . who are all these guys, Bob?' asked Liam as he struggled to keep up with him, striding across the snow-covered field towards the woods. There were men in their wake, dozens of them, waving their guns in the air, discharging them, cheering triumphantly.

'They keep following me,' answered Bob flatly.

Liam looked back over his shoulder at them: a grimy ragtag army of soldiers and civilians. Beyond them he could see the crisp white field was dotted with grubby prisoners fleeing the camp in all directions.

'The captain did it again!' cheered one of the fighters.

'Let's hear it for *Captain Bob* . . . hip hip . . .'

The men chorused 'hooray!', several of them firing their guns again in support.

Liam leaned closer, lowering his voice. '*Captain Bob?* You told them you were an army officer? Jay-zus . . . that was clever.' He was genuinely impressed with the initiative Bob had shown. 'I'm proud of you,' he said, slapping him on his broad back.

'I have told them nothing,' Bob replied. 'They have decided to call me this name.'

'Hey! You!'

Liam turned round. A dozen yards behind, catching up with them, was a small weaselly-looking man, who looked like the sort of dodgy debt dealer his mum had once warned him about.

'Hey, kid! Don't be crowdin' the captain like that. You want face-time with him, you come talk to me first, all right? He don't need to be troubled by no pesky little kid wantin' an autograph.'

Liam looked at the other fighters behind him, their eyes still glazed with the exhilaration of battle, panting plumes of winter breath and gazing at Bob with an intense . . . fierce . . .

What? Fondness? Love? No, it wasn't that . . . It was much, much more. It was *awe*.

'Hey, kid!' said the weasel in the suit. He jogged over. 'You wanna join Captain Bob's Freedom Force? Is that what you want? Then come talk to *me* back at the camp. The name's Panelli, *Vice-captain* Panelli. I'm the second-in-command around here. I'll sort you out with some food and a gun –'

'Uh . . . no, that's OK. I don't want to join your Freedom Force. I'm just –'

'Then if you ain't joinin' the force, kid, you better scram. We got us some more raids to plan, a war to fight. An' Captain Bob needs time to rest up before he leads us against them Krauties again.'

Liam looked up at Bob. 'This isn't what we're here for, is it? To fight Kramer's army?' he asked, ignoring Panelli.

'You are correct,' replied Bob. 'Mission priority now is to return home with acquired data.'

'So, how are we going to do that?'

Bob considered the question for a moment. 'I have no available plan. Suggestion: we await a signal from the agency giving us further instructions.'

'We just *wait* for them to call us?'

'Affirmative.'

'Hey!' cut in Panelli, grabbing Liam's arm. 'Hey, stop that! What sorta weird talk is that yer saying to the captain?'

Liam spun round angrily, shaking off his hand. 'Please! Can you leave us alone? We need to talk!'

Panelli looked at them both suspiciously. 'I heard you say something about an *agency signal*? You some kinda spy? Some kinda enemy sympathizer?'

'What? No!'

'You sound sorta funny to me. Got some kinda accent going on there. What do you think, men?'

'Oh, for cryin' out loud! I'm Irish!' replied Liam. 'I'm not a flippin' German spy!'

Liam looked up at his support unit. 'Bob, tell them I'm your friend.'

'He is my friend.'

Panelli looked surprised. 'You . . . you *know* this kid?'

'Affirmative. I know him.'

'So . . . so, what's the deal? You *family* or something?'

Liam shrugged. 'Yeah . . . that's right. We're family, aren't we, Bob?'

Bob cocked an eyebrow, uncertain what to say. Then, after a moment: 'This is the one I have been looking for,' his deep voice rumbled.

Panelli suddenly looked unhappy with that, jealous that his self-appointed status as Bob's right-hand man had seemingly been undermined by some scrawny kid.

'So, Captain Bob . . . you been looking for this kid, an' now you found him. What does that mean for me . . . us?' he asked, a look of growing concern on his face. 'Do we . . . do we still follow you?'

Bob frowned and looked down at Liam for guidance, again unsure what to say.

Good grief. These guys . . . they think he's some sort of a saint.

He almost giggled at the ridiculousness of it.

'Tell them, Bob. Tell them exactly what we're doing.'

'We are awaiting a signal.'

'A sign?' gasped the young corporal, standing just behind Panelli.

'Yes . . . that's it exactly,' said Liam, 'we're awaiting a *sign*.'

The word rippled around the gathered men, whispered with growing excitement and awe.

A sign. A sign.

'Do you . . . do you m-mean,' continued the corporal, 'a s-sign from the Lord?'

'From the field off–' added Bob helpfully. Liam elbowed him in the ribs and he closed his mouth.

'From the what?' asked Panelli.

'A sign,' repeated Liam, 'from, you know, from . . . *beyond*.'

Whispers spread like a breeze among the men. Liam spotted several anointing themselves with the sign of the cross.

'*Beyond*,' uttered the corporal, wide-eyed.

'That's right,' said Liam, trying to keep his voice even and his lips from creasing, 'from . . . you know who.'

A silence settled over the men.

At that moment a scudding cloud happened to pass out of the way of the sun, sending a burst of dazzling rays down on to the snowy ploughed field, bathing Bob in a warm light. The fuzz of coarse nut-brown hair growing on his coconut-like head seemed to glow for a moment, glow just like a halo.

A collective gasp passed through the gathered men, and one by one they began to kneel, even the weasel – Panelli – who Liam would never in a month of Sundays have thought was the church-going type.

Oh, just great. That's all we need.

CHAPTER 64

1957, woods outside Baltimore

The soup sploshed into Liam's bowl from a ladle smelled and looked almost as unappetizing as the gruel he'd grown used to eating in the prison camp.

He looked up at the man who'd served him. 'Thank you.'

The man offered an awkward smile and tugged his cap politely. 'Is there anything I can get for Captain Bob?'

Liam considered that for a moment. Bob was clumsy with a spoon. Chances were he'd end up dribbling the soup all down his front.

Not very inspiring. Not very saint-like.

'Our leader would like some bread, if you got any.'

The man smiled, delighted to be of service. He rummaged in a backpack and produced a long loaf of stale bread. Liam nodded a thanks, tucked it under his arm and began to head back to the tent before hesitating and turning back round to face the man.

'Uh . . . our leader sends his blessings for the food.'

The man grinned broadly. 'Thank you, thank you,' crossing himself as he spoke. 'God bless him.'

Liam made his way across the camp, illuminated by the glow of a crackling fire and silver shafts of moonlight, lancing down between the branches of the forest. He nodded politely to the others he passed, offering blessings from Bob along the way.

Over the last couple of days, the camp's atmosphere seemed to have changed from being that of the secret den of a band of patriotic freedom fighters to that of some kind of a monastery. Men who'd exchanged bawdy jokes one day seemed pious and reflective now.

They believe Bob is some warrior angel sent down by God. What do you expect?

Finally, reaching Bob's modest lean-to, he ducked under a flap of cloth and stepped inside. 'I picked up some bread for you. I'm afraid it's not that usual high-protein vomit-like gunk that you normally ingest back in the field office.'

'I have consumed this food type before,' said Bob, reaching for the offered loaf of bread and biting off the end of it. After chewing on it for a moment, his saliva breaking it down, his on-board computer analysed the protein content.

He nodded. 'This is adequate.'

Liam sat down on a wooden crate opposite. 'You know, I thought I was going to be stuck in that camp forever. I thought I was going to die in there.'

He shuddered at the memories of those months inside, the faces of prisoners he'd grown to know well. Wallace, he wondered, what had become of him in the chaos? Did he survive the massacre? Had he escaped? Liam hoped so.

He slurped noisily on the soup. 'I found myself wondering if I'd have been better off staying on the *Titanic*. Drowning to death would've been a lot quicker than starving to death, eh?'

'Correct,' announced Bob. 'Death by oxygen denial takes approximately three to five minutes.'

Nice. Soothing words.

Liam put down his spoon, reached out and patted one of Bob's meaty shoulders. 'I know this probably won't mean much to you, since Foster says your mind is just a little machine filled with codes and programs and stuff. But . . . I suppose . . . look, I just want to say thank you, Bob. Thanks for coming and getting me.'

He saw some kind of expression flicker across the support unit's rigid face. Was it some sort of involuntary muscle twitch, or was it a smile? Whatever it was, it almost looked convincing.

They ate in silence for a while. Silence that is, except for Liam's soup-slurping and the grinding of Bob's teeth – sounding not unlike the grating noise Liam remembered his Uncle Diarmid's cows made as they chewed on their winter maize.

'So you're suggesting we stay here indefinitely until we get a message?'

'Negative.'

'Just say "no", Bob. It sounds more natural.'

'No.'

'Then how long for?'

'We wait another seventy-eight hours, fifty-seven minutes.'

'Uh?' Seventy-eight hours and fifty-seven minutes seemed somewhat *specific*. 'Bob, why exactly that long?'

'By that time, I must have self-terminated.'

Liam dropped his spoon in the soup. 'Excuse me? *Self-terminate* . . . what exactly does that mean?'

Bob stopped chewing on the bread and turned his cool grey eyes on him. 'Basic operational requirement: six-month lifespan in the field. If I fail to return from a mission after six months, I must self-terminate. They know this. So they will not attempt to send me any messages after six months. If we are to receive a message it will occur before then.'

'Six months? But . . . but you're telling me you're going to *destroy* yourself in . . . in . . . in . . . ?'

'Three days, six hours and fifty-seven minutes' time,' answered Bob helpfully. 'I must terminate by then.'

'But why?'

'To prevent my computer technology being used.'

Liam suddenly realized he felt something for the big automaton in front of him. A fondness? He knew it didn't make any sense that he should care for what was basically a meat-and-muscle weapons platform with a personal organizer stored up top. Perhaps, in a way, it was because they were both new to this *timeriding* thing. Both new boys. Or maybe it was the thought of being alone in a world that should never have been without Bob to watch over him, to protect him.

'Bob, can't you decide *not* to destroy yourself?'

'Negative.'

'What if I were to give you a direct order? As the mission operative, I'm in command here, right?'

'This is correct.'

'So if I were to order you to cancel –'

'This protocol cannot be countermanded. It is firmware.'

'Firmware?'

'Built into the computer's design. It cannot be overridden.'

Liam looked up at his expressionless face. 'But that's stupid!'

'It is unavoidable.'

Liam looked down at his soup, growing cool in its bowl. 'Doesn't the thought of dying, well . . . does it not scare you?'

'Negative.'

'Bob, say "no" . . . not "negative".'

'No.'

'You don't have any strong feelings about . . . about *terminating* yourself?'

'My consciousness is merely procedural code; my memories are stored on my internal hard drive. My body can be regrown from a single cell. I can be endlessly duplicated, Liam O'Connor. I have no concept of death. So I have no concept of fear.'

'No fear,' Liam snorted humourlessly. 'Jay-zus, I wish I could say that. I've spent the last few months spending every waking hour in fear. Afraid I might be picked on by a guard to be made an example of. Afraid they'd decide to finish us all off. Afraid that –'

'I wish . . .' rumbled Bob.

The words stopped Liam's self-pitying ramble in its tracks. He set the spoon down in his soup bowl and looked up to see the support unit's eyes were glazed over, focused on some far-off, unattainable desire.

Did he just say 'I wish . . .'?

He remembered Foster saying the computer was linked to a small organic brain. Perhaps that tiny wrinkled part of Bob, that undeveloped nub of brain matter, was able to wish for something, to desire something, in an indefinable way?

'Tell me,' Liam said softly. 'What . . . what do you *wish* for, Bob?'

'I wish . . . I was . . . like you, Liam O'Connor.'

Liam cocked his head. 'Like me? Jeez! Look at me. A weedy little runt. I'm sixteen and I still don't have any bristles I can shave. And the best I ever managed to achieve, before I was supposed to have died, was to become a ship's steward. Just a flippin' waiter. Great, huh?'

'You were recruited because you have essential skills.'

'Essential skills? You kidding? I can tidy a cabin, make a pot of tea and deliver it without spilling it on a napkin. Big deal.'

'Your data records indicate you have a very high intelligence quotient, fast mental reaction times and creative cognitive skills.'

'Really?'

'These things are listed in your personal profile records.'

'What records?'

'I have your complete profile on my hard drive. This includes

White Star Shipping's personnel records, details on your family, your home town, your school reports –'

'You've got my *school reports* up there in your head?'

'Affirmative.' Bob's eyes flickered momentarily, a sign that he was retrieving data.

'*Liam O'Connor is quite clearly a clever lad,*' Bob began reciting words Liam recognized as being penned by his old headmaster, Father O'Herlihy, '*perhaps one of the brightest in his academic year. However, he is also prone to gazing out of the window, wool-gathering at the slightest opportunity and not applying himself as much as some of the other promising young boys in his year. Liam is something of a loner; it seems he does rather enjoy his own company during break times, not joining in* –'

Bob stopped dead. Frozen for a moment.

'You all right there, Bob?'

'One moment . . . one moment.'

The muscles in Bob's face flickered and tensed, his eyes blinked rapidly as, inside his head, every thought process came to a sudden grinding halt.

[Transmission particles detected]

His computer sifted the data coming in, sub-atomic particles winking into existence as if by magic and passing through solid matter as if it was air. Enough tachyons were appearing in his neural net – caught like flies in a web – for him to begin to decode some partial message fragments.

[. . . time cont . . . complete devastation . . . low energy . . . for one on . . . as follows: Lat: 38°54'24 . . .]

'Bob? What's up with you?'

'One moment . . . one moment,' he replied tonelessly.

More particles arriving, more fragments of message assembling. He waited until the passing wave of particles appeared to have finally ceased. Another minute in silence, waiting for a possible second wave of tachyons to be ensnared inside his head. But there seemed to be nothing more now. The signal beam from the future had briefly passed this way and moved on.

'I have just received a weak signal from the field office,' he announced.

'What?' Liam's face lit up. 'Just now?'

'Affirmative.'

'Oh . . . thank Mary-mother-of-Jay-zus they've found us! And they're OK, right? Of course they are.'

Bob became unfrozen and took another bite out of his bread.

'So don't keep me in suspense, Bob. What's the message?'

His eyelids fluttered. 'Message from field office: *time contamination in present. Result is complete devastation. Very low energy. Unsure of window size. Perhaps for one only. No second chance. Time-stamp as follows: Lat: 38°54'24.35"N – Long: 77°2'33.94"W – Time 23.50, 03-03-57.*'

Liam stared at Bob. 'I . . . I'm not sure I understood much of that. Did you?'

Bob nodded. 'Their timeline has experienced a significant shift resulting in much destruction. As a result, their external power feed has become compromised.'

Liam's eyes widened. 'So what does that mean? Their time machine doesn't work?'

'Incorrect. It works, but they have a limited supply of power.'

'*Window for one only* . . . That means . . .?'

'That means they have only enough power to return one of us,' Bob answered. 'That must be you.'

Liam shook his head. 'Surely they can get us *both* back somehow? If they fiddle around with their dials or something.'

'Negative. Body mass affects the energy required for timeriding. You are very small, requiring much less energy than myself.'

Liam sat in silence for a moment, then finally shook his head. 'I . . . I can't just leave you here on your own to . . . to terminate yourself, Bob. I just –'

'That is an illogical assessment.'

'Surely something can be done to boost the energy their end, or lighten the load our end? Something, surely?'

'There is something that needs to be done,' said Bob. 'The data on this timeline is stored in my hard drive and must be transported back with you.'

'Uh . . . I'm not sure I like the sound of that.' Liam swallowed nervously. 'Does that mean what I think it means?'

'You will have to break open my cranium and remove the soft tissue inside, including my organic brain, to access the computer. Disconnecting the computer and removing it will require me to provide detailed instructions before you do this in order to prevent you from triggering the self-termination firmware as you extract the computer.'

'Ugh . . . no . . . I'm not sure I can do that, Bob. Really . . . I'm –'

'You have no choice. It is a mission requirement.'

Liam shook his head, already feeling sick at the thought of hacking open Bob's head. 'So . . . so when would I have to perform this *operation*?'

'The extraction window is set for twenty-five hours' time.'

'And where is it?'

Bob blinked, retrieving data. 'The co-ordinates are for a street called Jefferson Place, in the city of Washington DC. It is approximately one mile from the location of our original arrival window.'

Liam's eyes widened further. 'A mile from the White House? But that's just crazy! That whole area is going to be thick with soldiers and those buzzing air-jet thingies.'

'We must make for this location within the time left. Once there you must extract the computer from my cranium, or alternatively remove my head and take that with you.'

'Cut your head off?' Liam blanched, his face turning sickly pale. 'I can't do that, Bob. I'm . . . I've never been good with blood and icky stuff. I'll faint . . . I'm telling you, I'll keel over and faint, so I will. And then I'll miss this window and we'll *both* be in a fix.'

He looked down at the tepid remains of lumpy soup in his bowl and put it to one side, no longer feeling hungry. 'Is there really no other way?'

'If you were smaller. If I was smaller. If the extraction window was opened *geographically* closer to the field office. If the extraction window was not so far back in time. These factors all affect the total energy required.'

Bob looked at him with his calm grey eyes. For some reason Bob tried out one of those pitiful smiles he'd picked up from Sal. As far as Liam was concerned, that didn't help matters. Didn't help at all. It made him look strangely vulnerable, like an oversized toddler.

'You will need to acquire a bone saw or blade with a serrated edge to remove my head,' Bob continued. 'Also, you may need to acquire a power drill with –'

'Jay-zus Christ!' Liam blurted suddenly. 'Enough! I need some air – think I'm going to puke!'

CHAPTER 65

1957, woods outside Baltimore

Liam stood outside breathing deeply, sucking in the cold air until the sensation of nausea began to ease. He took a few steps through the undergrowth away from Bob's shelter, trying to clear his mind of what needed to be done.

Past the slender sapling trunks and low fir tree branches he could see the flickering light of the campfire in the middle of the clearing. Around it huddled most of Bob's little army, nearly a hundred after that last raid. He wondered how betrayed and angry all those men were going to be when he had to announce that Bob was leaving with him; that they had other more important matters to attend to.

Men don't give up their gods or leaders lightly.

He imagined the scene was going to be nasty. Their eyes would be upon him, suspicious and accusing, wondering what poison he must have dripped into their leader's ear. But there was no time to delay if Bob's decoding of that message was right. Washington wasn't so far away from here. Just over an hour of driving. But there'd undoubtedly be roadblocks and guarded perimeters to figure their way through, once they reached the city.

Why'd they have to pick a place so close to the White House?

He wondered how on earth they came to the conclusion that that was such a good idea. But then it occurred to him that

Foster, Maddy and Sal could have no idea where they might be. So they were making a simple logical assumption – that they'd remained in the vicinity.

That's one hell of a big assumption.

A lot could have happened in six months; they could have ended up on the other side of the country in that time. Or even the other side of the world.

He shook his head. It was crazy and stupid that he and Bob couldn't communicate back. Not for the first time he cursed this insane time-travel technology. Just when you thought you'd managed to get your head round it, it just seemed to get even more complicated.

So, they had a time and a place now. At least that was something. Heading for the middle of enemy-occupied Washington DC sounded like suicidal foolishness . . . but it wasn't as if they had a choice.

'Oh well,' he muttered to himself. He was sure Bob would enjoy himself cutting a swathe through the bad guys. It's what he did best.

The sooner they got a move on the better, left these woods behind . . . *and Bob's loyal band of worshippers.*

Liam decided they'd be best setting off at first light. With a nationwide curfew in place, they'd look far more suspicious if they were stopped at a checkpoint travelling around at night than they would during the day.

Meantime, Liam decided, he'd better figure out a way for Bob to extract himself politely from his devoted followers. He had visions of those men lynching him for luring their messiah away from them.

CHAPTER 66

2001, New York

Day 5? (since the power went)
So now we're waiting. Waiting for the time machine to store up enough of a charge for us to try opening a window.

There's no way we'll know if they got the message we sent. No way of knowing until we open the window in Washington. If they got it, then they should step through and appear right in front of us. If they didn't . . . then we'll be wasting our energy for nothing.

Everything's off in here. All the lights, everything.

Maddy suggested we should put the 'field bubble' back on so that we'd flip back in forty-eight hours' time. If those creatures outside haven't managed to find us by then . . . we'd be safe from them. Because whatever progress they made in finding out where we're hiding would be lost when we 'reset'. But Foster said it would drain too much power from charging up the displacement machine. He said that's the only thing that matters right now – getting that thing charged up.

Jahulla . . . I'd rather have the bubble on, and have to wait a little longer. Every little noise outside makes me jump out of my skin.

'How much longer, do you reckon?' asked Maddy.

Foster studied the row of winking lights on the machinery's

charge display. 'I'd guess, four or five more hours.'

'That long?'

'Four or five more hours . . . we open the window and they should pop into existence right here.' He smiled encouragingly at her. 'Simple as that.'

Although it's not as simple as that . . . is it?

Foster really wasn't certain the thudding generator in the back room was going to have stored up enough of a charge for them to produce a window big enough for even Liam. So many factors to consider: the distance from here, the size of the window, the mass of the persons being sent – all variables that affected how much energy would be needed. While they'd been tapped into New York's electricity grid, these weren't considerations that normally had to be taken into account, but now running on what meagre energy they'd managed to generate . . . every variable was an important factor to weigh up. And getting Liam and Bob home wasn't the only window they needed power for – there was also sending them back to where they needed to go to fix this problem once and for all. Foster had to be sure to conserve enough of a charge to be able to do that too.

He cursed under his breath. Too many unknowns.

'So, they may have got the message, Foster,' said Maddy, 'but what if they can't make it to the location we specified? What if it's just not possible?' She tapped the monitor in front of her showing a street map of Washington DC. 'The city could be completely different. There might not even be a street there in their time. It could've been built over by the Germans or razed to the ground . . . or . . . or submerged beneath some large rubbish tip, or –'

'We have to take that chance.' Foster sat tiredly back in the old office chair with squeaky castor wheels and a faded threadbare cover. 'Liam's a smart lad. Between them they'll find a way, Madelaine. They'll find a way to make it there in time.'

'If they're still alive, that is,' she added grimly.

Foster could've replied irritably that her doom and gloom wasn't exactly helping things. But she was right. There were many reasons why this was just a desperate shot in the dark. If it failed . . .

Then this is it.

The world left forever like this – just ashes and rubble. And living within this ruined landscape, those pitiful mutated creatures feeding on the flesh of each other, scavenging like rats. In a few days' time they'd be out of water and canned food, then have to be out there scavenging for food just like them.

And how long before those creatures found them? Found their little archway? They may mewl and babble like babies, but there was intelligence in those pale eyes. He could well imagine them slowly but surely scouring the city for them, gradually zeroing in on them. The thought of it set the grey hairs on his forearms on end.

If those things managed to find them here . . . they'd work out a way to get inside. After all, their humble little base was little more than a crumbling bricks-and-mortar archway. Hardly impregnable.

They'll find a way in . . . and it will all be over very quickly.

He couldn't let the girls know what he was thinking, of course. He couldn't let them know that he suspected their plan was almost certainly doomed to failure. The chance of the message getting through was painfully slim, let alone Liam and Bob being able to make the appointed window in time. And listening to the faltering muffled chug of the generator . . . it sounded like it was on its last legs. Chances were there wasn't going to be enough of a charge on the displacement machine to get them out of this fix, anyway.

'You OK, Foster?' asked Maddy quietly. Quiet enough for Sal not to hear. 'You don't look so good.'

He smiled. 'I'm fine . . . just a little tired.'

'This *is* going to work, isn't it?' she asked.

He needed to put a brave face on things for now.

'Sure, of course it is. It's going to be fine.'

Fine?

If they failed to bring Liam and Bob home and they were stuck here alone in this ruined place forever, then he silently vowed he'd do the deed that was necessary. There were a dozen rounds of ammo in his shotgun. The first nine he'd use to defend them if those creatures found their base and decided to break in.

The last three? Well, there'd be one for each of them.

CHAPTER 67

1957, command ship above Washington DC

'Paul? What is this?'

Kramer looked up from the workbench. He smiled when he saw his friend standing in the doorway to the lab.

'Karl, good to see you.'

Karl stepped into the lab, his eyes darting across the assembled machinery, trying to make sense of the draping cables, the gutted machine parts strung together, the wire cage.

What is this?

'You've not been available for our daily status meetings for over two weeks, Paul. Your assistant said you were unwell . . . not taking *any* meetings at all.'

Kramer looked back down at his hand-drawn schematic. 'I have been busy, Karl. Very busy.'

'I can see that,' he replied, shaking his head, a bemused look on his lean soldier's face. 'What manner of thing are you working on now?'

Kramer answered the question with a dismissive shrug.

Karl stepped a little closer, ducking beneath a loop of power cables. 'I have a backlog of papers for you to sign, Paul. Important matters that need discussing. We have a growing problem in the New Jersey and Maryland state areas . . . more of those raids on prison camps.'

Karl squeezed past a rack of acetylene cylinders to join Kramer at his workbench.

'The American newspapers have printed stories of this superhero and his army. This isn't good, Paul. It's giving the American people something to rally round.'

'So, close the printing presses,' replied Kramer, distracted, returning to his task, scribbling amendments across his work.

'I have already done that on my own authority. But they have underground printing presses. Not just in Washington . . . but in New York, in Boston, other cities.'

Kramer continued scribbling in silence.

'Paul? This is a problem that could very quickly become serious. We don't have the manpower over here in America to deal with a nationwide insurgency. We would need at least three, four times as many men to cope if this resistance movement catches on.'

Kramer's eyes remained on the workbench. 'Do what you feel is necessary, Karl . . . I am busy here. I do not have the time to deal with this.'

Karl studied him silently. *He has not been listening to me.*

Frustrated, he reached across and placed a hand on Kramer's arm. 'Paul. You must –'

Kramer looked up at him sharply, grabbing his hand tightly and pushing it forcefully off him. 'You forget, Karl . . . that I am your *Führer*!'

'I'm sorry . . . I meant only to –'

'Be quiet!'

Karl flinched. He met Kramer's eyes and realized there was a hardness there, an iron-stiff resolve, none of the warmth of friendship he'd grown accustomed to over the years.

Paul is not himself.

Kramer began to say something, then irritably shook his head.

His gaze dropped impatiently back down to the papers splayed out across his workbench.

Karl remained standing stiffly to attention, waiting for Kramer to formally dismiss him from the room. As he waited, he looked around. This lab was Kramer's thinking space aboard the command ship. It was normally as tidy as his leader's mind, a place of order and calm, a place where Kramer's mind could comfortably work on refinements to their army's weapons technology. But right now it had the look of a troubled mind. Along the workbench, a meal started, forgotten and unfinished; a teacup half full, cold and growing a skin of congealed cream. Karl's eyes followed a loop of cables snaking across the floor towards a wire cage.

A cage.

His mind flashed an image of the museum basement . . . fifteen years ago. A desperate gun battle, then hastening into a cage similar to this. Static electricity, sparks, then a terrible sensation of falling.

'My God . . . you are making a time machine?'

Kramer muttered something in response.

Karl's eyes followed another thick string of cables away from the cage, across the lab towards what appeared to be a small beer keg suspended in the middle of a protective metal frame by an array of thick springs. The unfamiliar frame confused him for a moment. But the beer keg, he suddenly recognized.

'Paul! You have one of the atom bombs in here!'

Kramer sighed, and looked up. 'Indeed.'

'Is it . . . is it deactivated?'

'No, Karl, it is primed and ready for use.'

Karl immediately felt his scalp begin to prickle. 'You understand . . . you understand how dangerous it is to have this aboard the command ship, when it is primed for –'

Kramer's smile was cold and lifeless. But worse than that was the vacant look in his eyes. Karl felt his leader – his friend – was looking *through* him, beyond him, not at him. The muscle tics in his face he'd first noticed some weeks ago, the tremor of Kramer's jaw were more pronounced. His eyes looked deep, hooded and dark from lack of sleep.

'Paul, what is wrong? Will you tell me what is going on here?'

Kramer's eyes seemed to focus back on him. 'My old friend,' he said, some warmth finally returning to his lean face, 'I believe it is over for us.'

'Over? What is over?'

'Someone has come for me, Karl.'

'What are you talking about?'

'You saw that body. You remember it? On the day we took the White House?'

Karl cast his mind back. Yes, he remembered a curiously *fused* body. Remembered it had troubled him for a few nights, but then their high-powered weapons, their incendiary bombs, habitually produced all manner of twisted and unpleasant corpses. He'd had no time to reflect further on it; the business of governing a conquered nation had made sure of that.

'Do you see, old friend . . . that's *them*.'

'Them?'

'*They* know where we are . . . They know *when* we are. And they're going to come.'

'They? Who?'

Kramer shook his head, that tremor in his jaw uncomfortably exaggerated now. Karl realized Paul must have experienced some kind of a nervous breakdown.

'Our actions in history, Karl, have *angered* them. And now they're coming to exact payment. To take their pound of flesh.'

Karl frowned. 'You are talking of other time travellers?'

Kramer's eyes, red-rimmed and glistening, widened. 'I've seen it in my nightmares. Perhaps I glimpsed his face in the gap in space-time, Karl. When we travelled back to 1941. I must have seen his face then . . . in that swirling chaos between the present and past.'

'Face? *Whose* face?'

'The devil, Karl . . . Satan. Death. Chaos.'

He regarded his leader in uncomfortable silence.

He has gone quite mad.

'Paul, there is no such thing as the devil.'

'Oh, but there is. You and I stepped through a gap in space-time, a gap in the laws of physics . . . you and I may have stepped briefly, so very briefly, and placed our feet in Hell itself.'

This has to stop. Paul is not himself.

'And Hell has our *scent* now, Karl. It has our scent. It is *seeking* us and it will punish us.'

Karl's eyes stole away from Kramer's intense face, and darted again to the atom bomb nestled in its metal support frame. *He could kill us both with this device. Kill everyone aboard the command ship.*

Kramer turned and followed his gaze. 'Yes, Karl. This *device* . . . you want to know what it is?'

'You have an atom bomb linked to a time machine?'

Kramer shook his head. 'It's not a time machine. I'd need things I can't get my hands on in 1957 to make one of those. No . . . it's a doomsday bomb. An atom bomb magnified infinitely by Waldstein's displacement field.' He pointed at the wire cage. 'It will ensure a blast and gamma radiation that will wipe out every living thing.'

'My God!' gasped Karl.

Kramer's face creased with a playful grin. 'It *is* a God-like thing, is it not?'

Karl felt his heart thumping through his charcoal-grey tunic, through the silver eagle stitched on his left breast pocket.

'Paul, this is . . . this is madness.'

'I consider it a *kindness*, my old friend.'

'*What?*'

'Yes . . . yes, a kindness. We mistakenly let some dark force come into the past behind us. Something evil . . . chaos itself. It is *seeking* us. It will come for you and I, and will come for every other soul in this world. I can see that now.'

'Paul . . . listen. There are no angels, or demons, or –'

'It will come for every soul in this world . . . because this is a world that should *never have been*. Every person living right now is living a life that should never have been.'

Karl found his hand instinctively, slowly, reaching down for the pistol on his belt. Being merely decorative it was unloaded, but perhaps Kramer would not be aware of that.

Am I really going to pull my gun on him?

Yes. He needed Paul to come with him now, away from this contraption, where he could talk to him, where he could reason with him safely. And, if needs be, he would order a physician to provide sedatives for the Führer. The man needed to be calmed, desperately needed some sleep by the look of him.

'You know, Karl, I wanted to make a better world, a better future,' said Kramer, his tired eyes rimmed with tears. 'Instead –' he shook his head – 'I believe I've condemned us all to something worse than death itself.'

'But you are talking of *supernatural* things, Paul. Devils, angels, God, Satan – these are things that belong to the Middle Ages. You are a man of science, not some insane . . . priest.'

'Perhaps the supernatural is what lies beyond our science? It is in that gap in space-time.' A solitary tear rolled down Kramer's gaunt cheek. 'The fact is . . . I know the devil has arrived and is coming for us as we speak.'

He's gone too far.

'I have to ask this, Paul . . . Is this device functional?'

Kramer nodded. 'It is.'

I have no choice, then. Karl's hand stole into his holster and with one fluid sweep pulled out the pistol. He aimed it at Kramer. The gun was steady. His voice wasn't. 'Paul . . . I'm s-sorry. You must understand I cannot let this go any further.'

Kramer remained calm, his eyes on the gun. He smiled, not unkindly. 'I'm afraid it's something I have to do.'

Karl cocked his gun. 'Look, come with me, Paul. We'll talk about this in your quarters. You and I –'

Kramer calmly reached for the intercom on his workbench.

'Paul! Please stop! I will shoot!'

'I don't believe you will, old friend,' said Kramer softly as he thumbed a button on the intercom. 'Security detail to my private laboratory on the double, please.'

A tinny voice acknowledged the order over the desk speaker.

Kramer looked up at him. 'I'd hoped we could face this together, Karl. After all we've been through.'

'Do you not see? You're not well. You're tired. You're not seeing things clearly. Send the guards away and you and I can talk.'

Karl could already hear the clatter of boots on the hard floor outside the lab. 'Call them off, Paul. This is madness.'

A rap on the double door, a muffled voice outside. 'Security detail, sir!'

'Enter!'

Karl quickly lowered his gun. The SS Leibstandarte guards would shoot even him, the Reichsmarschall, if they saw a weapon raised at their beloved leader. The door swung open and five SS Leibstandarte entered. The oberleutnant leading them glanced at Karl, the pistol held loosely in his hand now aiming down at the ground.

'*Mein Führer?* Is everything all right?'

Kramer sighed, his shoulders sagging. 'I'm so very sorry, Karl.' He stepped around a nest of cables towards his friend, gently easing the unloaded pistol out of his hand and placing it on the workbench.

'Paul,' said Karl quietly, 'you must listen –'

Kramer put a finger to his lips, hushing him. He reached out and affectionately clasped his shoulder. 'I consider you my closest friend . . . perhaps my *only* real friend, Karl. But this is too important a thing.'

My God. He's going to place me under arrest.

Karl bit his lip, realizing it would be foolish to push Kramer any further right now. As second-in-command of the Reich's invasion force, he might still be able to reason with the guards, the higher echelon officers . . . but not right here, not like this.

Kramer took a step back. 'Trust me,' he said softly, barely more than a whisper for Karl's ears only. 'This is a kindness for you.'

'Paul? What are you –?'

'Oberleutnant?'

'Sir?'

'Execute Reichsmarschall Haas.'

The young officer's eyes widened in momentary confusion.

'Do this right now, please.'

What? He can't be . . .!

Karl was turning round to sharply bark a counter-order when two precisely aimed shots ended his life and scattered tissue and blood across Kramer's workbench.

CHAPTER 68

1957, woods outside Baltimore

'All right, Bob? You understand what you've got to say to them?'

'Affirmat–'

Liam raised a finger and cocked a scolding eyebrow.

'*Yes* . . . I understand, Liam O'Connor.'

'Better. This has to be convincing. You need to come across sounding sort of like some Old Testament prophet, and not like a bloody robot.'

'I understand.'

'You remember it all?'

Bob looked down at the tattered sheet of paper in his hands, and Liam's untidy handwriting littered with words crossed out, phrases rewritten, and written again.

'It is stored in memory.'

'Right, then I suppose we should get a move on.'

'Correct,' rumbled Bob, 'Washington is fifty-seven miles south-west from this location. We will need to travel quickly.'

Liam led the way out of Bob's shelter and blinked at the early-morning sun piercing the branches and pine needles above them and dappling the hard-trodden snowy ground with pools of warmth and light. The camp was already stirring with activity, some of the men already up and reviving the smouldering campfire to cook breakfast and heat an urn of coffee.

He could see Panelli interviewing more newcomers eager to

join the fight, even more eager to catch sight of the legendary Captain Bob in action.

Oh boy, they're really not going to like this.

'Come on,' he whispered to Bob, 'you better lead the way.'

Bob strode past him towards the clearing in the middle of the camp. When he stepped out from under some low branches, the camp's hum of activity died down to an expectant silence as they stared in awe at their magnificent heroic leader.

The newcomers, about thirty of them, surged forward excitedly, keen to get a closer look at Captain Bob.

'Hush!' cried out Panelli. 'It looks like he has something to say!'

Bob stood beside the fire, legs planted apart, his hands on his hips – just as Liam had demonstrated – his cold grey eyes panned slowly across the people before him with a solemn gravitas.

'The time has come for me to move on . . . O people!'

Liam winced at the way Bob's flat voice delivered the lines. It had sounded pretty good on paper as he was scribbling it out and reading it to himself. However, right now, with Bob belting it out in a one-tone voice, it sounded painfully embarrassing.

'I have received a calling from above, to leave you now that my work here is done . . . and I am to form other groups of fighters across the nation to fight this evil invader. This dark force of evil. Satan's army of minions and the devilry of their inventions and weapons.'

Liam felt his cheeks colour.

Maybe I should've left that bit out.

'But you will continue the fight here. You shall continue God's work. I, Captain Bob, captain of the Lord's army, will return again one day. I shall return . . . and together we shall destroy the enemy and return freedom to this great nation,' announced Bob with all the passion of a bored teacher taking morning registration.

The forest was still and silent for a long time. Too long for Liam, who wondered if between his appalling creative-writing skills and Bob's emotionless drawl, they appeared as ridiculous as he suspected they did.

Then one of the men, the pious young corporal, dropped down on to one knee and gruffly said, 'Amen.' As did another, and another.

Panelli looked down at them and, keen not to be outdone, did likewise. 'Amen.'

In ones and twos, the rest of the men standing there in the forest followed suit, dropping to their knees solemnly.

Good grief, we're actually getting away with this?

'Your leader has spoken and th–'

Liam nudged Bob's elbow gently. 'We should probably go,' he hissed out of the corner of his mouth. 'Whilst we're ahead.'

Bob nodded and stepped forward and gestured his hand in the way Liam had demonstrated in the tent. 'Blessings upon you,' his deep voice boomed to the man nearest him as he touched his shoulder. 'Blessings upon you,' he said to another as he strode past.

Liam followed in his wake, smiling self-consciously at the men he passed by. 'We're uh . . . we're going to leave now, to uh . . . you know, to spread the good word.'

Bob led the way past this morning's newcomers, all of them on their knees, all looking up at him with wide eyes.

'Blessings upon you all,' he growled tunelessly as he strode past them towards the camouflaged trucks.

Liam nodded. 'Yes. Keep up the good work, fellas,' he said, cringing inside at how stupid that had just sounded.

Bob was in the truck, turning over the engine with a loud rattling cough and a belch of exhaust fumes as Liam pulled himself up into the cab. Without a moment's hesitation Bob slipped it into gear and the truck began to roll across the uneven forest floor towards the twin muddy ruts of forest track.

'Ooh . . . that was awkward,' Liam uttered, looking in the rearview mirror as the pale ovals of curious faces emerged from the undergrowth on to the track behind them, watching them leave.

He felt something inside him. Sadness? Perhaps it was guilt. Those poor men would probably carry on the struggle without Bob, many of them dying as they did so, fighting for a future that wasn't going to be.

When they got back home, back to 2001, and Liam told Foster exactly where and when they needed to return to, to put history back on its correct course – and this Kramer was confronted and killed before he could change Hitler's destiny – when that happened, this *incorrect* history would cease to be. Just disappear. And all the sacrifices those men had already made and might yet make in the coming days . . . it will all have been for nothing.

Although Liam would never see it for himself, this world would shimmer and shift amid increasing waves of temporal instability, and then in the blink of an eye – *pop!* – it would become the 1957 it should be.

Bob turned to Liam. 'There is sufficient time to reach the rendezvous location in Washington DC. We have fourteen hours and fifty-two minutes.'

'Great, thanks, Bob.'

'However, there is a high probability that enemy units will stand between us and the rendezvous location. This reduces the estimated probability of our successfully getting to the rendezvous point to –'

'I'll stop you right there, Bob . . . if that's OK.'

The support unit looked at him expressionlessly. 'You do not wish to know the percentage estimation of success?'

Liam shook his head. 'Uhh . . . no, not really.'

CHAPTER 69

1957, Washington DC

It was after dark when they finally entered Washington DC. A curfew was in effect and the streets quiet and still, street lamps buzzing softly amid the hiss and patter of sleet drizzling down. They decided to ditch the army truck on the outskirts of the city when they spotted a roadblock ahead. The rest of the route into the city they navigated through DC's subterranean network of sewers.

Bob efficiently led the way, Liam following, grimacing at the stench of sewage and the sight of rats running alongside him on a brick ledge, eyeing him cautiously as they scuttled past.

Finally, Bob cocked his head, his eyes fluttered. He took a left turn off the main tunnel. 'We go up this access ladder. The co-ordinate stamp indicates a location fifty yards from this position.'

Bob clambered up the ladder. At the top he gently, cautiously, pushed aside a round sewage cover. He poked his head up to check the lay of the land, then ducked back down.

Liam was right behind him on the ladder. 'Is it clear?'

'There are no enemy units in line of sight. Please stay close to me.'

'How long have we got until the window opens?'

'Seventeen minutes,' replied Bob as he pulled himself up.

Liam nodded. A pretty close thing. But they were here in time and that's all that mattered.

He clambered up the ladder until his head was poking out of the manhole. He could see a four-laned boulevard. Nothing moved along it. The buildings on either side – rows of three- and four-storey town houses – looked occupied. Dull vanilla lights flickered beyond drawn curtains. Liam thought he saw the diffused silhouette of someone's head and shoulders crossing in front of a bedroom lamp.

People still living in the city, then.

But subdued, cowed . . . frightened.

Above in the night sky, still hovering like a dark thundercloud, he could see Kramer's command ship in position above the White House. Several dozen searchlights lanced down from it, sweeping the sullen and silent city, hunting for any citizens foolish enough to dare break the curfew and step out into the night.

'Come!' whispered Bob.

Liam pulled himself up, and scrambled across the empty road, joining Bob in the mouth of a dark and litter-strewn backstreet.

'This is the location,' said Bob. 'Twenty yards along,' he added, pointing to the end where garbage pails and boxes were piled against a wood-slat fence.

They made their way down to the end, carefully doing their best to avoid kicking any loose clutter across the ground.

'This is the location,' said Bob, squatting down. He began shifting aside several wet cardboard boxes full of rubbish. 'Recommendation: we clear this space of obstructions. Otherwise density warnings will prevent them from opening the time window.'

Liam nodded and eagerly began to help. He suddenly realized, for the first time since they'd been sent back into the past, since things had gone so completely pear-shaped on the White House lawn, that they were actually going to make it home to 2001.

'I owe you my life, Bob,' he said, slapping the support unit on the back. 'You got us here in one piece.'

Bob tossed a wet handful of mushed cardboard and rotting refuse to one side. 'Mission parameters will be met only when you and the data that has been acquired are successfully returned to the field office for analysis.'

Liam grinned. 'All right, Bob. I was just trying to say thank you, that's all.'

'Thank you?'

'Yeah, you know . . . *thanks*. You rescued me. I reckon you weren't meant to do that, were you? I'm pretty certain you should've gone through the back-up window six months ago, to be sure.'

Bob's eyebrows locked. His mouth opened and shut. 'My mission priorities were . . . *recalculated*.'

'*Mission priorities recalculated*, huh?' Liam's grin widened. 'What I think you mean is that you chose to rescue . . . a friend.'

Bob's confused frown became a loose approximation of a disapproving scowl. 'Negative. I do not have friends. I am a biological weapons platform, a field support unit.'

Liam pursed his lips and nodded. 'Fine. Sure . . . if that's how you –'

Bob's eyes fluttered. 'This location is currently being scanned for density packets.'

'That's them, isn't it? Foster? Maddy?'

'Affirmative.'

Liam clapped his hands together. 'Oh yes! Jay-zus-'n'-Mother-Mary, we're going home!'

'One minute until window opens,' said Bob. 'Please stand clear.'

Liam obediently stepped back, as did Bob. They both waited in the dark for the telltale pale flicker of light.

'Ten seconds.'

Liam grasped Bob's hand and shook it. 'We make a good team, don't we?'

Bob looked down at the young man's hand, folded in his giant sausage fingers. For a moment the gesture seemed to be lost on him, then he managed an unattractive smile.

'Good team,' he replied.

A pale spark appeared, flickering dimly like a firefly. Then a moment later Liam felt a gentle puff of displaced air against his face, a soft pump of air that sent several damp scraps of newspaper fluttering up the backstreet, and empty tin cans rolling noisily across the ground.

Some grit in his face – Liam was blinking and rubbing it from his watering eye when Bob's deep voice rumbled.

'This is not good.'

Liam rubbed the grit out, wiped the tears off with the back of his hand and gazed down at the window: an undulating sphere of soft, pale-blue light. It was no bigger than a football, bobbing gently a couple of feet above the ground.

'What the –?'

'They have insufficient power,' said Bob.

'That's it? They can't make it any bleedin' bigger?'

'They have insufficient power,' said Bob again.

'Oh no,' cried Liam. 'Oh Jeez, no, no, no . . . this can't be happening!'

Bob turned to look at him. 'Liam O'Connor, you *must* be very quick.'

'Quick? Doing what?'

Bob pulled a long knife from his belt. 'Neither you nor I can go back, Liam O'Connor. But the *data* that they need must go back.'

Bob pushed the knife into Liam's shaking hands. 'You must

be very quick,' he said again, dropping heavily to his knees so that Liam could reach his head.

'I . . . I can't,' said Liam, the blade trembling erratically in his hands. 'Bob . . . I can't do this!'

'I will not feel pain. Insert the blade between the top of my neck and the base of my skull, that is where the cranium casing is weakest, then press very hard –'

Liam nodded. He stepped round behind Bob, and raised the blade until it was pointing towards the dark mop of hair at the back of his head.

'You must do it now,' insisted Bob.

'I . . . I . . .' Liam could feel his whole body shaking. His stomach tightening, lurching, getting ready to eject the last meal he'd eaten.

'You must do it NOW.'

The small blue shimmering light hovering above the ground began to flicker and modulate uncontrollably. In the middle of the sphere, Liam thought he could just about make out the flickering, undulating form of someone . . . no, *three* people . . . waiting, beckoning for him, for someone, something . . . *anything* . . . to step through.

Then it was gone.

And once again the backstreet was dark and quiet, save for the soft pattering of sleet around them.

'I'm sorry,' mumbled Liam. 'I'm sorry, Bob. I just couldn't do it.'

CHAPTER 70

2001, New York

Maddy and Sal stared at the space in the archway where a moment ago the very air had been thrumming vibrantly, a pocket of space that shimmered like the heat veil above a barbecue or the hot tarmac of a sun-baked highway.

Foster had deactivated the time-displacement machine.

'I'm sorry,' he said. He leaned wearily against the computer desk, tired and finally looking like someone with no more answers left to give. 'I thought we had enough of a charge to get Liam through. I was wrong.'

Sal looked up from where the small ball of hot air had shimmered three feet above the ground. It had bobbed and undulated for less than a minute, and she was almost certain that through the flickering haze she'd seen Liam's and Bob's faces staring back at her.

'So, that's it?' she said quietly.

Foster nodded.

'Hang on! We've still got some charge left,' said Maddy, pointing at the row of little green lights on the machine. There were three green LEDs and an orange one; the rest were now red.

'Yes,' he replied.

'So . . . why couldn't you have used that power to widen the window?' she asked, a sharp edge of desperation creeping into her voice.

He took a deep breath. 'It was as wide as I could make it. There just wasn't enough to work with. I'm sorry.'

'Couldn't we have . . .' Maddy was looking for possibilities. 'Couldn't we have kept the window open longer? Maybe we could have communicated with them somehow?'

'We were just wasting energy, Madelaine. Just wasting it. It was obvious they couldn't come through.'

'So you closed it off?'

He nodded. 'At least we still have some charge left.'

She shook her head, a shrill, desperate laugh escaped her lips. 'For what, Foster? For what?'

He said nothing.

'Maybe . . . ' cut in Sal, 'maybe there's enough diesel left in the generator to –'

Maddy snorted. 'To what? Charge it up again so we can open up another midget-sized window?'

The muted chugging from the back room filled the long silence between them.

Foster finally nodded towards the small line of lights on the machine. 'We have a little stored power left. I suggest we should be thinking how best to save ourselves now that . . .'

'Now that it's too late to save history?' said Maddy.

Foster's smile was pinched and weak. 'Yes. What power's left will provide us with light for a while at least.'

'And coffee,' said Sal.

He laughed softly. 'And coffee . . . until it runs out.'

Maddy looked up at the ceiling light. 'And then eventually that will flicker out.' She looked at the other two. 'And then we'll be like those things out there . . . in the city, foraging in the dark for scraps.'

She immediately wished she hadn't said that. They all realized they'd run out of options. It hadn't needed spelling out quite so bluntly.

Sal slumped down on one of the armchairs around the breakfast table. 'I guess that's it.'

'I'm so sorry,' replied Foster. 'It does seem like that's it.'

CHAPTER 71

1957, Washington DC

That's it, then. We're finished.

Liam looked at the dark hulking silhouette of the support unit, standing in the alley beside him. Still, calm, as always – free of doubt and despair.

The sleet had turned to rain and pattered softly around them and the darkness flickered every now and then with passing light as searchlights from above panned routinely across the rooftops, across the top of their little backstreet.

'You must assign new mission parameters,' Bob's voice rumbled.

New mission parameters?

Liam could have laughed cruelly at that. There was nothing they could achieve now, not in the time they had left. In just under two days' time, a tiny explosive charge inside Bob's head would leave him little more than a comatose giant, a mindless, dribbling vegetable. Liam figured he might be able to keep Bob's body alive, feeding it like a big baby, keeping it going with protein and water. But to what end? Bob would be gone . . . unable to protect him any more.

'I don't know what to suggest, Bob,' whispered Liam. 'Do you?'

Bob was silent for a few moments. 'Negative.'

Go back and rejoin the freedom fighters?

Liam's smile was thin. He wondered what they'd make of their superman – *Captain Bob* – slumped against a tree trunk, drooling long strings of saliva and staring lifelessly at their crackling campfire. Hardly the stuff of legends.

He'd listened in on those men talking about Bob in hushed reverential tones, huddled in one of the tents. It was almost a form of worship. One of them told an exaggerated account to some newcomers of the raid in which Liam had been rescued, claiming he'd seen a shimmering 'godly' halo around Bob as he strode unharmed through the prison camp, protecting him from the guards' bullets . . . and angels in the clouds looking protectively down on him.

Liam wondered if that's how all the legendary figures in history began, as tales told round a campfire, then retold and retold through successive generations, grandfather to father, father to son, each time the tale growing more exaggerated.

An odd thought occurred to him. He wondered if the ancient Greek hero, Achilles, had merely been a support unit like Bob, caught up somehow in the Siege of Troy, his presence unintentionally becoming a part of history. Or how about the super-strong Samson from the Bible? Or Attila the Hun? King Leonidas of the Spartans? He wondered if any of those implausibly heroic characters from history were the unintended side-effect of a mission like theirs . . . some other agency team going about their work, leaving unavoidable footprints in time.

Footprints in time.

'You must assign new mission parameters.'

Footprints in time.

'Oh my God!' he whispered. 'Footprints.'

Bob remained silent.

'Footprints,' he whispered again. 'Bob?'

'Affirmative.'

'I think there's a way we can communicate with the field office.'

'Negative. Tachyon transmissions can only –'

'Shhh!' hissed Liam. 'Listen to me. How long will it take us to get to New York?'

CHAPTER 72

2001, New York

Maddy realized she'd nodded off. The steady muted chug of the generator in the back room had lulled her into a fitful sleep.

She'd been dreaming.

Dreaming of the day she'd been snatched from a doomed airliner, waking up on this same cot and opening her eyes to see Liam slouched on the bed across from hers. That daft, lopsided grin on his face.

She realized how much she missed Liam. Even Bob. If she added up the looped Mondays and Tuesdays they'd all been here in this archway together – before things had gone wrong, that is – it came to several weeks' worth of days. That's all. But it seemed like she'd known them both so much longer.

She missed them.

Another memory floated into her half-conscious mind. Foster taking them down to the Museum of Natural History. She'd been there before on school trips. But this last time had been different. This time not a bored schoolkid gazing at dusty old exhibits behind glass panels, but seeing these things as precious heirlooms of the past, mark-points of a history crying out to her to protect it, to preserve it . . . to keep it unchanged . . .

She remembered . . .

Maddy jerked herself out of her drowsy wool-gathering.

'Oh my God!' she whispered.

The generator was still chugging away in the background. She climbed off her bunk and looked around the archway. Sal was sitting at the long desk listlessly staring at the turned-off monitors.

'Where's Foster?'

Sal gestured towards the sliding corrugated door leading to the back room. 'In the back fiddling with the generator, I think.'

Maddy paced across the floor, slid the door to one side and stepped into the smelly darkness. 'Foster!'

Torchlight flickered towards her, and over the noisy chug of the generator she heard him make his way over. 'What's up?'

'Foster, I think . . . I think there's a way Liam can communicate with us.'

'Sorry. What's that you say?' he replied, cupping his ear. 'It's noisy,' he barked, 'let's step out.'

They emerged from the back room and he slid the door shut. The noisy percussive rattle of the sickly-sounding generator was once more a background thud.

'What were you saying?'

'Liam . . . I think there's a way Liam could try to contact us.'

Foster shook his head. 'You know Bob can't *return* a tachyon beam transmiss–'

'Yes, I know that,' she cut in impatiently. 'Listen . . . the museum. The Museum of Natural History . . .'

'What about it?'

'When you took us there, Liam and I were looking at the visitors' guest book. We were having a laugh at some of the comments.'

Foster shrugged. 'And?'

'Anyway . . . the museum has kept a guest book in the entrance foyer since the museum first opened. They have an archive of them that they kept in the basement. They've kept that archive since, like, the 1800s, I think.'

Foster's eyes suddenly widened. 'Yes!'

'If we go there –?'

The old man nodded. 'They might still be down there!' The hope on his face made him seem much younger. But only for a fleeting moment. Almost as quickly as it arrived, the hope faded away.

'But Liam doesn't know all this.'

Maddy grinned. 'But he does! The security guard there told me. Liam was standing right beside me at the time. He was telling us both! And if I remembered . . .?'

Foster's lined face rumpled with a wide lopsided grin. 'Then Liam would too.'

'That's what I figured.'

Foster nodded. 'Yes . . . yes, he would. He's a smart lad.'

'So,' she continued, 'if he made his way to New York and visited the museum in 1957, it's possible he could have left a message for us in there.'

Foster nodded. 'And that message could give an exact time and location for us to open a return window for them.'

'Closer to home? Maybe in New York? Would we have enough of a charge left to do that?'

Foster glanced at the blinking LEDs. Another red light had turned back to green. 'Generator isn't going to last much longer, by the sounds it's making. The fuel tank's virtually on empty. We need it to get the charge meter up to ten green lights, at a guess.'

'But if it can?'

Foster chewed his lip, deep in thought for a moment. 'If we open a window close enough to home . . . and even then, only for a few seconds. We'd need an *exact* time . . . I mean *exact*.' His eyes met hers. 'Then . . . yes, we could make a window big enough for Liam. Possibly even for Bob.'

'Then –' she chewed a fingernail nervously – 'then we have to go see, don't we? We have to go check out the museum?'

Foster took a deep breath. 'I don't think we have any other choice.'

Maddy felt her arms and legs trembling. *Oh God. Why did I have to open my mouth and suggest this?* The thought of stepping outside again terrified her. But the prospect of being stuck in this nightmare forever scared her infinitely more.

Foster turned to Sal. 'Maybe you should stay here, Sal. Madelaine and I won't be gone long. We –'

She shook her head. 'No . . . I'm coming with you.' She stood up, sucked in a deep breath, steadying her own nerves. 'We're a team, right? The three of us . . . *TimeRiders*.'

Foster's grin was infectious – both girls suddenly found themselves sharing it. 'The best, Sal,' said Foster. 'The very best.'

Sal shoved the office chair beneath the desk and zipped up her hoodie. 'Then what the jahulla are we waiting for?'

Maddy nodded. 'Atta girl.'

'What the *jahulla* are we waiting for, indeed,' replied Foster. 'I'll get the shotgun.'

CHAPTER 73

1957, New York

Liam gazed out of the window at the streets of New York, crowded with brown and grey stone skyscrapers so tall he had to scrunch down in his seat to look up to catch the very tops of them.

Some buildings he remembered seeing before when Foster had taken them through Manhattan: the Empire State Building – Foster said a movie called *King Kong* was made that featured the building and an eighty-foot gorilla swinging from the top of it. Liam suspected the old man was joking with him. The idea sounded too daft to be made into a real movie.

He noticed Kramer's influence was already stamped across the streets of the city. Large billboards seemed to hang on every street with the man's face smiling benignly down upon them. Messages such as 'We are here to unite the world in peace', 'Unity is Progress', 'I promise you a thousand years without war' were stamped beneath him.

Liam could see troops on the street, checkpoints at some of the busier intersections, soldiers stopping pedestrians and inspecting identification papers. Above the tall buildings either side of them, hoverjets patrolled the sky. And hanging motionless above the Hudson River he could see another one of those colossal grey command saucers – a clear reminder to everyone that the war was over, Kramer's forces had won and that continued resistance was . . . well, futile.

The uniform Liam was wearing was uncomfortable – the stiff collar made his neck itch. Bob wore a similar uniform – SS. Black with silver buttons and epaulettes, an eagle on the left breast pocket and a red armband on the left arm featuring the looped serpent.

Bob had managed to stop a German army automobile, a VW Kübelwagen, earlier this morning as it cruised down a quiet suburban road in Queens. The officers were both easily dispensed with by a quick edge-of-the-hand chop to the neck. The attack – Bob's suggestion – had been a calculated risk. Some civilians on the road had witnessed it, but hurried along on their way rather than remain at the scene and risk being questioned. Somebody might call it in. It was possible. Either way, the bodies were going to be found sooner or later.

Liam craned his neck to look up at the patrolling Messerschmitt hoverjets and wondered if the alarm had yet been raised to be on the lookout for the stolen vehicle.

Maybe. So far at least, the risk had paid off well. The uniforms and the vehicle had ensured they'd only been stopped at one checkpoint, and even then Bob's fluent German had got them through without a problem as the young soldier eyed the death's-head insignia on their collars and dutifully waved them on.

Up ahead, Liam recognized the grand front of the museum. It looked no different from the last time he'd seen it, except, of course, for the fluttering crimson pennants dangling from twin flagpoles above the main entrance. He could see a lot of activity out front: workmen going in and coming out of the building laden with boxes and crates.

'What do you think's going on there?'

Bob looked. 'I do not know.'

Liam leaned forward, squinting as the Kübelwagen slowly edged up the busy street through several traffic lights. 'Looks like they're emptying the place.'

That seemed to make sense of some of what they'd heard.

Last night they'd stopped off for food. As Liam enjoyed a plate of grits and bacon and Bob joylessly slurped a dubious-looking mixture of porridge and scrambled egg, they'd listened in on the quiet talk among the diner's regulars: truck drivers and local workers stopping off on the way home. There were cautious words being exchanged about some resistance leader down in Washington state '*givin' them Nazi scum a goddamn hiding*'.

One of the men perched on a stool, wearing a grubby old Yankees baseball cap and threadbare dungarees, piped up. 'I hear'd say them fighters is led by the ghost of none other than *George Washington*! Ain't no harm them Germans can do to him . . . seeing as how he's a ghost an' all. Bullets go right on through.'

'Ain't no *ghost*, Jeb. Shee'oot, that's the dumbest thing I hear'd in a long time,' said another. 'What I hear'd is he goes by the name of *Captain Fantastic*, or somesuch. Folks are sayin' he's some sorta . . . military superhero. Reckon maybe he's like some secret super weapon the guv'mint was holdin' back on.'

'Either ways,' said a third, 'them Jerries is gettin' kinda nervous 'bout him, ain't they?'

Murmurs of agreement.

Talk moved on to Kramer's recent grand announcement that mankind's history was to be completely wiped clean; all of history's past hatreds, religious intolerances, racial bigotry was to be put behind them . . . and *erased*. And that, more than anything else, seemed to be an issue that enraged the men gathered around the counter.

'They ain't gonna get away with it!' snapped one of them. 'We fought them British for this here country of ours. Then we fought us a civil war too! They cain't take that kinda history off of us . . . an' . . . an' . . . *burn* it!'

'I'm hidin' my books an' stuff; my encyclopedias what I

bought my kids for school. I'm hidin' that stuff in my attic in case them Krauties come house-searchin'. Sure as heck ain't *burnin'* it like they told us we got to.'

'Ain't right,' agreed the waitress behind the counter. 'Just ain't right.'

Now up ahead at the museum, it seemed Kramer's dictum was already being put into action. As Bob passed over the intersection, swung the vehicle right and parked on the kerb in front of the museum, Liam got a closer look at what was going on.

'Oh boy,' he uttered.

On the forecourt in front of the steps leading up to the museum's grand entrance, he could see what appeared to be a large pile of bric-à-brac, a rubbish tip of twisted wooden things, books and papers, frames and furniture, the tangled limbs of stuffed animals of all sizes. He watched in growing horror as half a dozen museum workers carried out an Egyptian sarcophagus. Faded flakes of blue and gold paint and shards of ancient dry wood crumbled away beneath the fragile object, leaving a trail of debris down the steps.

And then, under the watchful eye of several soldiers standing guard, they casually tossed it on to the pile, where it split and shattered, revealing the brittle, shrivelled carcass of a mummified pharaoh, snapping into several pieces as it tumbled stiffly down one side of the large pile.

A dozen yards away several drums of fuel were lined up and a soldier stood beside them waiting for the order to douse the exhibits and set them on fire.

'My God . . . they're going to burn it all,' he whispered.

'It is logical,' replied Bob. 'Kramer wishes not to be located by any future agency operatives. No history will mean no reference points.'

'I hope to God they haven't made a start on the things stored down in the basement.' Liam cast a sideways glance at Bob. 'How long have we got left before your brain explodes?'

Bob's cool eyes narrowed. 'Two hours and fifty-three minutes. We have little time to waste.'

Liam realized he was trembling from head to foot, and cursed the fact that he looked so young. Perhaps the SS uniform he was wearing would be intimidating enough to ensure none of the workers nor any soldiers they might encounter would dare to look too closely at him, dare to question why someone so young should have an officer's rank.

'We must proceed,' rumbled Bob.

'You're right.' He puffed out nervous breath. 'Bob, you go tell those soldiers we have come directly on Kramer's orders to supervise the job.'

'Yes.'

'And tell them we will be inspecting the basement area.'

'Yes.'

Bob climbed out of the automobile with Liam following in his wake.

Oh boy . . . this better work.

CHAPTER 74

2001, New York

They almost didn't find the museum. It was just another dusty grey shell of a building amid a landscape of them: jagged walls of crumbling masonry and cracked marble.

'That's it? Are you sure?'

Foster nodded. 'As best I can tell . . . that's what was once the museum.' He looked up at the sun, faint and sick, hiding behind scudding clouds. It was high in the sky. 'We've only got an afternoon of daylight left. Come on.'

As the three of them made their way up the rubble-covered steps and into the museum's main entrance, Sal spotted a pale face observing them from behind the rusting hulk of a car across the street.

'Look!' she gasped. 'They've been following us!'

'I never doubted that,' said Foster.

'But they're getting braver,' added Maddy. 'Fire off a shot to scare them away.'

Foster racked the shotgun and aimed it at the sky. But then he stopped.

'Actually, no. Probably best I conserve the ammo for when we really need it.'

The girls looked uncomfortably at each other.

'Come on, let's get this done,' he said, leading the way over the rubble and stepping into the gloomy, cavernous interior of the museum.

Maddy snapped on her torch, Foster another. Their twin beams picked form out of the darkness. Twisted beams of metal, dust-covered masonry, the scorched and charred remains of a grand woodwork staircase across the way.

'Where's the big dinosaur skeleton?' asked Sal.

'The museum must have been emptied before their nuclear war.'

'I suppose it makes sense,' said Maddy, her soft voice echoing around the inside of the entrance hall. 'If back in '57 people knew a nuclear exchange was on the horizon, they'd have moved all the valuables to special nuclear bunkers and stuff, right? Do you think they'd have taken everything? Those guest books too?'

'We'll have to see. Where did that guard say they stored them?'

'I think he said they stored them down in the museum's basement. Some sort of an archive down there.'

Foster panned his torch across the floor. There were doorways leading to other wings of the museum, but he knew where the basement doors were; he'd visited this place often enough over the years when not busy saving history.

'Follow me. Up ahead on the right there's a double door that leads down to the basement.'

Maddy followed him as he stepped lightly across the dusty marble floor. Sal cast one last glance over her shoulder at the outline of the front doorway, expecting to see the hunched silhouette of one of the creatures curiously peeking in.

She turned back to see Maddy and Foster a dozen yards ahead. 'Hey, wait for me,' she whispered.

Foster's torchlight picked out a faded sign on double doors: TO STORAGE BASEMENT: STAFF ACCESS ONLY. He pushed against them, and with the gritty sound of rubble and debris being pushed across the floor on the far side, they stiffly yielded.

He poked his head and torch through the gap. There was a stairwell beyond. He pushed against the doors until they were open enough to squeeze through and stepped inside. His torch picked out smooth concrete walls and steps leading down.

'Come on,' he said.

Maddy reached out for Sal's hand and could feel it trembling uncontrollably. 'Hey, it's OK, Sal. Just down here, we'll get what we're after and be back home again,' she whispered.

'I . . . I can't go underground again . . . I can't,' she hissed in reply.

Understandable really. The sensation of feeling trapped, cornered – especially after their run-in on the subway. Maddy wasn't too keen either.

'I'm not going to leave you *alone* up here. Come on, Sal. We'll be quick.'

Sal gritted her teeth.

'O-OK.'

They made their way slowly down the stairs, finally joining Foster at the bottom. He was playing his torch around the entrance to the large basement floor beyond the stairwell. Unlike above, the floor wasn't thick with piles of rubble and debris, but instead coated in a silt-like carpet of fine dust. Across the floor and along the walls lined with racks and racks of empty shelves was a thick layer of decades' worth of dust.

Foster turned to look at the girls. 'There's nothing here. It's gone. All gone.'

CHAPTER 75

1957, New York

The museum worker led Bob and Liam down the steps.

'So we store them down here,' he spoke slowly, 'along with all the other valuable things due to be *destroyed*,' he added, his voice barely managing to conceal the bitter hatred he obviously felt towards the pair of them.

They followed him down the last few steps and into the basement where Liam could see endless crates and boxes stacked tidily across the floor, grouped in orderly categories, silently awaiting their turn to be carried out and tossed on to the bonfire outside.

Liam studied the man's face and all of a sudden realized there was something familiar about it. He was good with faces.

How can I possibly know him?

'So.' The worker looked up at them with an expression that told him he'd happily stab them to death if he thought he could get away with it. 'You need me for anything else?'

Bob dutifully faked not being able to understand him. It was Liam who was going to pretend to speak barely passable English. '*Ja*. Ve are seeking . . . zerr visitorrs' guest book.'

The worker's eyebrows lifted curiously. 'You want the *guest books*?'

'*Ja! Das ist* corrrect.'

He shrugged. An odd request. He gestured for them to follow him.

He led the way along a passageway between shelves that ran from the floor to the ceiling. Twenty yards down, the worker stopped, pulled a short stepladder out of a nook and climbed it to the top.

'They're all kept up here,' he said, patting a cardboard box.

'Verry good,' said Liam with a clipped, emotionless accent.

'You want me to get them down for you?' the man asked.

'*Ja*. Get zzzem down.'

The man pulled out the box, unleashing a small shower of dust motes. 'All in here, going all the way back to 1869. But . . .' he added with contempt, 'I suppose this'll be going up in smoke along with everything else, I guess.'

Liam cocked his head. There was something about the worker's voice too that was vaguely familiar.

I'm sure I've met this fella before somewhere.

The young man placed the box on the ground and pulled out the top book, leather-bound with pages of thick cartridge paper, the handwriting of recent visitors scrawled across every page. Recent, that is . . . up until eight months ago when the invasion of east-coast America had begun.

'The guest book,' the man said, passing it over to Liam. 'Every visitor is free to sign it and write a message.'

Then it came to Liam, right then, where he'd seen the man before.

The security guard?

He looked once more at the young face of the worker, more closely this time – the heart-shaped mole emerging from his brow. This man looked to be in his mid-twenties. The security guard who'd spoken to him and Maddy, he must've been in his mid to late sixties. The worker standing before him was . . . related somehow.

Not related, fool.

The resemblance was unmistakable.

It's the same man.

Liam felt an irrational urge to reach out and hug him. The man was a connection through time, a link to where they wanted to be. He could almost smell home . . . almost glimpse the world back in 2001. It felt good.

'Ah, sod it,' Liam blurted, all of a sudden, 'I'm no bloody Nazi.'

Bob cocked his head curiously and looked at him. The worker did likewise.

'Neither of us are. I'm Irish, actually, and he . . . ' He pointed at Bob. 'And he's . . . well, he's not German either.'

The worker's expression remained frozen, perhaps suspicious that this was some kind of a devious test.

'Truth is, we're from the future and we're here to put history right. Aren't we, Bob?'

Bob shrugged. 'That is correct.'

Liam grinned. 'I've actually met you in the year 2001. Guess what? You're still working here. You're a security guard, guarding these very books, so it happens.'

The worker's eyes narrowed. 'I . . . I don't understand.'

'You don't have to understand. I just wanted you to know that.' Liam reached out and grasped the man's arm. 'I want you to know that we're going to make things right again. It's all going to change and when it does it'll be like this invasion never happened.'

The young man's expression changed. 'Hang on, are you fellas resistance fighters?'

Resistance fighters. It would make explaining things a lot easier than trying to convince him they were time travellers. Liam nodded. 'Yes . . . as it happens, that's exactly what we are.'

'Well, why the heck didn't you say? The name's Sam Penney!'

Liam held out a hand. 'My name's Liam.'

'So what . . . uh . . . what were you sayin' about *meeting* me before?'

'Sorry, forget that . . . I was thinking of someone else. Now listen, can you help us?'

'Sure! Sure . . . anything I can do, anything at all I can –'

'Could you keep a watch on the stairs for me? Let me know if anyone's coming down?'

'Sure.'

'We'll be just a few minutes here, Sam Penney. Then we'll be gone again. Can you keep this a secret? Not tell anyone?'

'Sure.' The young man looked from Liam to Bob. 'So what're you fellas gonna do?' His expression changed. 'You're not putting a bomb or anything like that down here, are you?'

'No. Nothing like that. None of these precious things will be damaged. All right? You have my word, so you do.'

'Oh . . . OK. So what are you –?'

'I can't tell you that, Sam. All I can say is . . . that it's part of the fight back, all right? You have to trust me on this.'

Penney gave it a scant moment's thought, then nodded. 'Guess that's good enough for me.'

'So you keep watch at the top of the stairwell, all right? Give us a few minutes.'

'You got it.'

Liam watched the man walk back up the stairs, then he looked down at the open visitor's book in his hands. He turned to Bob. 'So what do I write?'

'They will need to know an exact geographical location. I will give you the co-ordinates down to a yard in accuracy. Also they will require a time-stamp: year, month, day, hour and minute.'

'Right. And the other thing . . . How do we make sure they're going to be able to find this book in over four decades' time, you know, when everything's about to be torched?'

Bob stared at him blankly. 'I have no suggestions.'

CHAPTER 76

2001, New York

'There's nothing left,' whispered Maddy, panning her torch around the basement. Her voice was a weak, defeated croak. 'I thought maybe . . . just maybe –'

'There are a lot of shelves down here,' said Foster. 'We should spread out and check them all.'

'They're *all* empty, Foster! Don't you see? If that guest book was stored down here along with all the rest of the museum's paperwork, then it was probably looted long ago, along with everything else. Maybe used as fuel for a campfire by the survivors, or those things outside.'

Foster's face tensed as he looked around. 'Liam's a clever lad. He would have made sure it was somewhere hidden, somewhere safe.'

'Yeah? Where exactly? And how're we going to find out where?'

'A sign,' whispered Sal.

The others turned to look at her standing outside in the stairwell on the bottom step. 'A sign,' she said again.

'You see a sign?'

'No, I don't *see* one, but that's what he would have done. If he came down here, he would have left us some sort of a sign.' Her face looked hopeful. 'Wouldn't he?'

Foster nodded. 'She's right. Some marker that would have

survived this amount of time. Something permanent.' He walked back into the stairwell and panned his torch around. 'And right here somewhere, that's where I'd leave a sign. Come on,' he said, 'everyone look.'

They did as he instructed, their torch beams snaking along the rough breeze-blocks of the stairwell walls, looking for something etched into the concrete, something scratched on the piping running down the side, something carved into the wooden double doors leading on to the basement floor. Something that might last forty-four years and never be completely erased.

'Come on, Liam,' whispered Foster, 'if you've been down here, let us know.'

They searched in silence for a few minutes, carefully sweeping their torches across the walls, the stair handrail, heating pipes running up the side of the doorway, an electrical junction box . . . even a fire extinguisher, still sitting on its wall mount, but . . . finding absolutely nothing.

Maddy sighed. 'Maybe he left a sign but it was scrubbed off, or plastered over, or worn away. It's been a long time.' She shook her head, frustrated. 'Or maybe he *didn't* come back this way. And he and Bob stayed in the Washington area. Or . . .' The words hung in the silence between them, unsaid.

Or maybe they just died back then.

Sal's head dropped, her dark fringe flopping down over her eyes. 'It was a waste of time,' she muttered. 'We're never going to find them.'

'Maybe Sal's right.' Foster nodded. 'We should probably think about heading back whilst it's still light outside.'

Her dark eyebrows were locked with a frown as she gazed down at her feet.

'We could always try again tomorrow morning as soon as the

sun comes up,' continued Foster. 'We'll have eight or nine hours of sunlight to look around down here. Actually, Liam may well have left us a clue *upstairs* in the main hall, for all we know. We'll have more time tomorrow.'

Maddy reached out and patted Sal's shoulder. 'Hey, Sal, Foster's right. We can try again tomorrow. Don't cry, it was just a –'

'I'm not crying,' she replied, shrugging off her hand and squatting quickly down to the ground. She reached for the floor, her fingers splayed out in the dust, probing a faint groove in the concrete floor.

'Sal?'

'Give me your torch,' she said to Maddy.

'What is it?'

'Just give me the torch!' she snapped.

Maddy passed it to her and watched curiously as the young girl leaned closer to the ground, blowing the dry plaster dust away from the floor. She shone the torch at the small groove etched into the concrete.

'What is it?'

'I think it's letters . . . letters scratched into the floor.' Peering closely, she tilted the torch's beam so that it played obliquely across the faint, worn grooves, throwing them into much sharper relief.

Foster squatted down beside her. 'What is it, Sal?'

'An *I* and an *H*, it looks like. And I think it's an . . . an arrow.'

Maddy dropped down beside them and studied the letters. Then she gasped. 'That *I* is an *L* . . . see? The foot of the letter's faint, but it's there. Can you see it?'

'My God, yes,' said Foster.

Sal traced the second letter with her finger. 'And that *H*,' she said, 'that could be . . .?'

Maddy grinned. 'Yes, a *B* . . . I'll be damned. It IS a *B*. L and B. Liam and Bob.'

'That's it!' said Foster. He pulled himself tiredly to his feet, wincing with the effort, but grinning like a schoolboy. 'He's been here! That means –'

'He *has* left a message for us. Oh God, Liam!' yelped Maddy with joy. 'You're a star!'

Sal jumped to her feet, her face lit up like a jack-o-lantern. 'They're coming home!' she squealed with delight.

Foster nodded. 'OK, then,' he said, hushing them with his hand, 'the arrow . . . He's telling us to go in and we make a left turn.'

They stepped into the basement, turning left and seeing ahead of them a wall of rusting metal brackets and empty shelves.

'But there's nothing on the shelves,' said Maddy.

'There'll be another message somewhere,' said Foster. 'Check the floor.'

Both girls on hands and knees swept aside the light silt on the floor around the entrance to the basement, probing the ground with their fingers for any more distinct grooves. Foster meanwhile ran his torch slowly up the breeze-block wall to the left of the double doors. Long ago painted a joyless mint green, it was now flaking off in patches where a creeping damp had seeped down from the museum above. His beam picked out a litany of scratches and gouges, endless decades of careless knocks by careless porters wheeling the museum's heavy exhibits in and out of storage.

Come on, Liam. Talk to us.

The paint covered over some older acts of clumsiness, and was gouged away by newer ones. But none of these marks, Foster guessed, had happened in recent decades. Certainly not since the world ended sometime in the past.

His finger ran over a faint curved groove, an indistinct and incomplete curve that might once have been part of a letter or a number. He traced the curve, dislodging a fine shower of dust, exposing more of it.

C.

Lightly blowing on the wall, more dust curled away in a light cloud, revealing a string of what looked like . . .

Numbers.

'I think I've got something!'

The girls clambered to their feet and a moment later were standing beside him, peering closely at the faint string of figures scratched into the concrete wall.

'It looks like . . . a code of some sort.'

'C . . . S . . . P, then a dash,' said Sal. 'Five, three, seven . . . then another dash . . . nine, eight, one, zero . . . then another dash and then five, seven, nine. What does it mean?'

Foster shook his head. 'I don't know.'

'We need to know,' insisted Maddy. She stepped back from the wall, panning her torch around. 'If that's Liam again, it's got to mean something. The answer's got to be something we can see as we're standing here, right?'

'That would make sense,' replied Foster.

She walked a few yards along the wall, sweeping her torch along the empty shelves. 'But there's nothing here,' she whispered under her breath, frustrated. 'Nothing.'

Her torch beam lanced up and down the rusting vertical support struts. And then came to rest on a small square tag.

'Wait a sec.'

She stepped forward, examining it more closely. A small metal frame, attached to the bracket with screws that were now little more than flaking nubs of rust. Contained within the frame, a yellowed strip of damp-stained card, numbers, almost too faint to read, printed on it.

She flicked the torch along to the next vertical strut. Nothing. But the one after had another tag like this. She hurried over to it and found another curled vanilla strip of card with a fading sequence of numbers printed on it.

'It's their filing system!' she called out. 'Three letters, three numbers, four numbers then three numbers.'

'That's right,' said Foster, shining his torch on the wall.

Foster smiled. *He's telling us which shelf to find.*

CHAPTER 77

2001, New York

It took them the better part of an hour to find it. There were quite a few tags with numbers too faded to read, and others where the cardboard insert had long ago fallen out.

But two hundred yards down from the basement entrance, on the opposite wall, on a shelf that required Maddy to climb up to reach, they found the correct tag.

And nothing else.

Maddy wiped dust and sweat from her forehead, and slumped against the metal support. It creaked and groaned softly, dislodging flakes of rust and motes of dust.

'Nothing here,' she called down to them. 'Nothing at all.'

'There must be *something*,' said Sal. More a plea than a comment.

'It's bare. Somebody made a clean sweep a long time ago.'

The three sat in defeated silence for a moment, the coarse rasping of their breathing echoing down the empty basement floor, accompanied by the sound of dripping water somewhere far off.

'We'll be losing daylight soon,' said Foster. 'We've done what we can.'

'I don't want to be outside in the dark,' whispered Sal.

'Then I suggest we leave.'

Maddy nodded. 'All right.'

She pulled herself up on to her feet and carefully swung one leg over the side of the wooden-slat shelf. She reached for the torch, casting a cone of light, thick with swirling, dancing motes of dust, towards the wall. As she did, she noticed within the circle of light on the wall, one particular block of concrete more clearly outlined than the others.

No. Surely not.

'Wait a moment,' she said to the others, swinging her leg back on to the shelf. On all fours she crept carefully across the creaking slats of wood, mindful to place her weight where the metal support brackets passed underneath. She reached out for the block and optimistically gave it a nudge. It shifted with a sharp gritty scrape that echoed loudly like the lid of a stone sarcophagus shifting aside.

'What have you found up there?' asked Foster. He must have heard.

'Would you believe it? There's a loose breeze-block . . . I'm just . . . just going to pull it –'

She eased it slowly out of the hole in the wall. Heavy, it slipped through her hands, landing on the shelf. She heard a wooden slat crack under its weight, and the entire metal frame rattled and complained loudly.

'Be careful, Maddy!' said Sal.

'I'm OK.'

Oh my God, this has to be it.

She ducked down, thrusting her torch towards the foot-wide hole in the wall, peering into the swirling dusty space beyond. It was a small space, just a cavity between walls littered with fossilized rat droppings and strung with webs. But nestling in the middle of it, unmistakable, was a large leather-bound book.

Oh my God.

Grimacing, she reached in and gently took hold of it, lifting it out through the hole in the wall. She wiped dust from her glasses and shone her torch down on the leather cover.

And grinned. 'It's here! I've got it!'

She heard both Sal and Foster yelp with excitement.

Pulling the stiff leather cover open, she quickly flipped through the thick pages of the book. 'What's the last possible date that Liam and Bob could have come here, do you reckon?' she asked.

'With Bob terminating six months after mission inception, – that would make it a couple of days after the window we tried opening in Washington. That would be . . .'

'Fifth of March 1957,' said Sal.

Maddy leafed through the pages, noting the dates left by various guests. There were many from the previous year. But they quickly dried up in the late summer of 1956.

Perhaps the museum was closed then.

She reached the last page and a last entry from a visitor by the name of Jessica Heffenburger. '*The museum must close today. The enemy is about to take our city. I could cry.*'

She scanned the other entries on the page. They all shared the same sentiment: sadness, bitterness and defeat . . . a broken people seemingly accepting the inevitable. Paying one last visit to their beloved museum.

But then, in a fainter ink, she spotted it: written with a different pen in the gap left between one comment and another, scrawled in the untidy hand of a person writing quickly . . .

Me and Bob would really like to come home now, please.
Lat: 40°42'42.28"N
Long: 73°57'59.75"W
Time: 18.00, 05-03-1957

She crawled across the slats with the book cradled in her hands and looked down at Foster and Sal standing in the aisle below, both of them staring up at her with expectant expressions.

'You find anything?' asked Foster.

She tore the page out of the book, grabbed her torch, swung her legs over the side and jumped down on to the floor, creating a small mushroom cloud of dust.

'He's right here!' she said, flourishing the page in front of her face, then her voice caught and she found her shoulders shaking as adrenaline-fuelled laughter filled the silence of the basement.

'He freakin' well did it!'

CHAPTER 78

1957, New York

Bob and Liam took the steps up and found the museum worker, Sam, dutifully standing guard at the top of the stairs, just as they'd asked him to.

'We're all done down there,' said Liam quietly. 'Thanks for looking out for us.'

'Look –' the man eyed them both – 'you said something about everything changing to *how it should be*?'

There really wasn't time for a full explanation, although Liam would have liked to have given the man that for helping them out.

'Time is going to correct itself.' Liam smiled. 'And everything is going to be all right once more. I promise you.' He reached out and patted Sam's arm. 'And guess what?'

'What?'

'Sometime in the future, I reckon I'll be seeing you again, so I will.'

Sam Penney watched them go, scratching his head, dumbfounded, trying to make sense of the nonsensical things the young lad had just said, and beginning to conclude that he must be quite out of his mind, when a guard barked at him to help some of the other workers lift a heavy display case down the hallway to be stacked ready for burning.

Liam and Bob stepped out through the double doors on to

the museum's main entrance floor, busy with workmen in boiler suits toiling under the gaze of stern-faced soldiers. Bob dutifully returned the clipped salute from the guard standing in the main entrance with a barked '*Heil Kramer*'.

Outside, the bonfire had already started and tongues of orange flame chased dancing flakes of ash up into the overcast sky. Liam could feel the searing heat on his face as they made their way down the grand front steps across the forecourt towards the street. Amid the heat-shimmering pile of burning antiquities he spotted the end of the Egyptian sarcophagus sticking out of the pile, the dry wood blackening and paint work, four millennia old, smouldering and peeling off the side.

The workers stood in a pitifully sad group watching the exhibits burn. Beyond the forecourt, on the street, citizens were gathering, sombrely witnessing the valuable relics of history and their national heritage disappear in a column of acrid smoke.

On the skyline, Liam noticed the pall of other plumes of smoke drifting up into the cold winter sky, and guessed that across the city books were burning, priceless paintings were burning, historical documents, journals and records were all burning, pulled from public libraries and private galleries. He imagined the very same spectacle being duplicated in America's other main cities in the next few days. And duplicated across the cities of Kramer's Reich over the next few weeks. History being wiped clean, purged wholesale from the face of the earth.

He felt physically sick.

They stepped on to the street, pushing past silent faces filled with hatred as they glared at his and Bob's black uniforms.

Liam was relieved to see the Kübelwagen still parked up outside and no soldiers standing around it on the lookout for the culprits who'd stolen it.

Bob climbed in quickly and turned on the engine.

'Do you think they'll find our message?' asked Liam as he settled into the passenger's seat and Bob eased the vehicle through the crowd back on to the street. 'I mean, we've hidden it away pretty good . . . maybe *too* good.'

'We will know this in approximately seventy-nine minutes.'

They proceeded south down an orderly Central Park West, on one side of them the city's park, all winter-bare trees and drab ochre grass, on the other endless office blocks and traffic nudging forward between red traffic lights. It started to rain. Joyless greasy drops spattered against the windscreen and soaked dispirited, plodding pedestrians outside.

Liam truly wouldn't be sorry to leave this drab brow-beaten world behind.

We're on our way home now . . . hopefully.

He wondered what the archway looked like, who might be occupying it here in 1957, if indeed anyone was. More to the point – he wondered what the girls and Foster were up to right now.

CHAPTER 79

2001, New York

Foster noticed them as they jogged quickly down the steps outside the front entrance, not just a couple of dozen of them peering curiously from the dark interiors of gutted buildings . . . but a hundred or more of them.

Fresh meat . . . the word's spreading.

'Oh God!' uttered Sal. 'There's so many.'

Maddy grabbed her hand protectively. 'Foster, fire your gun.'

He shook his head. 'I don't think the noise will scare them now.'

'But maybe these are ones who *don't* know your gun kills.'

'Oh, they know all right . . . otherwise I'm sure they'd already be on us.'

The street leading south, Central Park West, was thick with them . . . like some bizarre silent rally. To their left was what was once Central Park, now nothing more than a dust bowl dotted with the charcoal skeletons of scorched tree trunks, or the frazzled stumps of long-dead bushes. If the devil was given a say in how a city park should be landscaped, Foster imagined he would go with something like this.

It was wide open terrain, though. Nothing for the creatures to hide behind or jump out from. Far better than picking their way along some narrow street strewn with rusted vehicles.

'We should cut across the park,' he said. 'Then we're on the east side. It's a short way through to the East River.' They could then follow the river down to the bridge. The riverside boulevard was broad all the way down to the Williamsburg Bridge and they'd only need to keep an eye out for anything coming at them from their right.

'Let's go,' he said, leading the way down the last of the steps, across the forecourt, through twisted and collapsed iron railings over an intersection all but hidden by the tangle of rusted carcasses of abandoned cars.

The late-afternoon sun poked through dirty brown clouds as they pushed their way through the fossilized remains of a decorative hedgerow and into Central Park.

'They're following,' said Sal, her voice trembling.

Foster glanced back over his shoulder to see the creatures moving together as a giant pack, hundreds of them shifting across Central Park West, and climbing railings, squeezing through dead hedges to enter the park in their wake.

'OK, they're following, but at least they're keeping a distance.'

Although, as he said that, he noticed that the distance seemed to be narrowing as some of the more courageous of them edged out several dozen yards ahead of the herd. He wondered if they were ringleaders – pack leaders, individuals with something to prove to their followers.

The girls picked up their pace, swift strides quickly turning into an untidy jog, kicking up clouds of dust and ash. Foster brought up the rear.

The gap between them narrowed further as the creatures' hunched-over scuttling became more of a hunched-over trot. The braver creatures came closer still, now thirty or forty feet from them. Foster turned and glanced at the nearest of them – male by the look of him, tall and painfully thin, a few tufts of pale hair growing in isolated islands on his scalp and rags of clothing dangling from his powder-white body. He could hear the creature's laboured breath and a keening whimper as it yearned to close the gap between them. Yet, understandably, it feared the dark metal object in Foster's hand. Perhaps its mind remembered a solitary word from a long-forgotten language.

Gun.

And it knew the metal tube could spit death in an instant.

For what seemed an interminable age, they maintained this moving stand-off: the girls jogging across the dead park, Foster struggling along several yards behind them, his ragged breath growing ever more laboured, and the silent herd of creatures easily keeping pace – but slowly, warily, closing in.

'The other side of the park, look!' shouted Maddy.

Across the empty concrete bowl of a duck pond and the corroded A-frames of what had once been swings, he could see a row of stunted black trees and dark metal railings. Beyond that was 5th Avenue, running north to south down the side of the park.

Fifty yards along, he could see a way out that wouldn't require them to stop and scale the railings – a gateway. Then, across 5th Avenue, they'd be on to East 72nd Street. Half a dozen blocks of ruined buildings on either side and then they'd hit the river.

But this is where they may jump us, he decided. As they picked their way over rubble and weaved through abandoned cars, those creatures would finally close the gap and be upon them. He decided now was as good a time as any to demonstrate once more what his gun could do. He turned round, stopped and levelled his gun at the nearest creature.

He fired, throwing the pitiful thing on its back with a shrill high-pitched scream. It lay on the ground in a growing pool of its own blood, bony legs thrashing the ground wildly. The rest of the herd immediately turned on their heels and fled across the ash-grey park like rabbits startled by a farmer's gun.

'Just reminding them we're dangerous.'

Maddy nodded. 'Good.' But then she looked at the weapon. 'Eleven shots left?'

Foster racked another round into the shotgun. 'Yes, eleven.'

They made their way quickly along East 72nd and ten minutes later emerged on to the broad dual-lane expanse of FDR Drive, heading south, parallel with the East River.

Ahead of them were the shattered remains of Queensboro Bridge, collapsed in the middle. Beyond that, Foster could see the tall metal support towers of the Williamsburg Bridge, and on the far side of the river, the squat brick and industrial buildings, chimney pots and cranes of Brooklyn's dockside.

They rested for a moment on a wooden bench, overlooking the muddy bank of the river below, all three of them catching their breath.

'Just over the bridge . . . and . . . then we're home and dry,' rasped Foster.

'You OK?' asked Maddy.

'I'm fine . . . just a little winded. Let me grab some air.'

They hung on for a moment, looking back the way they'd come. For the moment it seemed like they'd lost the creatures.

'You girls ready?'

They both nodded.

He led them down the wide boulevard, all three of them happy to have the broad river to their left, and four lanes of wide, empty road to their right.

Another ten minutes and they were hurrying up a narrow brick stairwell to the Williamsburg Bridge's pedestrian walkway. The sick orange sun was now low in the sky and looking for a place to settle among the broken horizon of ruined buildings.

Long violet shadows were spreading across the river, reaching for the building on the far side.

'Nearly home,' gasped Sal. 'Looks like we're going to make it,' she said, grinning at Maddy.

The walkway, just wide enough for three to walk abreast and caged by high sides of basket wire, ran above the traffic lanes over the bridge. As they hurried along, they looked down on two lanes of crumbling tarmac filled with the ancient rusting hulks of bumper-to-bumper traffic. A soft wind moaned through shattered windscreens and across car seats and the bones of those who'd died at the wheel suddenly, mysteriously, decades ago – a vehicle graveyard filling the bridge with hushed whispers of torment and pain.

Foster concentrated on the way ahead. Just another three or four minutes across the bridge, down the steps on the far side, a turn into the backstreet at the base of the bridge, then they'd be home.

He'd checked that the generator was ticking over when they left. Provided the thing had managed to keep on going while they'd been out and not choke or stall on them, he guessed the displacement machine would be ready to use by now. He hoped.

Liam's message had given them an exact time. And once they'd entered the co-ordinates into the computer they'd know the exact location. If the lad was thinking smart, he knew precisely where that location should be.

Despite all three of them being exhausted and winded, their pace quickened as the far side of the lifeless, sluggish, polluted river below loomed. The prospect of safety was just ahead, just minutes away. The prospect of bringing home Liam, of bringing home Bob – a heroic tower of muscle who could protect them from virtually *anything* – urged them on ever faster.

They were nearly there. And Foster had begun to allow

himself to think that this nightmare might just be nearly over.

There was a scream.

He spun round to see a twisting branch of lean milk-white arms pulling at Sal through a large hole in the basket-wire cage.

'Oh no!' screamed Maddy. 'They've got hold of her!'

CHAPTER 80

2001, New York

Sal's arms and legs thrashed manically in their grasp. 'Oh God no! He-e-elp me! Help me!'

Foster shouldered his shotgun but realized he couldn't fire for fear of hitting Sal. Maddy rushed forward and began kicking, punching and scratching the arms pulling at Sal. Through the cross-hatch of rusting wire, he could see a pack of half a dozen of the creatures fighting each other to get a grip on her. They were standing on the roof of a truck's cab; the large hole in the rusting wire, he guessed, had been made recently, perhaps only in the last half an hour.

It was a trap.

He realized some of the creatures must have rushed ahead, must have known they were heading this way, must have known they crossed the bridge using the raised pedestrian walkway. They'd found a place they could reach up to, they'd made a hole in the wire . . . and waited.

More of the creatures scrambled up over the truck and on to the cab's roof. They slammed against the wire noisily with their fists, snarling at them through the gaps.

Sal's legs were being pulled out from beneath her, and through the gaping hole in the wire. 'He-e-elp me!'

Maddy desperately tried to peel off the long, pale fingers wrapped tightly round her ankles, her legs, her waist. But then found them snatching at her hair, roughly pulling the glasses from her face, attempting to find a firm hold to pull her through as well.

Sal was all but through the hole now, nothing left but her hands wrapped tightly round the sharp ends of wire. The creatures' clawed fingers snatched and twisted at hers, trying to wrench them free as she screamed and screamed and screamed.

Foster aimed the shotgun at the pack of creatures, no longer concerned that Sal might catch some of the blast. The cross-hatched wire would deflect some of the shotgun's blast, but most of it would certainly fly through and inflict damage on their tightly packed bodies.

He fired.

One of the creatures was thrown off the roof of the cab. Others screamed angrily as the scattered pellets from the shotgun cartridge painfully lashed their bare bodies. But they continued their eager work, their long claws twisting Sal's fingers off the wire, one by one, as Maddy desperately punched and scratched and screamed at them.

The last of Sal's fingers were suddenly wrenched free.

Foster's eyes met the girl's for one frozen moment in time. Wide, confused, terrified – her mouth an elongated 'O' from which a shrill high-pitched '*No-o-o-o-o-o-o!*' erupted like the whistle of a steam train.

The creatures carried her away between them with alarming speed, down over the truck's shattered windscreen, over the engine hood down on to the road, holding her body aloft between them like some squirming trophy.

She disappeared from view, her thin, desperate, screaming voice fading as they carried her down the bridge, weaving through the vehicle graveyard back towards Manhattan.

Maddy turned to look at Foster, her pale face frozen with shock and dawning realization of what had just happened.

'Foster?' she managed to whisper.

'We . . . we have to –'

'Foster,' she said again, unable to say anything else.

'She's gone, Madelaine. She's gone,' he replied. He tried desperately to blank out of his mind the fate that awaited her.

'We . . . we h-have to go after her,' gasped Maddy, already beginning to squirm her way through the hole in the wire.

Foster took a step forward and grabbed her wrist. 'No! Maddy. No!'

She struggled to pull herself free. 'We can't leave her!' she screamed, tears rolling down her scratched and dirt-smudged cheeks.

A part of him wanted to follow her through, to give chase down the road. If not to rescue Sal, then at least to get close enough to take aim and attempt to give the poor child a quick and painless death.

But that would be foolish.

It was obvious to him now. Obvious that those creatures had been biding their time, waiting until the three of them were boxed in on the bridge, had dropped their guard and were certain they were home and dry. They were clever enough to set a trap. What's more, they must have known all along where they'd been holed up.

'Madelaine!' he snapped as she squirmed in his grasp. 'They set this up! This was a trap!'

She continued to struggle. In the distance, echoing down the bridge, they heard Sal's faint cry, pleading for help once more.

She shuddered, her shoulders shaking convulsively as she sobbed. 'I'm coming, Sal . . . I'm coming!'

Foster struggled to pull her back. 'We have to go, Maddy . . . There's nothing we can do for her.'

'I'm not leaving her behind!'

Foster grabbed Maddy's jaw and turned her face to look at him.

'Come on!' he snapped. 'If they get a hold of us too . . . then it's *all* over! Do you understand? It's all over . . . for everyone!'

CHAPTER 81

1957, New York

Bob parked the Kübelwagen down the backstreet as Liam looked out of the windscreen at the row of brick arches running underneath the Williamsburg Bridge.

'We're home,' said Liam.

'Incorrect,' replied Bob. 'We are back *where*. We are not yet back *when*.'

Liam shrugged. It *felt* like they were almost home, sitting outside on the kerb looking at the familiar old brickwork. In place of the sliding corrugated door were two large wooden doors. Across them both was painted the sign DANG LI POH LAUNDRY. Plumes of steam spouted from a pipe beside the wooden doors out into the cool late-afternoon air.

Bob consulted his internal clock. 'We have seventeen minutes until the time we specified for them to open the window.'

Liam leaned forward to look up at the sky. There were more hoverjets circling the skyline above Manhattan, patrolling in pairs. He wondered if anyone was looking for them yet.

'You're right, no time to waste.'

He opened the door and climbed out, adjusting the black uniform and putting the cap on his head, tugging the peak low to shadow as much of his boyish face as possible.

Bob joined him on the cobbled pavement strewn with rubbish from a kicked-over garbage pail.

Liam rapped his knuckles on the wooden door. He waited anxiously for a minute before rapping again on the wood. A moment later a small service hatch in the left-hand door slid open and a ruddy-faced oriental man in a white apron peered out.

'Yeah?' he snapped irritably before registering the death's-head insignia and pitch-black uniforms.

Liam cleared his throat. 'You will let us in immediately,' he said, affecting a clipped officious tone.

'Whuh? . . . Er . . . What – what wrong?'

'We have reason to believe these premises are harbouring a criminal.'

The man's eyes widened. 'We not have bad man here!'

'You will let us enter NOW or I shall have you all arrested.'

The man's eyes widened still further. 'I let you in. One moment.'

He slid the hatch closed and then a few seconds later they heard bolts slide and the wooden door creaked open. The man waved them in.

'You come in . . . see. No criminal here.'

Liam and Bob stepped inside and almost immediately felt a fug of warm moist air against their faces. The arch was dimly lit by several bulbs dangling from the arched ceiling.

'You see . . . no bad man here!' snapped the Chinese man.

Liam looked around the gloomy interior. There were about a dozen men and women standing over tubs of steaming water, stirring clothes with ladles, scrubbing them with bars of soap. Strung across the archway were laundry lines from which clothing and bed linen hung to dry.

'We laundry. Make super-clean for customer,' the man explained.

'You will tell your people to leave the building *immediately*,' ordered Liam.

The Chinese man's eyes narrowed. '*Why* you want us leave?'

Hmm. He hadn't actually thought that far ahead. Liam hesitated a moment too long as he struggled to conjure up an answer.

The Chinese man squinted suspiciously. 'You just boy . . . not *real* soldier pig. You steal uniform an' try rob my laundry!'

Liam stared at him helplessly. 'Er . . .' was all he could manage.

The man continued to glare at him. 'This is *trick*. You leave now!'

Bob stepped in to help Liam out. He reached for the gun in his holster, wrenched it out and aimed it at the man's forehead in one fast and fluid motion.

'This is not a trick.'

The man's suspicious expression was instantly wiped away and replaced with wide-eyed fear as he stared down the barrel of the pistol.

'You will instruct the personnel here to leave these premises immediately or you will be terminated!' Bob's deep voice thundered.

The man swallowed nervously, then, eyes still anxiously locked on the hand gun, he shouted out in Cantonese over his shoulder at the others. Through the gaps in the hanging laundry Liam could see fear on their faces as they spotted the gun levelled squarely at their boss. Quickly they dropped their bars of soap and their stirring ladles, and filed out, ducking under the laundry lines and heading for the open door.

They disappeared outside and a moment later the wooden door swung shut, leaving Liam and Bob in the faint, familiar gloom of their arch.

Bob once more consulted his internal clock. 'Seven minutes and twenty-nine seconds until our specified window.'

'And how long have we got until your brain explodes?'

Eyes fluttered. 'Sixty-four minutes and three seconds.'

Liam pushed his way past a damp bed sheet and found a stool on which to sit down. 'So if this fails, if there's no window, you and I will have less than an hour left together?'

'Affirmative.'

'I guess that's enough time to say our goodbyes.'

Bob cocked his head, curious. 'You will be sad?'

'Sad? That you're going to be left a vegetable? Of course I flippin' will! I mean . . . after all this time you've just about worked out how to appear less like a complete idiot, and more like a human. It'd be a waste, to be sure.' He sighed and shook his head. 'Hang on. What am I saying? I guess maybe it's the humans that are the idiots.'

Bob shrugged, not entirely understanding what Liam was muttering on about.

Liam laughed at that. *Such a human gesture.*

'Six minutes.'

CHAPTER 82

2001, New York

The generator was still chugging when they got back. Foster slapped the vibrating and warm cylinder head, relieved. He'd been half expecting to find it still and silent on their return, having either become clogged up and choked to death on dodgy diesel, or the fuel tank having run dry.

He emerged from the back room to check the time machine's charge display. They were nearly there. Two LEDs were still red. He guessed the machine had to be powered-up enough to try opening a window in about twenty minutes.

He booted up the computer system, waiting for it to finish its start-up routine properly before opening the geo-positioning interface software and tapping in the co-ordinates that were scribbled in faded ink on the yellowed page before him. He whispered a prayer that Liam had written down the numbers correctly.

The screen zeroed in on a portion of a map of New York.

'Oh . . . good lad!' he gasped over the noisy chug coming through the open door of the back room. 'There's a smart lad!'

Maddy looked up, slumped in one of the armchairs around the communal table. Her voice sounded tired and small and defeated. 'What . . . what is it, Foster?'

'Right here!' said Foster. 'They're right here! Right inside the archway! The co-ordinates . . . they're saving us as much power as they can. Opening the window right here – that might just conserve enough power for us to bring them *both* back!'

She smiled weakly.

He got up out of his seat to join Maddy at the table. On his way over he pulled the door to the back room shut, reducing the deafening rattling chug of the generator, clearly struggling on the last dregs of fuel, to a muted background rumble.

He sat down heavily in an armchair beside her. 'It's almost over, Madelaine.'

'It's over for Sal,' she replied.

'Not necessarily.'

She looked up at him. 'How do you mean?'

He rubbed his face tiredly. 'Time travel is very muddy stuff . . . It's an unpredictable science. If Liam and Bob can go back and fix things second time round, then, it's possible . . . just *possible*, that the corrective wave of time realigning, shifting everything back to normality, might also return Sal to us.'

She sat up. 'Do you think so?'

'It's possible . . . just that.'

She grasped his hand. 'Poor Sal.' Tears cleaned fresh tracks down her grime-covered cheeks. 'I can't bear to think what . . . what –'

'Then *don't* think about it. If she comes back to us . . . IF . . . she comes back to us, those things that happened to her, well . . . they won't have happened. She'll have absolutely no memory of what's been going on here these last few days, she'll –'

'Foster.'

He stopped talking. Maddy's head was cocked, her eyes narrowed, squinting as she listened to something. 'Did you hear that?'

'Hear what?'

'I thought I heard . . .'

Then he heard it himself – something moving in the backstreet outside. The skittering of a loose chunk of rubble kicked carelessly across the ash and dust-covered cobblestones. The light brush of *something* against the corrugated-iron shutter door. Then tapping.

Their eyes met and both knew what it meant.

'They've found us, haven't they?' whispered Maddy.

'I think so.'

The tapping on the shutter door suddenly became a frustrated bang. Maddy jerked in her seat and whimpered.

'They're trying to find a way in,' said Foster.

'Can't we open the displacement window right now?'

He looked anxiously across the floor at the row of LEDs on the time machine, eleven of them blinking together . . . awaiting a twelfth to turn green.

'Not yet . . . we open it too soon and we could blow this one chance.'

Scratching. He could hear a scratching . . . scraping noise.

Maddy held her breath, listening to the soft noise slowly growing louder, more intense. 'What're they doing?'

'I don't know.'

But he did.

They're probing the walls for a weak area. Perhaps they've already found some loose bricks and they're now scraping out the crumbling mortar between them.

He looked again at the LEDs, willing that last one to flicker over to green.

They both heard the clatter of a brick falling to the ground outside. 'Oh God no!' Maddy hissed. 'They're coming through the walls!'

Foster reached for the shotgun on the table. Maddy snapped on a torch and studied the walls for a sign of their handiwork. Her breath rattled and fluttered noisily in the quiet stillness.

'I . . . I don't want to go like . . . like S-Sal.'

'Don't worry,' he said, panning a second torch along the base of the arch walls, 'I won't let them take us. I promise you that.'

His beam passed over a small mound of dry grey powder on the floor.

'There!'

She moved her beam over to the pale dust, then worked it up the wall until she glimpsed a hairline crack of daylight and a solitary brick shuffling in the wall, dislodging more crumbling mortar on to the ground.

'Oh my God . . . you see that?'

'Yes,' Foster replied. Getting to his feet and stepping across the floor towards the front wall, he aimed his gun at the loose brick. The brick fidgeted again and then shuffled inward, falling on to the floor with a heavy thud. Foster glimpsed one of the boiled-fish eyes through the hole left behind . . . and fired.

They heard a high-pitched scream and anguished cries of rage outside. The scratching intensified, now coming from several other places along the wall.

'Oh God, Foster! . . . It's everywhere! It's –'

There was a bang and the sound of something heavy clattering on to the floor in the back room.

'Jesus!' snapped Foster. 'They're in!' He ran across the floor and quickly rammed home a locking bolt on the sliding door.

'*What?*'

'They were distracting us at the front, meanwhile working on the brick walls at the back.' His eyes locked on hers. 'They're in the back room!'

There was a heavy thud against the sliding door, leaving a bulge in the thin metal sheeting. The hinges anchored to the old brick wall rattled loosely and rust-coloured brick dust cascaded down.

Maddy screamed.

Another heavy thud left another jagged dent.

'This door isn't going to take too much more of that,' shouted Foster.

'Oh God, no! Foster! I don't want to die like this!'

He looked again at the charge display, cursing that last red LED.

Please change colour!

'W-what . . . what if we open the window now? Foster? Can we?'

He grimaced as the door rattled again from another blow and more brick dust settled on his head and shoulders. Through the thin metal door he could hear them, whimpering, crying and snarling . . . frustrated by this last obstacle.

'Foster? Now! Open the window now!'

'OK . . . it's got to be nearly there. Near enough.'

He handed her the gun and shifted to one side so that she could replace his weight against the door.

'Hold this as long as you can. If they break through, you've got nine shots left. Do you understand?'

She nodded. 'I understand . . . seven for t-them . . . a-and –'

'That's right.' He smiled grimly. 'Two for us.'

Another heavy thud. The top hinge rattled loose from the brick wall, showering Maddy with grit and dust.

Foster grasped her hand tightly and squeezed, then he scrambled across the floor towards the computer terminals, quickly opening up the interface dialogue box with the time machine and tapping in the co-ordinates on the keyboard.

The door rattled from another heavy blow and the second hinge, halfway down the door, lurched off the wall, showering her again.

'Foster! *Hurry!* HURRY!'

He scanned the numbers he'd typed, checking them against Liam's untidily scrawled figures.

God help us if I've got this wrong.

He hit ENTER on the keyboard.

CHAPTER 83

1957, New York

Liam fiddled with the stiff starchy collar around his neck, irritated by the stitching of the oak leaves and the death's-head insignia. He undid the top button.

'How much longer now?'

Bob was standing in the middle of the floor, surrounded by laundry lines draped with linen sheets. His eyes blinked.

'Scheduled window imminent. Precisely fifty-seven seconds from now.'

Liam realized his stomach was churning with nervous anticipation. In less than a minute they were going to know whether Maddy had remembered the museum's guest book. In less than a minute Liam would know whether he was going to be stuck in the past forever.

'You see anything?'

'Negative. No sign of density probing yet.' And, of course, if the window *didn't* arrive, then Bob was due to self-terminate shortly, leaving Liam all alone. He wasn't sure he was going to be able to cope with that, wondering when the men in dark uniforms were going to round him up and put him back in one of those camps. Or, worse, execute him by firing squad for killing their soldiers, stealing the car, stealing the uniforms.

'Ten seconds,' said Bob.

Come on, Maddy . . . please remember the museum guest book.

He stood up, ducking under a laundry line to join Bob in the middle of the floor.

'So this is it, Bob . . . cross your fingers.'

'Why?'

'It's meant to be lucky.'

'Why?'

'It just is . . . It's . . . oh, forget it.'

'Window due in six seconds . . . five . . . four . . .'

Liam clenched his chattering teeth, his fingers crossed tightly round each other for good luck, knuckles bulging beneath his pale skin. 'Come on . . . come on,' he whispered.

'. . . three . . . two . . .'

Here we go.

'. . . one . . .'

Nothing.

Liam looked around them, snatching the linen sheets to one side in case they hid the shimmering outline of the displacement window. 'Where is it?'

Bob looked at him. 'There is no window.'

'What? You sure?'

'I would detect tachyon particles in the vicinity if there was one.'

The nervous energy that had Liam trembling moments ago drained out of him like water from an emptying bath tub. His legs felt wobbly and he found a wooden stool to slump down on to.

So that's it, then.

He looked up at the support unit, standing motionless, looking back down at him with a calm expressionless face.

'So how much time do you have left before you have to terminate?'

Bob's brow flickered for a moment. Liam thought he almost

detected sadness in that expression . . . almost. 'I have fifty-six minutes left on my mission clock.'

Fifty-six minutes left to live. Liam wondered what a person could do with fifty-six minutes. Not a lot. Time for a cup of tea and some cakes. A bath and a shave maybe.

'I'm really sorry, Bob,' he said quietly. 'I think I was getting to quite like you, you know.'

Bob's stern face seemed to shift, soften. Liam was certain that behind the flesh and bone, at some level, the unit was experiencing something beyond simple binary numbers and logical functions.

'I am . . . ' His deep voice searched for unfamiliar words. 'I . . . am sorry too . . . Liam O'Connor.'

'We made a good team, didn't we?'

Bob tried one of Sal's smiles. It worked pretty well this time. Still ugly as sin, though.

'Yes. We made a –' Bob froze mid-sentence. His eyes focused beyond Liam, then he was blinking rapidly.

Is he getting something?

'Information: I am registering tachyon particles in the vicinity,' said Bob all of a sudden.

'Is it another message?'

'Negative.'

'One of them density probes?'

'Negative.'

Liam got to his feet, ducking under a laundry line. 'A window?'

Bob turned round, reached out for a laundry line and yanked it aside. The line snapped, crisp and clean sheets and shirts fluttered to the ground and there, in the middle of the archway, he could see it – the heat shimmer of a time window, flexing and distorting like a pool of water. It was a much smaller sphere than the one they'd stepped into returning from the assassination of

John F. Kennedy. But bigger than Washington's aborted attempt, big enough to carefully step through this time.

'Why's it still so small?'

'They must have limited power. Or this window has been projected by machinery that is not fully charged.'

Liam stepped eagerly towards it.

'Caution: you must be entirely *within* the sphere. Any part of you not within will be left behind when it closes.'

Liam carefully ducked down low and eased himself within the shimmering envelope of energy. Once he was in, crouching because the sphere was low, Bob joined him, stepping in and hunkering down, wrapping his thick arms around Liam to prevent him wobbling out of the envelope.

'Remain completely still,' said Bob.

Then all of a sudden it felt like the ground beneath their feet had been whipped away from them and they were tumbling through air.

2001, New York

His feet hit hard, cold concrete. Familiar concrete. Oil-stained concrete. The first thing he noticed was that the arch was pretty dark. The second thing he noticed was Maddy screaming and then the deafening, echoing boom of a shotgun fired just a few feet away.

He looked up to see Maddy cowering on the floor with the smoking gun in her hands and something he thought was a skeleton at first fly back like a rag doll against the wall. There were plenty more of them: skeletons in tattered clothes, pushing through the sliding door from the back room, long claw-like hands stretching out to grab her. Across the room Foster was staggering from the computer terminals to join her.

Bob's reactions were much quicker. He was already on his feet and sprinting with the speed of a bird of prey towards Maddy. His huge muscled arms thrashed violently at the nearest of the skeletal things, shattering bones and tearing muscle tissue.

He grabbed another and twisted its head with a flick of his wrist. The creature flopped to the ground like a rag doll.

The shotgun fired again, sending another one of them sprawling against a wall.

Liam realized he was doing nothing and then remembered he had a gun. He fumbled at the holster on his hip, pulled out the pistol and tried his best to aim at the confusing tangle of pale limbs picked out by a dancing beam of torchlight.

He fired a shot into the confusing scrum, producing an exploding puff of crimson on Bob's left shoulder. The support unit glanced back at him and growled.

'Oh Jay-zus, I'm sorry!'

Bob turned back to the task at hand and tore the limb off another one of them and proceeded to swing the flopping thing like a club at the others. Their high-pitched screams made them sound like startled children and they began to scramble back to the door through which they'd entered.

As Bob pursued them into the back room, the sound of crashing, a heavy perspex tube rolling across the floor and further shrill screams of terror echoed out through the doorway. Liam joined Foster and Maddy.

'What's happening?'

Foster looked at him. 'Bad things, Liam. Bad things.'

He reached down to Maddy, wide eyed and in shock on the floor.

'You OK, Maddy? You all right?'

Her eyes drifted from the contorted pale bodies either side

of the doorway and on to Liam's face. For a moment she seemed confused, looking at him as if he was a stranger.

'It's me! Liam!'

Recognition flickered into her squinting eyes. Recognition . . . followed by gradually realized relief. Her mouth opened and closed. Opened and closed. 'Oh God,' she finally managed to whisper. 'Oh God . . . I thought I was going to . . . thought those things were . . . were –'

Foster reached out and held her. 'Shhh. It's OK now. They made it back. Both of them. We're safe now.'

The sound of struggling in the back room had ceased. Bob appeared in the doorway, his face spattered with dark droplets of blood, his SS uniform ripped and soaked with even more blood.

'Information: the field office is now clear,' he said matter-of-factly.

It was then Liam registered that they were missing someone.

'Where's Sal?'

CHAPTER 84

1957, command ship over Washington DC

Paul Kramer sat alone in his lab. Truly alone.

Karl's dead. All those other men, Saul, Stefan, Rudy, Dieter . . .

Others whose faces he could remember, if not their names.

Now I'm the last.

He looked up from his lap across the messy floor, thick with snaking cables, towards the atom bomb in its frame, nestling inside the small wire cage.

There you are, my little friend.

In his hand, he held a simple toggle switch wired carelessly into the complicated device. A loosely soldered red cable descended from it, linking the switch to his jury-rigged version of a Waldstein field-displacement cage. His thumb rested on the tip of the toggle switch.

Kramer felt so incredibly tired. A solid week now without a moment's sleep. Not since he'd had Karl killed. If he'd had the courage, he would have activated his device right then. Joined Karl in the *hereafter* moments later.

Karl's adjutant, and several other senior invasion-force generals, had petitioned to see him, over and over. Problems mounting up, issues that needed to be resolved, paperwork that needed signing.

He could face none of those things right now.

And there'd be no sleep either. Because the moment his eyes closed the nightmares came. His assassin was no longer some time-policeman from the future, but some dark, formless entity from Hell . . . hungrily seeking his soul, ready to drag him down through a rip in space-time to burn for eternity for daring to step, albeit briefly, into its dimension.

'Burn . . . for eternity,' he muttered quietly.

His thumb toyed with the toggle switch.

Paul, it's time.

'You're back,' he said flatly. The voice had been so quiet these last few days. Paul thought it had abandoned him.

I never left you.

'I thought I was going to die alone.'

No. You and I, we'll face destiny together.

Kramer gently applied pressure to the switch.

Just a little more, Paul . . . an ounce more pressure on this tiny little switch . . . and all life on this world will be gone.

He smiled weakly. There was poetry in that – to create a new world, a new history, and then be the one to destroy it. Like a child builds a sandcastle, then in a moment of vainglory tramples all over it.

That's right. We achieved so much, didn't we?

The toggle switch clicked over . . . and the world turned white.

CHAPTER 85

2001, New York

Foster finished telling Liam their story as they stood in the backstreet just outside the open shutter door and gazed upon the ruined city.

'My God,' Liam whispered. 'What do you think happened to this world?'

'A nuclear war of some sort is the only thing I can think of,' said Foster. 'I was hoping you might have a better idea, though.'

'I don't know,' said Liam. 'Kramer's army had finished the job of conquering America. I heard of no other wars going on. He still had Russia and China to take . . . but that wasn't happening yet back where we were.'

Foster shrugged. 'Then something must have happened not long after you left. Perhaps this Kramer started a nuclear war. Who knows?' Foster offered him an encouraging smile. 'We get things fixed in the past and we'll never need to know what happened after you left because . . .'

'Because it never will have happened,' Liam finished.

The old man patted his arm proudly. 'You're getting the hang of it, lad.'

They stepped back inside and cranked down the shutter door. Inside, Bob had been busy fixing up the holes in the brickwork as best he could and hefting the bodies of the creatures outside.

They sat down at the table, joining Maddy, who quietly

nursed a mug of coffee in both hands, still clearly very shaken by the attack.

'Foster, you said it was possible we might get Sal back? If things right themselves?'

The old man shrugged. 'It's just a possibility, Liam. One of many possibilities.'

Liam reached for a mug and sipped some of the tepid brew. 'But right now, out there somewhere, you're absolutely certain she's dead?'

Foster sighed. 'We can only hope so. Whatever she went through . . .' He shook his head tiredly, his eyes briefly meeting Maddy's. 'Well, I'd like to think it's over now. It's done. She can't suffer any more.'

'But if we fixed things and she came back . . . Would she remember?'

Foster shook his head. 'I don't want to raise your hopes. Even if we get the timeline corrected, she may just stay gone for good. There are no guarantees.'

'She was so . . . so terrified,' whispered Maddy. 'I saw them carry her away . . . I . . . I saw the look in her eyes. I –'

'There was nothing you could have done,' Foster sighed. 'Absolutely nothing. If I'd not stopped you going after her, then you'd have shared the same fate as her.'

'But she was just a kid!' cried Maddy angrily. 'Just a kid! I told you we should have gone after her!'

'If we had, we'd be dead too,' he replied softly. 'I'm sorry, Madelaine, I truly am, but this is what it is. We just have to get on with it.' He turned back to Liam. 'Our focus has to be on one thing now. One thing only: correcting time. That literally is *all* that matters.'

A moment of silent reflection, then both Liam and Maddy nodded. He was right.

'Now, Liam, you said you've identified a possible point in time for us to send you back to?'

'Yes. It was in that Hitler fella's second book.'

'In the *correct* timeline Adolf Hitler wrote *Mein Kampf* in what? 1925? And he shot himself in 1945, so he never got to write any more books.'

'Yes,' said Liam, 'but in the past that we were sent to Hitler lived on and wrote this second book. And shortly after that he was kicked out of the job by this Kramer fella who became the new Führer.'

'OK, so in this second book . . .?'

'There's this chapter where he describes receiving inspiration from God in the form of an angel. Apparently it's a well-known chapter. Hitler never actually mentions Kramer's name specifically, but it's assumed that when he refers to a "guardian angel" and "divine inspiration" it's Kramer he's talking about.'

'Go on.'

'I learned a lot about this guy, Kramer, whilst I was in that prison camp. He was a very mysterious man who seemed to sort of pop up out of the woodwork from nowhere. No family history, no details of a childhood. A real mystery man. He took credit for steering Hitler away from launching an attack on Russia in 1941. He claimed to have personally invented most of the modern weapons that helped them win the war, that allowed them to invade America and wipe out their armed forces within just a few weeks.

'His people worshipped him almost like a god. And I think he encouraged the idea that he was extraordinary in some way. Apparently, up until he launched his invasion on America, he was the most written-about man of his time. Hundreds of books about him . . . all trying to work out who he was and where he'd come from.'

'And you recall the *when* and *where* of Hitler's first encounter with him?'

'Yes,' replied Liam. 'There was a fella who told me, a man called Wallace. If he remembered it correctly that is . . . then, yes, I can tell you the time and the place.'

Foster considered that in silence for a moment. 'So, this *Kramer* is our target, then. We can only presume he's some foolish technician from the future who fancied the idea of going back in time and ruling the world. Somebody who decided to step into the past at a crucial tipping point . . . and make his own history.'

'I suppose.'

'Liam, you understand what you're to do?'

'Locate him and . . .?'

'And *kill* him. *Execute* him. Before he meets Hitler . . . before he has a chance to change *anything* to affect history.'

'Sure.'

'All right then. Give me those details of time and place.'

CHAPTER 86

2001, New York

Liam looked at the empty perspex cylinder. 'There's no water in there. It's empty.'

'We don't have a water supply. You'll have to go back dry this time.'

'So . . . do I still climb in the tube thing?'

Foster shook his head. 'I'll open the time window right here on the floor. It'll mean a scoop of our lovely concrete floor will be going back with you . . . but I'm afraid that can't be helped.'

'But you told me nothing but ourselves can go back?'

'That's right. The less potential for contamination, the better. But, look, on this occasion there's not a lot we can do. There's no tap water. Anyway . . . I'm not sure we'd have enough charge left to shift thirty gallons of water as well as you two back into the past.'

Foster returned to the console. 'I have the fifteenth of April 1941 set as the time-stamp. The co-ordinates will place you in some woods near a road that leads up to where Hitler's Obersalzberg retreat once stood. This is the *only* road in.'

He turned to face Liam and Bob. 'It's the only way in for this Kramer too. Now, I'm assuming he arrived as some sort of a special guest. Perhaps he managed to convince an influential general or a Nazi bigwig to arrange an audience for him with Adolf Hitler.'

'Would he not have opened a window right inside the building? Right in front of the man?'

Foster shook his head. 'If it were me, I wouldn't. What if you appeared right in front of a guard? You'd be gunned down on sight. No,' he said, stroking the grey-white bristles of his week-old beard, 'far safer to have appeared somewhere quiet. Then make an approach through some official channel – that's how I would do it – an offer of untold wealth, or strategic knowledge of the enemy . . . something to bluff my way into the offices of some senior Nazi official.'

He turned back to the console. 'You say Hitler wrote that his profound moment of inspiration occurred at nine thirty p.m. on that night. I have set your time-stamp for eight thirty p.m., an hour earlier. If Kramer managed to arrange for an audience with Hitler, then it's a reasonable assumption he arranged to be punctual. His meeting might have been for nine thirty p.m., but he presumably would arrive a little earlier to ensure he was there on time to go through whatever security procedures they carried out back then.'

'If we miss him?'

'If you fail to intercept Kramer,' sighed Foster, 'then we've missed our chance.'

'What then?'

The old man shook his head. 'It means it's game over. History remains changed. God help us all.'

'We'll be stuck back in 1941, won't we?'

'Yes, Liam. And Maddy and I will be stuck here.'

They stared at each other in silence. Liam realized their fate would be worse than his. 'What about those creatures . . .?'

Foster waved his hand and smiled grimly. 'Let's forget about them for now, shall we?'

Maddy stepped across the floor, over snaking cables. She

grasped Liam's arm and looked at him with red-rimmed eyes. 'Just make sure you get him, OK?'

He nodded.

She looked up at the support unit. 'I've downloaded all the historical information we have on Obersalzberg and the surrounding area from the database on to Bob's hard drive.'

Bob stirred. 'Affirmative.'

'If . . . *if* . . . you're successful, Liam,' said Foster, 'and history realigns, we'll have a power feed once more. We can bring you home. The initial return window will be nine thirty p.m. from the same co-ordinates. The first back-up will be ten thirty p.m. The second back-up will be twenty-four hours later. Is that clear?'

'Yes, sir,' said Liam.

'If you fail,' said Foster, stepping towards him, 'if it doesn't work out, lad, then don't throw your life away on some foolish gamble, eh?' He placed a hand on Liam's shoulder. 'Find a way to survive. You'll have Bob to help you for the first six months. Find a way to survive . . . and live your life as best you can.'

'What about you two?'

Foster reached out and squeezed Maddy's hand. 'Don't worry about us, Liam. We've got something arranged.'

Maddy nodded and offered him a thin smile. 'That's right.'

The four of them stared at each other in silence for a moment, understanding the stakes, knowing this was their one and only chance to set things right.

She looked up at Bob, standing stiffly to attention in his blood-spattered SS uniform. 'Oh, that's definitely you.' She punched him softly on the chest. 'Look after Liam, you dumb ape.'

'Affirmative.'

She grinned, a rim of moisture beginning to spill from her eyes. 'And you, Liam, come back safe, OK?'

He nodded. 'That's the plan.'

CHAPTER 87

1941, woods outside Obersalzberg

Falling again. Falling through a dark void.

Liam had just enough time to wonder whether he was ever going to get used to the stomach-lurching sensation before he found himself waist-deep in a drift of powder snow.

'Oh, great!'

Liam looked around at the snow-covered pine trees, glowing almost a luminescent blue by the light of the quicksilver moon. Thick branches of fir needles were weighed down beneath a heavy shroud of fresh-fallen snow.

Beneath the thin material of his SS uniform, he shivered. 'Jay-zus, it's bloody f-f-freezing,' he hissed under his breath, sending a plume of condensation out before him. 'Glad we're not just wearing wet p-pants right now. Hang on, isn't that going to cause a contamination problem?'

'Acceptable level of contamination at this point,' replied Bob. 'We will return with our clothes.' He stopped mid-stride for a moment, consulting data in his head. 'Information: two hundred yards ahead is the road leading to the Eagle's Nest.'

'Right.'

'Recommendation: we attempt to acquire better weapons and appropriate clothing and disguise.'

Liam nodded eagerly at the suggestion of appropriate clothing.

The support unit led the way, pushing through the wood's undergrowth, dislodging hissing showers of shifting snow from the low branches above them. They walked quietly through the hushed winter forest until finally Liam could make out a narrow road, snow shovelled to either side to keep it passable.

Bob squatted down, surveying the way ahead, and Liam joined him. The road, little more than a dirt track, climbed the hill gently. Fifty yards up they could see a guard hut picked out in the glow of a swivelling floodlight, sand bags either side, and a raisable barrier blocking the way. A small smile crept across Liam's quivering lips.

Nothing Bob can't handle there.

'If you can take out those guards,' said Liam quietly, 'we could wait right there for Kramer.'

Bob nodded. 'Affirmative. That is a good plan. I shall –'

He froze.

'Bob? What is it?'

'I have just detected emerging tachyon particles in the vicinity.' His grey eyes swivelled on to Liam. 'A time window has just been opened nearby.'

'What? You sure it's not traces of our own time window you're picking up?'

'It is not us.'

Liam glanced at the trees around them. 'Nearby?'

'Very close. Within three hundred yards of our position.'

Foster's guesswork must have been wrong. This guy, Kramer, hadn't already been back in 1941 for some time working at getting an audience with Hitler. He'd only just arrived.

'I am detecting a significant number of decaying particles.'

'And that means?'

'One large displacement window or many smaller windows.'

Liam bit his lip with dawning realization. 'It's not just Kramer on his own, is it?'

It was then that they heard movement through the trees: faint at first, the swish of a snow-laden branch pushed aside, the soft clink and rattle of webbing and carried equipment, the hushed whisper of several voices. All of it coming their way.

'Recommendation: we should hide.'

Liam looked around in the darkness. The glow of moonlight made everything that wasn't snow-covered stand out in stark contrast. Unless they could quickly bury themselves, they were going to be spotted. He looked up at the tree they were squatting beneath.

'Up there.' He pointed. 'In the tree.'

Bob nodded. Without a moment's hesitation he grabbed Liam and effortlessly hefted him up on to the lowest branch. Silently, and with the grace of a gymnast on parallel bars, he swung up beside him, the branch creaking worryingly beneath his immense weight.

The noises grew subtly louder, closer, until Liam was able to see movement. Dark shapes warily emerged from beneath the shadow of trees, stepping cautiously across the glowing snow below, then – almost unbelievably – coming to a halt beneath the very tree they were hiding in.

They squatted down and surveyed the track heading up the hill just as Bob had been doing a moment earlier. Then he heard one of them talking softly.

'This is it, Karl. This is it! Hitler's winter retreat!' An accent he vaguely recognized. He recalled the precise tones, the voice of recited speeches endlessly broadcast over the prison-camp speakers.

Kramer?

A second voice. '*Der Kehlsteinhaus*. The Eagle's Nest. It does not appear that heavily guarded.' This one had a clipped, foreign-sounding accent.

Liam strained to hear what the men said next, their voices quieter still. Then Kramer spoke more clearly: 'A little further up the hillside, only a few hundred yards away, is an SS garrison housing four or five hundred of them. They will happily die to defend their leader. Your men will have to be very fast, Karl.'

His voice dropped again, then the second murmured a response.

Liam turned to look at Bob, perched perfectly still on the branch beside him like a night owl watching the progress of some small rodent and poised ready to leap.

'Switch to night sights, gentlemen,' hissed the second man. In the darkness below them, Liam saw something glowing a soft ghostly green among the gathered men. Then several more. He realized they were goggles of some sort.

'Mr Kramer, sir?' whispered one of the men.

It is *Kramer!* Liam felt his heart suddenly flutter.

'What is it, Rudy?'

'Will we actually get to *meet* Adolf Hitler tonight? For real?' Another heavily accented voice.

'Yes, Rudy, you will. Tonight, gentlemen –' Kramer raised his voice from a whisper to a soft murmur for them all to hear – 'we are going to write a brand-new history together.'

Bob tapped Liam on the arm. They were too close to the men below to be able to talk. Instead the support unit gestured at them. An unmistakable gesture that told him . . .

I am ready.

Liam swallowed anxiously, feeling his gut churning once again with fear. Gritting his teeth, he nodded.

Do it.

CHAPTER 88

1941, woods outside Obersalzberg

Bob dropped silently down out of the tree on to the men below. Liam heard the heavy thud of his solid body and the unmistakable crack of bones.

Then all hell broke loose.

Voices brittle with alarm and confusion. The dark swirling scrum of figures below illuminated for a freeze-frame second by the single muzzle-flash of a silenced weapon. Bob, a bloodied knife in one hand mid-slash across the chest of one man, his other big hand crushing the throat of another of them.

Several more strobing muzzle-flashes in the confusing darkness, accompanied by the muted puff of a silenced rifle. The fleeting light showed four tangled bodies on the ground already, blood pooling across the snow. Bob thrashing at another man with lethal speed and agility, and at least another dozen men around him recovering from the moment of surprise and cocking their guns to fire.

I have to help him.

Liam pulled the pistol out of his holster and aimed it at one of the dark outlines – one of the men who looked nearest ready to fire – and pulled the trigger. The loud crack from his gun echoed through the trees, no doubt rousing the SS guards up the track.

One of the men below him grunted and went down, clutching his thigh.

My God, I actually hit something.

Having now given his position away, he realized he couldn't sit perched up on the branch any more. Grimacing and gritting his teeth, he dropped down to the ground into the thick of the fight. He landed heavily on the back of one of the dead men. Around him all he could hear was the grunting, the laboured breath of a dozen or more men, shrill words barked in German, accented English and one or two other languages.

'There . . . shoot him!'

'Shoot! Shoot!'

'Out of the way, Schwartz!'

A machine gun spewed a salvo of muzzle-suppressed *taps* and lit the scene with flickering light. Liam saw Bob take half a dozen shots in the chest, his black tunic erupting with exit wounds and geysers of dark blood.

Not enough to stop him, though. In an instant he was upon the one who'd fired, his blade a lethal flash of quicksilver death across the man's throat.

Another short burst from someone else caught Bob from behind and once more his uniform tunic danced, tattered, ripped and bloody.

Liam fired several rapid-fire rounds at the dark shape. It buckled and fell to the snow.

Bob leaped forward at another man, his hand twisting the blade into him, but he was slowing down now. Still a deadly force, but no longer with the devastating whip-tail speed of a lethal predator. Instead he had the lumbering energy of a cornered and exhausted mammoth, his flesh-and-blood body weakened by too many wounds to recover from.

Another short, silenced burst of gunfire, sounding like a walking stick dragged across a wooden picket fence. Bob staggered back heavily.

'Scheiße!! Töten Sie ihn!'

Another rattle of suppressed fire.

Bob collapsed to his knees, wavered for a moment, before falling face forward into the snow.

A torch snapped on to Liam. Caught in its glare, he instantly tossed the gun aside and raised his hands. 'Don't shoot! P-please!'

The torch panned across his face, blinding him. 'On your knees!'

Liam dropped down into the snow.

'Who the hell are you?'

'I'm . . . my name's Liam.'

'Who sent you?'

There was no official name for the agency. None that Foster had been prepared to tell him anyway. 'I'm . . . I'm an agent f-from the future.'

The torch beam dropped down, out of his face, and Liam could now see from the glow that only four of them remained standing. The man holding the torch spoke again.

'From the future? So soon?' said Kramer. There was bitterness in his voice. Bitter and resentful that his bid to change history had already, after mere minutes, been intercepted.

Liam knew for certain his life was now going to be measured in minutes . . . if not mere seconds.

'But this is impossible. Waldstein's was the *only* machine,' snapped Kramer.

You have to keep him talking, Liam. Keep him talking.

'No, Kramer. You're wrong. The people I work for have machines. We're here to protect history.'

Kramer took a step towards him. 'But why?' He shook his head angrily. 'Why? The world we've come from . . . it's dying. We killed it with our pollution, we over-populated it, sucked it dry of resources, wiped out almost every other species.' He squatted down in front of Liam. 'Why would *anyone* want to preserve that kind of future?'

Liam looked up at him. He realized from the haunted expression on Kramer's face that perhaps he wasn't driven by greed or an insatiable thirst for power, but perhaps by better intentions. 'Why would anyone want to protect that?' he asked again.

'I . . . I've seen the future you made,' uttered Liam, 'with my own eyes. It . . . it's a world of ashes and . . . and ruins.'

Kramer's eyes narrowed. 'What?'

'You will end up doing something terrible. And it will destroy the world . . . leaving nothing. The future may be bad. But what you do makes it far worse.'

One of the other three men stepped forward and stood beside Kramer. 'We came back here to make a *better* world,' he said adamantly. 'Not to *destroy* it.'

It was the heavily accented man. The one called Karl.

Liam shook his head. 'But somehow . . . somehow that's exactly what you will end up doing. Something will go wrong. Something you do will lead to a . . .'

What was it Foster said?

'. . . a . . . a *nuclear* war. And there'll be nothing left.' Liam looked from one of them to the other. 'God help me, I've seen what's left of humanity. Pitiful ghouls . . . living on each other's flesh.'

Karl's eyes widened. For a moment he looked lost, confused.

'If there is a Hell, if there really is . . . then I've seen it,' said Liam. 'And it will be *your* actions that create it.'

'Paul?' Karl turned to Kramer. 'Paul? Could this be true?'

Kramer shook his head, his eyes searching for truth in Liam's face.

In the distance, they heard a siren begin to wail. Liam's

unsilenced gunshots had clearly alerted the SS guards. The entire regiment would be roused and combing the woods soon.

'You say you have *seen* this yourself?' asked Kramer.

Liam nodded. 'And I think I'd rather die here . . . than go back to that.'

Clouds of vapour filled the space between them, caught like fleeting pale ghosts in the beam of torchlight.

'Paul,' said Karl, 'this must be a lie.'

Kramer's face was shrouded with conflicting thoughts, conflicting emotions. In the distance they could hear the barking of dogs over the mournful wailing of the sirens. Voices raised and growing closer.

Kramer shook his head. Something in the expression on his face, the glint of his haunted eyes, told Liam that deep inside his troubled mind a decision was being made.

But what it was, he'd never know.

A burst of silenced gunfire ripped through the stillness. Kramer's Arctic-camouflage jacket spat blood and then he flopped to the ground.

Karl and the other two men turned round to open fire on Bob. The support unit was splayed on his back, holding one of their machine guns loosely in its left hand. Most of their unaimed shots sent divots of dry snow into the air. But all of Bob's shots hit home, dropping each of the three men with surgical precision.

'Bob!' gasped Liam, scrambling across the ground wet with blood, snow stained dark as night.

'Bob . . . I thought you were dead.'

Up close he could see the support unit had taken too many chest and stomach wounds to possibly survive.

'Information . . .' He gurgled blood out of the side of his mouth.

'No . . . shhhh, Bob,' whispered Liam, cradling the support unit's head in his lap. His coarse dark hair, grown over the last six months and long enough to lose a fist in, was matted and wet from a head wound.

Bob's grey eyes blinked and fluttered. He was doing some housekeeping on his hard drive – collating files, compressing data.

'Bob?'

His eyes cleared and locked on Liam. 'Mission priority one: must destroy the weapons . . . advanced weapons technology.'

'Yes . . . yes, of course.'

'Gather the weapons together . . . destroy them with a grenade,' he said, pointing towards an equipment satchel lying on the snow nearby. 'Grenades are in that bag. Use one . . . set off the others.'

Liam nodded and realized there were warm tears running down his cheeks. Realized he was shedding tears for a broken machine.

'Bob . . . I –'

'You must be quiet and listen!'

He could hear voices now, dozens of them calling out to each other, and baying dogs eager to be let off the leash. In the distance, torches flickered faintly through the woods. Floodlights up on the hill, where Hitler's Berghof was located, sent beams into the sky.

The entire hillside seemed to be alive with activity.

'Mission priority two: you must leave, Liam O'Connor. You must not be captured alive. Hide, await the return window or back-up window. You must leave immediately.'

'Just help me get you up! I'll not leave you here to –'

'Negative. Self-termination must be activated.'

'No! Don't you do that, Bob! I mean it, don't you do it!'

Bob gurgled more blood. 'Mission priority three: support unit cannot fall into the hands of –'

'No! That's crazy, we can get you out of here . . . if you'll just get off your backside, you big lump!'

'Negative. You must leave now. You should leave now.'

'Bob . . . will you shut your mouth for just a second?'

'Leave now! Leave Now!'

'Bob! Please . . . You don't need to terminate! I'll do it! I'll do it!'

He looked around the bloodstained snow and saw what he was after.

CHAPTER 89

2001, New York

Still. Quiet . . . but for the rustling of a lifeless breeze across the barren landscape. Tall spires of rusted metal and crumbling concrete stand over the lost remnants of a place once called Times Square.

The creak of a long-faded sign swinging from a lamp post. The squeak and bang of a window shutter somewhere, caught and played with by the haunting wind.

A sickly yellow sun behind scudding brown irradiated clouds casts pallid beams down on to ashes and dust. From the darkness inside gutted and scorched buildings, milky eyes look out hungrily for some other meagre supply of food . . . a rat, a dog – if any are left – perhaps another of its kind.

Not a dying world, but a *dead* world . . . just waiting for these last pitiful skeletal survivors of mankind to realize the time has come for them to die.

But, gently at first, the breeze freshens.

That loose window shutter across the square bangs ever more heavily; small clouds of dust whip along the ground. The wheel on a rusted and upended pram turns slowly with a *click-click-click* of bearings.

Then, faintly – blink and you'd miss it – the slightest shimmer. Like the ripple across the hot tarmac of a motorway on a midsummer's day, the flicker of hot air above a bonfire.

A shimmer, flickering, undulating . . . changing.

The tallest dead spire overlooking Times Square now has windows, unbroken. As do the other buildings, one after the other. One can see clear roads and faint ghostly apparitions moving along them. Clearer now . . . not ghostly but solid. Cars, buses, trams . . . people.

The sky has changed from an unhealthy poisoned brown to a wet-Tuesday grey and the persistent drizzle of mean-spirited rain.

Tall crimson-coloured banners with the emblem of a snake eating its tail suddenly adorn every lamp post. Placards appear above shop entrances, featuring the face of a leader who promises to unite the world under his rule. Soldiers in grey and black uniforms and tall leather boots patrol soulless ordered streets full of soberly dressed civilians quietly, obediently, turning up for work.

This at least is life. Not a dead world any more.

The breeze freshens again.

The banners flutter, as if sensing something more is on its way.

Another shimmer.

Another change is coming, rippling forward through months, years, decades of time as events realign, destinies change and possibilities find correct versions of themselves.

The wet grey sky slowly clears, the rain stops.

The pennants and banners vanish with a whisper, the placards disappear.

With a final flourish and twist of reality, Times Square becomes noisy, garish, busy, impatient, filled with rude people on mobile phones organizing their day ahead, jostling each other for pavement space, queuing for breakfast bagels and Starbucks coffee.

A giant green ogre called Shrek peers out from a poster.

A homeless man pushing a shopping trolley full of cardboard boxes and topped with a tarpaulin takes a moment to sit down on a bench and watch the busy world go by.

A lovely blue sky. Unseasonably warm sun for this time of year . . . and the distant drone of an approaching plane on the far horizon.

CHAPTER 90

2001, New York

Maddy lay on her cot in the dark. Opposite, she could hear Foster's laboured breathing, the wheezy rattle of an unwell man.

All was quiet in the archway save for the drip of water from the brick ceiling somewhere out in the darkness. The generator had finally stopped thudding. She had lost track of how long that had been now.

Hours . . . a dozen? More?

No power, no light. They'd used their last candle as they'd sat either side of the table and discussed their options should Liam and Bob fail. Not many options, if truth be told. The choices available to them boiled down to just one, really.

When to do it . . . when to use the last two rounds in the shotgun.

When they'd both be ready to admit that all was lost.

She'd not been foolish enough to let herself think this was actually going to work. That some foggily remembered date from an autobiography that should never have been written would lead Liam and Bob right to the cause of all this? No.

That was the kind of unlikely happy ending that belonged on some cheesy TV show or some rubbish FX-laden blockbuster movie, the nick-of-time last-minute reprieve for the Good Guys that you *always knew* was going to happen right from the moment the opening credits rolled.

Maddy's face was buried in the pillow when the ceiling lights in the field office winked silently on. Half asleep, it wasn't until her ears registered the soft hum of the machinery that maintained the time bubble quietly initializing itself that she stirred and turned her face to one side.

It took another long moment for her to realize the power had come back on. That the archway was bathed in a flickering clinical light.

Is this for real? Or am I dreaming?

She sat up quickly on her cot, almost banging her head against the rough springs of the bunk above. And smiled.

It's not a dream.

'Foster!'

She reached across and shook his shoulder. 'Foster!'

His rustling breath caught and with a moan of painful discomfort he roused and opened dark, sallow eyes. 'Whuh . . . what is it, Madelaine?'

She pointed up at the bulb in the wire cage above them, glowing brightly. 'Foster, I think they did it.'

Several minutes later they were standing outside in their rubbish-strewn backstreet savouring the return of a familiar world. A lovely sunny day in September, the rumble of traffic over the Williamsburg Bridge above them, the honk of impatient horns, the distant wail of a police siren.

Life. Impatient life.

'I've never seen anything so beautiful,' cried Maddy, her cheeks unashamedly wet.

'Nor I,' replied Foster.

She stretched an arm round his sloped shoulders and planted a kiss on a cheek as dry and wrinkled as parchment.

'We made it,' she whispered.

Foster smiled. 'Then let's bring them back home, shall we?'

*

The lights in the archway flickered momentarily as a result of the drain of power. The hum of the displacement machinery rose in pitch and then, all of a sudden, there it was. Maddy could see the shimmering outline of the window in the middle of the floor, appearing in exactly the same place it had when they'd sent both of them back to 1941.

Within the window she could see a faint rippling image, like a reflection in a disturbed pool of water – it looked to her like a world of trees and snow. Then into view the wavering silhouette of something dark merged into the puddle-like image. Unmistakably a human figure. Someone coming to them.

A moment later . . . Liam stepped alone on to the floor of the arch.

'Liam!' screamed Maddy with initial delight. Then she saw that his hands and arms were slick with wet and drying blood, his uniform, his neck, his face, pale like a ghost, were spattered with dark droplets.

'Oh my God . . . what happened? Liam, are you OK?'

He turned to look at her, his mouth struggling to reply, searching for words.

Foster stepped forward. 'Liam, lad . . . are you all right?'

He looked at the old man, frowning, struggling to take things in, blinking back the brightness from the strip lights above him. Finally he nodded as he opened the palm of one hand and held out something metallic. It was the size of a small mobile phone and coated with clots of drying blood.

'I . . . managed to . . .' He took a breath and tried again. 'Well, anyway . . . Here's Bob.'

Foster reached for the object, taking it from him gently. 'You did well, Liam,' he replied softly, knowing full well the grisly deed that Liam had just carried out. 'That's no easy thing to do.

Come sit down, lad,' he added, leading him over to the table and chairs.

'Did . . . did we do it?' Liam asked.

Maddy grinned and hugged him tightly in answer to his question.

'Yes, Liam,' replied Foster, 'you did it.'

CHAPTER 91

2001, New York

A couple of hours later, after Liam had given a more detailed account of his time in the past, he was fast asleep on one of the cots. His snoring seemed to reverberate through the arch even more noisily than the generator had.

Foster worked over at the computer desk. Having scrubbed Bob's neural processor clean of brain tissue and blood, he connected it up to the computer system and began downloading the entire content of its hard drive.

'Bob's AI is in there amongst that,' he said, nodding towards the loading bar slowly creeping across the screen.

'That's a lot of data uploading there,' said Maddy.

'Well, he was away for nearly six months; all the time, his eyes and ears recording everything that was going on.'

'So, what's the deal with Bob? Is his AI intact?'

Foster shrugged. 'I'm no computer expert. So I don't know how it works. But the code that makes up Bob's AI will merge with the computer system's.' He tapped the keyboard. 'You'll be able to communicate with him in there.'

'Right. Six months of learning . . . I guess that AI code's a lot smarter than the idiot that plopped out of the birthing tube.'

Foster chuckled. 'Oh yes.'

She looked at him. 'How are we going to grow ourselves

another support unit? Those tubes are smashed, the gunk they were growing in has all gone off –'

He raised a hand. 'There's going to be a lot of work to do to get this field office online again.'

'I'll help you with that . . . You look tired.' If she was being honest, she would have said he looked ready to keel over and die.

'New clone embryos and growing solution. The generator needs replacing. The walls fixed up. You need to replenish our supplies,' he added.

'A new generator. That's going to cost money.'

'Fine,' said Foster, 'just go find a hardware store and buy another.'

'We've got enough money?'

'As much as you'll ever need. It's in a bank account.'

'Cool. Do we get a debit card with that or something?'

He turned to her. 'That's one of many things I'm going to need to go through with you . . . before . . .' His voice trailed off.

'Before what?'

Foster looked uncomfortable. 'Before I leave.'

'Leave? Leave! You can't leave us! Neither of us know what the heck we're doing just yet. Jesus, I . . . I certainly don't –'

'You did fine.' Foster smiled. 'You did just fine. I'd say right now there's no team better trained to do this than you. You survived the ordeal. You'll be able to cope with pretty much anything else this job has to throw at you. Of that I'm sure.'

'*Team?* There's no team. There's just me and Liam now.' She cast a glance at the bank of monitors in front of her and the upload bar, now inching past the halfway mark. 'Oh . . . and a computer system that's very soon going to start insisting we call it *Bob*.'

It was then they heard the soft scrape of feet behind them. They turned round to see Sal standing in the middle of the archway, a shopping bag in one hand, looking curiously down at the small crater of scooped-out concrete in the floor.

'So what happened here? This place is a real mess,' she said, shaking her head disapprovingly. 'I go out for a couple of hours to get some milk and bagels for breakfast and come back and it's like someone's been drilling holes in the wall outside . . . and someone dropped a bowling ball on the floor here.'

'Sal?' Maddy's jaw dropped. 'Sal!'

A dark eyebrow arched quizzically. 'Uh . . . yeah, and?'

'You're alive!' Maddy leaped up from the desk and swept the confused girl into her arms. 'Oh my God, you're alive! You're alive!'

Foster could see Sal's bewildered face over Maddy's shaking shoulder.

'Uh . . . is someone going to tell me what's been going on while I was out?'

CHAPTER 92

2001, New York

Monday

They haven't told me everything that happened. I can tell some things went on that they're keeping from me. But I know now that while I was out buying milk and bagels a time shift happened, the world changed and Liam and Bob went into the past to fix it.

Liam told me he and Bob were actually stuck in the past for six whole months! And I know about none of it. Time travel is such a strange thing to get your head round.

They said our field office was attacked, but no one's told me by who or what yet. There are scratch marks everywhere on the wall outside, like someone took a scouring brush to the bricks. Maybe we were attacked by an army of porcupines or something.

Many of the things in the back room were broken, shards of glass and stuff everywhere, so I guess there was a bit of a struggle back there. I wish they'd just tell me everything instead of trying to 'protect' me just 'cause I'm the youngest.

And Bob died. I know that's affected Liam. He's missing him. I see him typing to Bob on the computer system every day. Maddy tells him not to be so cut up about it – he's not actually 'gone'; he's just in the computer instead. She said it's no different to, like, chatting to a friend on MSN.

I miss the big guy too.

Foster says we can grow another Bob once the birthing equipment has been sorted out. I'm not sure how I'll feel, though, about a Bob Version 2. It just won't be the same Bob. Or will it? I mean, they're clones, so I suppose it will be exactly the same.

Maddy's been kept very busy. Foster says she's the team leader and needs to do a lot of learning while we rest up and recover. The birthing tubes in the back room have got to be replaced, and we'll need new cloned foetuses and supplies of that gooey soup they float in. Foster's getting Maddy to sort out those things. We also have to get a new back-up generator installed to replace the old one and supplies of food and water and diesel and so many other things.

We're all going to be kept busy for the next few days, that's for sure.

You know, I hate that I completely missed out on whatever happened. I feel like I'm still the newbie here and the other two are now sort of like old hands.

In fact, all three of them seem a bit different, like what happened changed them somehow. Like, for example, Liam. He's sort of older now. I swear he's grown an inch or two taller. He seems bigger, firmer. Less boyish and a bit more manly. Obviously he's six months older than he was . . . but it's actually like he's two or three years older. It's weird.

Maddy jokes around a little less now. She seems to have so much on her mind all the time . . . like she's about to sit a whole load of exams and she hasn't done any revision.

And then there's Foster.

I worry about him. He looks so-o-o-o sick and so-o-o-o much older. Coming back from my shopping trip, it was like he'd sort of aged a hundred years in the time that I was out.

I figured it would be rude to blurt something out about how he looked really old all of a sudden. So I haven't said anything about it these last few days. I guess it's a time-travel thing.

So incredibly weird, though, this time-travel business. It really messes with your head.

Sal looked up from writing her diary and slurped a spoon from her breakfast bowl of Rice Krispies. The cereal had gone soggy in the milk as she'd been scribbling away. She stared disinterestedly at one of the banks of computer monitors in front of her. She'd tuned the signal feed from CNN to the Disney channel, and right now *Toy Story 2* was on – Buzz and gang desperately trying to cross a busy highway disguised as traffic cones. Sal had seen it many times over. It had been one of her dad's favourites.

The arch is quiet right now. Liam is on his bunk, his nose stuck in a history book all about the Second World War. He does a lot of reading. Says he never ever wants to be stuck again in a time he knows nothing about.

Maddy and Foster went out earlier. He told her he had a number of things to discuss with her 'confidentially'. I don't like that. That there are things he's telling her and not me and Liam. It doesn't seem fair. After all, we're a team, aren't we?

Sal had watched them both step out under the open shutter door a couple of hours ago. Foster had waved a goodbye. But there was something about the way he'd done that, a rueful smile as he'd surveyed the scruffy place.

In fact, the old man had been acting very oddly these last few days. She wondered if it was because he was tired. Foster seemed to have too much on his shoulders, too much to do. She decided, when they returned, she'd insist he sit back in one of the tatty old armchairs they had around the table, put his feet up and she'd make a fuss of him. Make him some coffee, some beans on toast. Whatever he wanted.

He looked like he could do with some TLC.

CHAPTER 93

2001, New York

'So,' said Foster eventually, 'so now you know everything you need to know, Madelaine. *Everything*.'

Maddy stared back across the table at him. It was mid-morning, and Starbucks was relatively quiet. The morning rush for take-away lattes and frappucinos had been and gone and now the coffee shop was half empty.

'And now you know *why* I'm dying. Why I can't risk riding time any more. Why I can't live in the field office's time bubble any more . . .'

'You're sure?' She looked at him. 'You're sure the technology is killing you?'

'Yes,' he replied. 'The damage it does builds up slowly over time. You don't notice it at first, but it catches up on you really fast eventually. I don't know how much longer I'll be able to live outside the bubble, but it'll be longer than if I remain inside with you.'

'If you did stay?'

'Stayed with you . . . *inside*?' He shrugged. 'It's hard to tell. Maybe I'd live on a few more days, a week or two at most.' He sighed. 'It's not an exact science. And I'm no doctor.'

Maddy bit her lip. 'I'm sorry.'

'Don't be.' He smiled weakly. 'It goes with being an operative. I was told early on, when I first started out and I was a fit, young lad, that being a TimeRider would eventually kill me.'

'But you carried on regardless?'

'Given all the wonderful history I've seen, Maddy, all the history I've touched, smelled, tasted, all the experiences I've had, the things I've learned? Jesus . . . I'd do it all again. I really would.'

'You were given the same choice that you gave us? Join up or go back and face your predestined death?'

'Yes,' he replied, 'and I don't regret a moment of it.'

'So, what about Liam?'

Foster pursed his lips in thought, then eventually, reluctantly, he nodded. 'Yes, I'm afraid Liam will end up like this. Time travel will age him faster than you or Sal. Time travel will sooner or later kill him . . . riddle his body with cancers.'

She shook her head and looked down at her coffee and her muffin; all of a sudden she had no appetite for either.

Poor, poor Liam.

It was going to be down to her, as the team leader, to tell him some time, to let him know each occasion he stepped through a displacement window and was sent back into the past that the cells of his body were going to become more and more corrupted, until finally they turned on themselves and became tumours that would eventually eat him up from the inside.

'So,' she said after a while, 'where will you go?'

'I don't know.' He shrugged. 'I guess I wouldn't mind feeling the sun on my face whilst I enjoy a good hotdog.' He grinned. 'Make the most of whatever time I've got left.'

'Will you stay in New York?'

'They say it's the city that never sleeps . . . and, as somebody once told me, you can do all the sleeping you want when you're dead. So I guess New York's the place for me.'

They both laughed. A dry, sad noise that filled the space between them.

He finished the last of his coffee. 'Anyway, it was always my plan to visit New York and see the sights. I just got waylaid for a little while.'

He reached for a bag at his feet, a small overnight bag with a few personal keepsakes and mementoes.

'Foster, wait,' said Maddy. 'I'm not sure I can do this. I'm not sure we're ready to cope on our own.'

'You're more than ready. I *know* you'll make a great team.'

'How can you *know*? There's still so much we need to –'

'I know,' he said firmly as he rose from his seat slowly, painfully, grimacing wearily from the effort.

'Will we see you again?'

'You have all the information you need, Maddy. It's there in your head, in what I've told you, what you've learned, what you've experienced. Anything you don't know . . . Well, there are notes on the computer's database, answers to all the questions you're ever likely to ask.'

'How do you *know* what I'm going to ask?'

He winked. 'This is time travel, Maddy; *what goes around, comes around.*'

She cocked her head, confused by his cryptic answer. 'Yes, but if I needed your help . . . could I find you out here somewhere?'

His frail, liver-spotted old hand squeezed her shoulder lightly. 'You'll do just fine, Maddy, so you will.'

He turned away and shuffled towards the glass front of the coffee shop with his overnight bag slung over one shoulder. He looked like the world's oldest traveller, pulling the door open and stepping out on to the busy Manhattan pavement. She stifled an urge to call out, to chase after him and beg him to stay on a while longer with them.

But then he was gone from view, lost amid the busy pavement

traffic. For a while she watched the bustling street outside, pondering all the things Foster had told her. Wondering how much of that information she ought to share with the others, how much of it was best she keep to herself. Already she was beginning to feel the burden of responsibility settling all too heavily on her narrow shoulders.

'Top you up?'

Maddy looked up at the Starbucks waitress standing beside her booth holding a decanter of steaming coffee in her hand. A girl the same age as her. For a moment she wondered what troublesome dilemmas kept *her* tossing and turning at night . . .

. . . *Go skating with Sheena and Kayisha tomorrow? Should I accept Danny's invitation to Jimmy's house party? Or shall I go out with Stevie instead? Should I do an overtime shift Tuesday or shall I make it Wednesday? . . .*

'Top you up?'

Maddy nodded, distracted. 'Sure . . . yeah, please, fill me up.'

The waitress poured till the cup was filled and she moved on to the next booth to ask the same question.

Maddy watched her go, envious of what she supposed was an untroubled life of petty decisions. She realized right then that if she could wave a magic wand and swap places with the waitress – she could pour coffee and Miss Starbucks Waitress could go and worry about keeping history the way it is – she'd do it in a heartbeat.

But, she realized, rubbing her tired eyes and thinking she needed to get a new pair of specs, someone's got to do it, you know? Someone's got to keep an eye on the time.

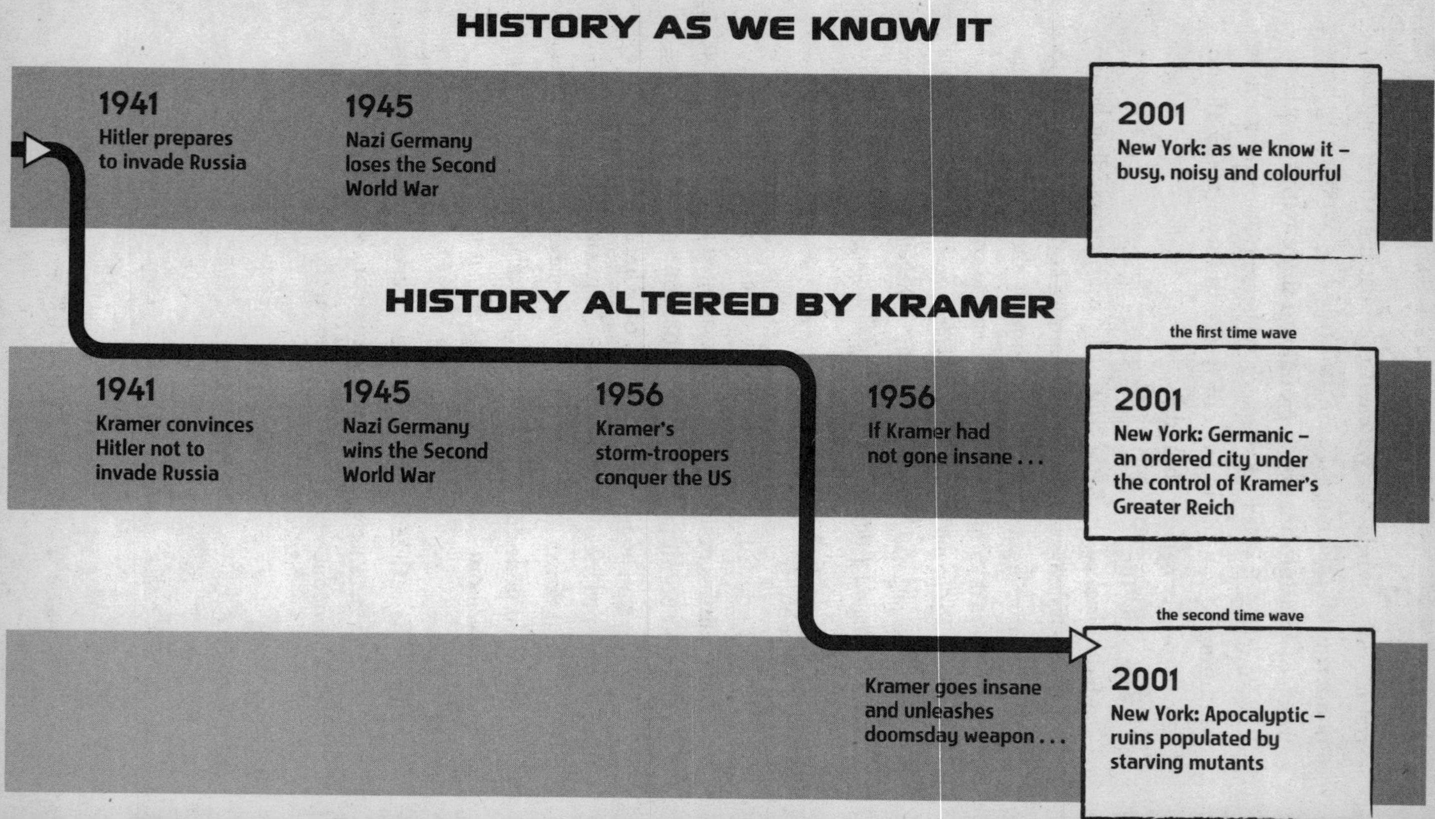
HISTORY AS WE KNOW IT
1941
Hitler prepares to invade Russia
1945
Nazi Germany loses the Second World War
2001
New York: as we know it – busy, noisy and colourful
HISTORY ALTERED BY KRAMER
1941
Kramer convinces Hitler not to invade Russia
1945
Nazi Germany wins the Second World War
1956
Kramer's storm-troopers conquer the US
1956
If Kramer had not gone insane . . .
the first time wave
2001
New York: Germanic – an ordered city under the control of Kramer's Greater Reich
Kramer goes insane and unleashes doomsday weapon . . .
the second time wave
2001
New York: Apocalyptic – ruins populated by starving mutants